791.440941 GAR

The Nation's Favourite

Just how difficult can it be to run a pop radio station?

Very.

In 1993, BBC Radio 1 gained a new controller. Matthew Bannister said he was going to reinvent the station, the most popular in Europe. But things didn't go exactly to plan. The station lost millions of listeners. Its most famous DJs left, and their replacements proved to be disasters. Radio 1's commercial rivals regarded the internal turmoil with glee. For a while a saviour arrived, in the shape of Chris Evans. But his behaviour caused further upheavals, and his eventual departure provoked another mass desertion by listeners.

What was to be done?

In the middle of this crisis, Radio 1 bravely (or foolishly) allowed the writer Simon Garfield to observe its workings from the inside. For a year he was allowed unprecedented access to management meetings and to DJs in their studios, to research briefings and playlist conferences. Everyone interviewed spoke in passionate detail about their struggle to make their station credible and successful once more. The result is a gripping and often hilarious portrait of a much-loved national institution as it battles back from the brink of calamity.

'Brilliantly observed and screamingly funny . . . It's the ultimate fly-on-the-wall documentary, full of gaffes, bitchiness and all-out stupidity . . . An indispensable document of those times, a thoughtful fable on media and celebrity, and a great read even for those of us who switched off long ago.' *Uncut*

'The author lucked into this assignment at just the right moment. The year he spent at Radio 1 eavesdropping on its movers and shakers spanned the period when Matthew Bannister binned DLT and became involved in (Chris) Evans Gate – the months of transition from the station of Smashie & Nicey ("I love Tuesdays, don't you mate?") to the station of Pete Tong and Tim Westwood ("Having it large for the weekend!"). The clash of egos was titanic, with more intriguing and backstabbing than a Medieval court, and Garfield's account of the upheaval makes for engrossing reading . . . Poptastic!' *Mojo*

'What emerges is a strange and intriguing parallel universe, a place where tabloid showbiz editors talk intelligently and in sentences, and the wisdom of the ages comes from the mouth of Simon Bates. But the most gripping moment in *The Nation's Favourite* comes when its miasma of conflicting egos is suddenly shot through with the real stink of fear . . . *The Nation's Favourite* not only weaves a fascinating tapestry from its thread of public and private utterance, but supplies many insights into the way power is wielded in the media. The endlessly mutating cabals and spheres of influence, the cruel slights and shameless sucking up, have rarely been better dissected.' Ben Thompson, *Independent*

'We might remember Dave Lee Travis as the man who liked to be known as The Hairy Cornflake, a man who pioneered a snooker quiz on the radio and went drag racing at Santa Pod. But we forget his support for seals, he reminds us, and the nurses. Clearly, there was more to him than met the eye, so it is with frustration that he complains: "We're in such a ludicrous business." . . . *The Nation's Favourite* is a shrewd and clear-sighted account of precisely that.' *Times Literary Supplement*

Simon Garfield was born in London in 1960. He is the author of *Expensive Habits: The Dark Side of the Music Industry* (1986), *The End of Innocence: Britain in the Time of AIDS* (1994), which was awarded the Somerset Maugham Prize, and *The Wrestling* (1996).

The Nation's Favourite

The True Adventures of Radio 1

Simon Garfield

faber and faber

First published in 1998
by Faber and Faber Limited
3 Queen Square London WC1N 3AU
This edition first published in 1999

Typeset by Faber and Faber Ltd
Printed in England by Mackays of Chatham plc, Chatham, Kent

A CIP record for this book
is available from the British Library

ISBN 0-571-19735-3

10 9 8 7 6 5 4 3 2 1

Contents

Preface

In May 1997, I approached Radio 1 with the idea for a book about the inner workings of a pop radio station. I explained that I would need to attend management and other meetings, and to spend considerable time with staff and DJs. I said that I wished to write a fair and detailed picture, and that this might reveal certain aspects of the station that previously had been concealed from public view.

To my delight, Matthew Bannister, then Radio 1's controller, and Polly Ravenscroft, the station's head of publicity, agreed to the proposal, and facilitated my approaches to their colleagues. Clearly this was a brave and trusting decision on their part, particularly as they held no veto over the text. Further, they were extremely supportive and helpful in the many months I subsequently spent with them, even when it came to talking to their detractors. Why should this be? In part, I believe, it was because they wanted their work recognized and vindicated; no one finds it easy to turn down the offer of being at the centre of a book, particularly if they believe their image has suffered from unfair treatment in the past. Perhaps it also had something to do with their desire to have a complete document detailing what, even in the context of modern media upheavals, had been a tumultuous and turbulent time. Or maybe they just wanted to see what others thought of them. Whatever their reasons, it is clear that I owe them a great debt of thanks.

Although I observed Radio 1 at first hand for about a year, the real story began four years before, and so I am also indebted to a great many people who have helped me reconstruct events. Most of them appear in the text, but several others gave up much of their time and took the trouble to help me without appearing in the final narrative. I would like to thank them all, and hope they accept my assurances that their contributions were valuable and much appreciated.

In addition to those interviewed, my thanks for their all-round assistance and advice to Adrian Deevoy (*Q*), Tim Hulse (*Arena*), Rebecca McGinn, Sue Terry, Luke Vinten, Rebecca Hardy (*Daily Mail*), Paul Simpson, Nicola DiTullio, Ann Matura-Graville, Georgina Armstrong, Julie Dawson, Jeff Walden, Ruth Parrish, Naresh Ramchandani, Venetia Williamson-Noble, Jo Pilkington, Jo Lamb, Tola Lamont, Emma Farmer, Matt Priest, Simon Willis, Mark Kermode, Phil Lawton, Ian Parkinson, Tarrant Steele, Kate Marsh, Richard Murdoch, Paul Donovan, Sonya Gooderham, Ben Cooper, Sarah Carrington, Gail Nuttney, Mark Goodier, Tracie Tungate, Raymond Duck and Clare Marvin. My editor at Faber, Julian Loose, and my agent, Pat Kavanagh, have been as unfailingly helpful and encouraging as ever.

This book is for Diane.

Cast of Characters

The DJs
Zoe Ball
Simon Bates
Nicky Campbell
Chris Evans
Kevin Greening
Andy Kershaw
Steve Lamacq
Simon Mayo
Chris Moyles
Annie Nightingale
John Peel
Peter Powell
Mark Radcliffe
Marc 'Lard' Riley
Pete Tong
Dave Lee Travis
Clive Warren
Tim Westwood
Jo Whiley
Steve Wright

Chris Evans:
'I'm never going to broadcast again'

The Producers

Pat Connor
Rhys Hughes
Barrie Kelly
Dan McGrath
John Revell
John Walters

The Management

Matthew Bannister, Director of Radio and Controller of Radio 1
John Birt, Director-General, BBC
Trevor Dann, Head of Music Entertainment
Liz Forgan, former Director of Radio
Chris Lycett, Executive Producer, Live Music
Sue Lynas, Chief Publicity Officer, BBC Network Radio
Sophie McLaughlin, Head of Radio 1 Marketing, now Head
    of Strategy and Broadcast Analysis, Network Radio
Andy Parfitt, Deputy Controller of Radio 1, then Controller
Polly Ravenscroft, Head of Radio 1 Publicity
Jeff Smith, Head of Radio 1 Music Policy
Jo Watson, broadcast analyst

The Media and Others

Steven Armstrong, broadcasting writer
Johnny Beerling, former Radio 1 Controller,
    now freelance producer and technical adviser
Harry Enfield, comedian
Matthew Freud, public relations director
Paul Robinson, former Head of Music Policy at Radio 1,
    now Managing Director, Talk Radio
John Robson, advertising executive
Francis Rossi, singer/guitarist, Status Quo
Phil Sutcliffe, *Q Magazine*
Nigel Sweeney, promotions executive
David Walker, manager, Status Quo
Matthew Wright, the *Mirror*

The Nation's Favourite

The Christmas Party: 'We used to have an awful lot of fun'

Chapter 1

Sheep, Chickens

John Peel (Disc Jockey): I lived in the States for seven years in the sixties. In the days before we knew about sexism, me and a couple of mates used to follow the fortunes of a young woman who performed under the name of Chris Colt, the Girl with the 45s. We used to follow her from grisly strip joint to strip joint. I was driving back from a particularly exhilarating performance in New Orleans, having left my friends down there, and I was crossing what they call the Piney Woods of East Texas, which cover an area the size of Belgium, as all big woods invariably do. I was driving along this long road in the middle of the night, and the moon was at the far end, so it was like driving along a silver ribbon if you want to be poetic about it, and the hills were rising and falling, and there was a small town before me, and on the radio came a record by Elmore James called 'Stranger Blues'. The first line was, 'I'm a stranger here/ I just drove in your town'. I just thought it was a perfect conjuncture of time, place and music. You always hope in the course of doing a programme that somebody somewhere may experience a moment like that.

Matthew Bannister (Director, BBC Radio): The controller's job was advertised in the middle of 1993, and I wrote a formal application, a lengthy paper. The interview panel was the Chairman of the Board of Governors, Marmaduke Hussey; Sir Kenneth Bloomfield, the National Governor for Northern Ireland; John Birt, the Director General; Liz Forgan, the managing director of Network Radio; Margaret Salmon, the director of personnel; and Mark Byford, the controller of regional broadcasting, who I think had been invited along because he was the only person under forty, and he knew a bit about music. I was third to go in.

To be confronted by such a high-calibre line-up was pretty nerve-wracking, but the interview itself was pretty fair and equable. They asked me what I thought about the current output. The bulk of the interview was conducted by Liz Forgan with John Birt. Marmaduke Hussey only asked one question at the end of the interview. He said, 'How do you feel about the prospect of being Mr Nasty in the newspapers?' I said, 'Well, if it's an inevitable consequence of following through the change we're about to embark upon, I'm prepared to put up with it.' I don't think I understood at that point quite what it would feel like, or exactly how much I would be vilified, or the exact nature of the difficulties in trying to transform a radio station. But certainly it was interesting and prescient of him to have asked me the question.

Liz Forgan (Former Director, BBC Radio): There were three or four candidates, not the biggest field in the world because it was clear that Radio 1 was in for a tough ride and anybody who wanted an easy number would not come anywhere near it. At the end John Birt said to me, 'You can have whoever you want.' People always think John is deeply manoeuvring and pulls every string, but he said the choice was entirely mine.

I knew nothing and cared less about pop music. I did like the Beatles, but then everybody in the universe liked the Beatles. I don't think that counts as liking pop music. I listened to the Rolling Stones, and I used to go to parties, but I never had any interest or liking for it; I would never have willingly bought a pop record or turned on a pop music station ever. Which made me in some ways a very unsuitable person to be in charge of Radio 1, but in other ways this made me a very wonderful person to be the managing director, because there was no risk of my interfering.

Matthew had a tremendous advantage from having just done all this work on programme strategy at Broadcasting House, because he'd thought about all the things that needed thinking about at Radio 1 at that very moment: not incidental stuff like what sort of DJs it had, but a completely strategic change in the network.

It was clear that all the radio networks needed a strategic rethink for one simple reason. Commercial radio was getting itself together and there was competition of a sort that there hadn't been before, and it was clear the world was changing. Radio 1 at that time was so genuinely hard to distinguish from any of the commercial pop stations that there was a real and quite legitimate argument for privatizing it.

Matthew Bannister: At lunch time I was called back in by Liz, who offered me the job. That was an emotional moment, but then we went straight away to a staff meeting at Radio 1, into the infamous Room 306, where that dreadful typing pool used to be in Egton House. People were hanging from the rafters, crammed with DJs and all the staff. They were so agog with the announcement as to who the new controller would be, that as I walked through the door Jonathon Ruffle, who produced Simon Bates, was on the phone to the on-air studio, and said 'It's Matthew Bannister!' The news was then broadcast live on air without anyone approving it, and no press release ready.

I told the meeting how proud I was to be in charge of Radio 1 and that I intended to get round and meet all of them – an entirely anodyne ten-second speech. All those people looking at me rather worriedly and rather aggressively – a foretaste of things to come.

To be honest, the atmosphere in the building was appalling. There was no doubt from the staff meeting I attended that these people by and large didn't want to work with me. They were going to resist change. There were a lot of barrack-room lawyers, and a lot of people sitting with their arms folded saying, 'Well, we've seen off five controllers now – Bannister won't last long.' I think I entirely underestimated the power of the entrenched production teams, and their desire to dismantle everything around me and to stop change happening.

You can understand why DJs are mercurial, and have their egos, and want to be treated in a particular way, but I assumed that members of BBC staff working in the most popular radio station in Europe, and with long experience, would be capable of being professional enough to do their job under new management in an interesting way. But there was a lot of leaking of nasty stories, and I was convinced there was hacking into computer records.

Simon Bates (Disc Jockey): Matthew once said to me, 'Everyone here hates me and wants me to fail.' But I said to him, 'They don't want you to fail – they want you to succeed.' Even the staff who were leaving wanted the station to succeed because they had put a great deal of effort into it and cared desperately about it. But I think Matthew became a victim of the Year Zero principle – 'Is that the way Bates did it, is that the way the last controller did it? Then let's change it.'

Matthew Bannister: Radio 1 was run by blokes in blazers and suits and ties, and the women did typing and put up balloons at parties. That's what they were for; the men were for shifting trucks around, and getting into a field with Status Quo. There was also a good deal of sexism and patronizing on the air. On the roadshow there was a lot of throwing of cream cakes and water over women. When I went to a string of leaving parties for long-established Radio 1 producers, in my capacity as chief encourager of their leaving, there were these incredible speeches about how sexy Alice had been their wonderful PA and made the best cups of tea and had great legs. The women were there to look pretty, and they didn't seem to have much aspiration other than to get free tickets and records. I once went into the typing pool, as I called it, where they sat entering record details, and I was asked, 'What the fuck do you want?' I asked someone, 'Well, what's your ambition?' and she said, 'Oh no, I don't have no ambition, mate – so long as I keep getting the free tickets I'm really happy.'

Apart from the management, the other big strata of influence was the big DJs. Simon Bates was hugely influential, and used to run a web of gossip and intrigue from his studio in the morning. He'd get the *Golden Hour* underway, and then he'd be on the phone most of the show plotting and doing deals and trying to undermine the management. Being summoned to Simon Bates's studio was like being summoned to see the boss. Most of the DJs detested each other. Bates hated Wright because Wright was a threat. Wright hated Bates because Bates was a threat. They both hated DLT. The clashing of titanic egos was rather like *Jurassic Park*. Did John Peel tell you about the time he tried to attack Simon Bates?

John Peel: As a Radio 1 DJ you were expected to do ludicrous things. We had these Radio 1 funweeks, which usually consisted of travelling the country with a bunch of other DJs and Noel Edmonds filling people's hotel rooms with chickens. In more enlightened days than ours you'd be burnt at the stake for doing that. There was always a lot of shouting and showing off – awful events. I was put down, no doubt by somebody trying to settle old scores, to take part in and judge a disco-dancing competition in a shopping centre in Livingstone, Scotland. In the lunch hour. If ever there was anyone who would be physically and spiritually disqualified from doing that it would be me, and so I had to say to management that I'd love to be the sort of insensitive oaf who could do it, but I wasn't. All sorts of memos and faxes then went flying down to London saying I was being arrogant and uncooperative.

But these things did have compensations. Perhaps the best moment for me took place in a multi-storey hotel in Birmingham, in something called The Dickens Bar, lots of dark-wood booths full of people who no doubt travelled around the country selling Dickens Bars to other hotels. Tony Blackburn got up with Paul Williams, a Radio 1 producer who used to play the piano tolerably well, and sang for about half an hour. There was massive indifference to his efforts, if not downright hostility, yet he went through the whole thing as if he was Barry Manilow at the Copacabana, as if everyone was absolutely adoring everything he did. He soared in my estimation after that. I thought, He's not such a tosser after all.

People like Mike Read and DLT would often complain that they couldn't go anywhere without being recognized, but of course would go everywhere in a tartan suit carrying a guitar, so they would have attracted attention in a lunatic asylum. In the streets of London people would go, 'Who the fuck is that? Isn't that that Mike Read bloke?'

Phil Sutcliffe (*Q Magazine* Journalist): Back then Radio 1 owned time: 'At 17 Radio 1 minutes to 9 a.m. this is Culture Club.' It owned the weather: '76 Radio 1 degrees this afternoon and here's Kajagoogoo.'

John Walters (Producer, Presenter): I was Peel's producer from 1969. There were very clearly two Radio 1s – the third floor versus the fourth floor. The mainstream playlist Radio 1 – which was Noel Edmonds and the welly boots sticker Radio 1, the fun Radio 1 – was on the fourth floor. Whereas Tommy Vance and Peel and the people concerned with live recordings were on the third floor, where it was about music. On the third floor the management were total aliens from us, and we from them. They left us to our own devices, never came in and said, 'What's happening, talk us through this week's programmes . . .' They didn't give a fuck one way or the other.

I once had to go with Peel to some event like a roadshow in Plymouth. We came down to breakfast in our hotel, and at one big table were the producers and jocks, perhaps Andy Peebles and DLT, and there was Doreen Davies, Radio 1's head woman. It was our instinct, without being awkward, to sit on a separate table for two. But Doreen went, 'Hey! John!

The Two Johns! Come on over here . . .' They wanted to show us it was one big fun family. But we didn't feel part of that crowd at all. They'd all be up until three at the hotel bar, and then they'd be letting sheep into each other's rooms and doing apple-pie beds.

Culturally we were so different to that crowd. Peel once went on a social event at DLT's house. Why was he asked? Well they must have thought, 'He's the weirdo, but he has been here since day one . . .' So Peel went out of curiosity. He went round the house and suddenly realized that DLT didn't own any records. He asked him, and DLT said, 'Oh no, it's too much trouble and the dust . . . Anything I really like I've copied on tape. I've got quite a lot of tapes and I play them in the car, you see?' Peel, of course, to keep his records, had to have an extension built on to the side of his house.

One conversation I had with Derek Chinnery [former controller] seemed to sum up the difference between us. There was a time on Radio 1 when it came off the air at about seven in the evening, and then started up again with Peel at ten. They soon realized that their listeners would desert Radio 1 at that point, and go to Capital or somewhere, and maybe not come back the following morning. So they decided to keep on air all the time up to Peel, and set about finding programmes to fill the gap.

I went to see Chinnery and said, 'Peel and me have achieved a certain status over the years, and we know what it is we're doing. I'm just pointing out that we're not going to change just because you might be playing the New Seekers at 8.30.' Then I said, 'Well, what sort of music are you going to put in there?' I knew pretty certainly that Derek didn't know a crotchet from a hatchet. He knew famous names, more of a career BBC man. So he didn't know any names, frankly, and he didn't want me to laugh if he said the wrong ones. He said, 'On Noel's breakfast show, for the kids going to school, on a scale of 1 to 10, he's playing music that's 1 and 2. With Bates it gets to 3 and 4. Throughout the afternoon we move on to 5 and 6. But John's show, as you know, is perhaps a little too much 9 and 10.' Then I said, 'But we're back to the same question: What sort of music will you instruct producers and disc jockeys should be used in that in-between period?' He looked at me as if I'd gone mad and was a complete idiot and said, 'Well it's obvious – 7 and 8!'

Johnny Beerling (Former Controller): I think it was clear that after twenty-five years it was time that I did actually make a move. I'd been there since the first programme, and for a young person's rock and pop station there needed to be changes made, and clearly I was too close to it to make the sort of changes that were needed. At the same time there were a lot of political things going on – the BBC's charter was coming up for renewal, there was a school of thought, I think led by the new incoming Director General John Birt, that Radio 1 wasn't sufficiently different or distinctive from its commercial opposition. He once said, 'I can't hear any difference between the Radio 1 breakfast show and Chris Tarrant.' Well I think that shows quite an ignorance on his part about the style of the network. I proved conclusively that we were different in terms of the social action campaigns, the amount of time we gave to news, the number of documentaries we did, the commitment to live music and all the rest of it, but that was not noticeable in John's eyes to the opinion-formers in the country. I think one of the reasons he wanted Bannister to replace me was that he deliberately wanted it to attract a lot of publicity and get people, the opinion-formers of the country, the MPs and the people who made these decisions, particularly on the right wing of the Tory party, to understand that Radio 1 was different from its rivals, and that was one of the reasons why I had to go in the end.

John Walters: I don't mind Beerling today, and we're all friendly. He made sure I got a good send off, and he didn't have to. I wasn't in a position that I had to have the governor's dining room and a black-tie do with Ned Sherrin and Peel and Fluff and one or two telly people.

But me and Peel didn't like him in the first instance, in fact saw him as the Prince of Darkness. Johnny was a wheeler-dealer, who also didn't know anything about the music. His favourite music was Kenny Rogers. His thing was getting the show on the road, the roadshow. He didn't really care who appeared on the roadshow, so long as it was a big name.

The management weren't the brightest or the best. I used to feel that even if I was wrong, even if what I was saying was crap, that I could still beat them in an argument. If I was defending the Yorkshire Ripper I'd still get him off as far as they were concerned.

We saw Beerling as having a different agenda from us, and we tried to put a curse on him. The curse of Snibri. This came up when we went on honeymoon with our wives, although Peel hadn't yet married his at the time. We went down the Nile, great to see the mummies and pyramids. Peel, of course, went off with his missus to find a record shop. He had no idea what the records were, had to take them home to find out. We'd go up to people and ask, 'Excuse me, where is the temple or the bus depot?' and the locals would always answer, 'Ah, snibri, snibri.' So we started to talk to each other, just saying, 'Snibri, snibri.' Very politically incorrect. It could have meant anything. When we got back home there were even more free records in our pigeonholes than usual, and we started wondering who sends us these free records. We'd arrive every day, and get our free records, and then a few hours later we'd look again and there would be more free records. Where would they come from? We decided they all came from the God of Snibri.

I still have two packets of unopened records, they've still got brown card around them, and I don't know what they are, but they became the Ark of the Covenant, the Snides. Snibri had sent them to us, and they became holy. On these holy things we actually said, 'Oh Snibri, bring down your wrath upon Beerling.' The next day I went in, up to the management area, and said to one of the girls, 'Is Johnny in today?' She said,

'Oh no, he was getting off the train in Kent, and he slipped and twisted his ankle.' I told Peel, and we were apprehensive. It did seem to be working.

Matthew Bannister: The building itself, Egton House, was the least creative building of any place I've had the misfortune to work in. A horrible building, consisting of a rabbit warren of tiny offices, and people just shut away and quite unapproachable. In one of the first conversations I had with John Peel he said that the place operates like a series of Italian city states, and there were baronies within the place, and they never talked to each other; they all hated each other and did the best to undermine each other. That rabbit warren of offices was absolutely conducive to shutting yourself off and getting on with your own empire. It may also be, beneficially, one of the ways that people like John Peel and Andy Kershaw survived. If I ever had to go and see somebody, I'd have to knock on their door, find they were in the middle of a meeting, apologize and retreat, or make a formal appointment. There was no sense of wandering the floor and saying hello to people.

The extent of this came as a shock to me. I thought that this was the biggest radio station in the UK, probably in Europe, possibly the world. It had a long and proud record, at least for the first fifteen years of its existence, it's part of the BBC, and it was instantly clear to me that the sort of overhaul it needed was far greater than anyone outside it had recognized.

It had become separated from the rest of the BBC both physically and mentally, and it had been allowed to go its own way, because the BBC had never really understood Radio 1. It had developed a very powerful culture of its own, separate from the rest of the BBC – powerful because almost everybody who had worked there had almost always been promoted from within.

All the people had been there for many years. So there was a real inward-looking feel, and people's eyes had started to get a bit close together. It was quite a shock to encounter that, and to encounter the genuine hostility from the staff to some-body coming in from outside. And of course I was thirty-six, and some of the guys there were famously sound-mixing rock bands throughout the world when I was in short pants. Many people could see that it needed to change, but it had gone way beyond the need for just minor tweaking.

John Peel: When Radio 1 was established the whole idea was that the DJs would go on, as indeed a lot of them did, to become enormously well-known public figures. You were supposed to use Radio 1 as a device by which you could pro-cure a remunerative outside living – as a talk show host, or do a lot of voice-overs.

Radio 1 was regarded as something the BBC had to do just to supply pop music when the government closed down the pirates in 1967, but which it approached without a great deal of enthusiasm. In the early days, being controller of Radio 1 was by and large not seen as a terrifically significant job, but something you would drift into in the twilight of a rather undistinguished career.

When Radio 1 started it was genuinely regarded as rather unhealthy for presenters to show any interest in music, as it was believed that this would lay us open to unscrupulous promotions people offering fast cars and women. Of course these things never happened, but you did have to keep your interest in music very much to yourself.

John Peel *circa* 1969: 'You did have to keep your interest in music very much to yourself'

13

In earlier days there were times when senior management at Radio 1 seemed to be rather surprised that I walked upright and used knives and forks. I never saw my programmes as all that radical – more an alternative to what was on at other times of the day. It was perfectly all right to like what's going on in the charts, but there also exists this other area of activity which you may find interesting. But at one time I was regarded within the corridors of the BBC as being the Baader Meinhof Gang of British broadcasting, and treated with a certain amount of terror.

It used to be that we had a controller, name of Muggeridge, who was joint controller of Radio 1 and 2, quite a good idea. When the BBC was looking for the man to do this job they quite naturally chose someone who until that time had been head of the Chinese section of the BBC World Service. Once he had got the job he interviewed various DJs one after another, and I was last in. I think he thought I would do something unpredictable and startling, like rub heroin into the roots of his hair. He was sitting at his enormous desk, a sort of Dr Strangelove position. At some point in the conversation I mentioned public schools, and he brightened up a little at this idea, as if at some stage in my life I had actually met somebody who had been to a public school.

I said, 'Actually, I went to one myself.'

He went, 'Extraordinary! Which one?'

He was assuming it was some minor public school somewhere on the south coast. I said, 'Shrewsbury.'

He said, 'Good heavens!' At this stage he was getting quite elated. 'What house were you in?'

I told him, and he said, 'How's old Brookie?'

It was clear that he thought, Whatever he looks like, and whatever sort of unspeakable music he plays on the radio, he is still one of us. I think for a long time it was this factor that sustained me at the BBC.

Annie Nightingale (Disc Jockey): I came in in 1970 as the token woman. There was an incredible atmosphere of sexism, and for three years they resisted having a female DJ, until the outside pressure became too much. They ran it as a boys' club, and even when I started they were hugely intimidating, and I was very scared about making technical mistakes, playing a record at the wrong speed, when they would inevitably pounce and be terribly patronizing and think 'woman driver . . .'

For years I'd have to do clubs as a sort of DJ celebrity. So humiliating, being on after the Miss Wet Teeshirt contest. You had to give money away – fivers. At the end the manager would take you aside to pay you and say, 'Well we had so-and-so in last week, and he pulled in far more people than you did.' I'd bring my own records, and they'd say, 'Oh no, you don't need those, we've got the top twenty, all you need do is take this microphone and walk up and down the stage and give away money.' What was I? Not a comedian, not a music person, some weird hybrid. I did one with Leslie Grantham, where the audience were just screaming at him, 'I'll have your babies!' They would have done anything for a free teeshirt. Radio 1 DJs were a weird novelty.

Annie Nightingale:
'I'd survived a few
shake-ups before'

John Walters: In the 'fun days', entire Radio 1 series seemed to spring from an idea inspired by a sign that somebody might have seen coming to work on a bus. On one occasion I think what may have happened is that Doreen Davies [a senior Beerling lieutenant] sat up in bed with her curlers going pink, and she suddenly thought of the phrase Ticket to Ride. 'Hey!' she must have thought, 'We can do a show called Ticket to Ryde in the Isle of Wight . . . Ticket To Ryde . . . We can do a whole two-hour radio show on the ferry journey to Ryde . . . What a new idea.'

But my mother lived in Ryde, so I had to say to them that the ferry journey only lasted about twenty minutes, so there was no way you could get a radio programme out of it. Then she thought we could do one from a venue in Ryde. There was a competition to be in the audience – you had to write in a little essay saying why you wanted to be present and what you thought about Radio 1. I asked where it was being held, but they said, 'If we say where it is, there'll be a lot of unemployed yobbos turning up.' That summed it all up for me, their attitude to the audience.

There was that thing with the Christmas calendar. One year one particular producer was in charge of the calendar, and the novelty idea for the picture was for the DJs to be photographed with their idol. Others were being photographed with pop stars, and the obvious thing for Peel was to pick someone like Kenny Dalglish. But instead I thought it would be better for him to pose with a listener, because that was what he was about – man of the people. So the idea was to get people to write in, answer a simple question, like name the drummer with the Fall, and then if they were picked out of the hat they'd be on the calendar with John. I told this producer, and he said, 'I'll need to have a veto on it.' I said, 'No, it's just whoever we pick out, gets it.' He said, 'Ah no, it's a commercial calendar, man, I've got to be able to sell this damn thing.' I said, 'Well, the whole idea is that it's like the unknown soldier, but the unknown listener.' He went, 'Yes, but we might get somebody who's crippled or something.' That summed it up for us. Of course after that we were hoping that the God of Snibri would ensure the winner was an Asian woman with one leg from Dunfermline. It turned out it was a leather-clad kid whose whole family listened to the show. So it turned out all right.

Andy Kershaw (Disc Jockey): I've got a file called 'The Nation's Favourites', which is one of Radio 1's old slogans. I thought I might find you a copy of the Mandela memo in there. Somewhere here . . . Well, this is the legendary Dear Mr Madigan letter. Gary Davies had this feature called *Willie on the Plonker*, and this bloke took exception. It was found on the photocopier – you know that thing where you copy a thing and then walk away and leave it in there. It's from Doreen Davies, from March 1987. Doreen was famous for being Doreen.

Dear Mr Madigan
I am so sorry you find the piano character 'Willie on the Plonker' offensive. I can assure you it is meant as pure fun, and our programmes are not in any way planned to aggravate, offend or outrage any of our audience. I wonder if children really do think it is 'garbage' as you suggest. I do think in this case the suggestion of a smutty phrase is in the mind. It may surprise you to know that we literally get hundreds of letters each week asking Willie to play a particular tune on the piano.
   The piano is situated just outside Gary Davies's studio, and his producer, Paul Williams, to whom he refers, plays the piano each day. Paul Williams is a Cambridge University music graduate, and has three children, two daughters and a young son. You can believe me that in no way would Gary Davies or indeed Paul Williams set out to present the listener with any more than a bit of harmless fun. Radio 1 policy, generally speaking, is to make the audience feel a bit better, look at life lightheartedly and enjoy themselves whenever they switch on. Yours is the first letter of complaint I have received.

I completely go along with you when you suggest that the next stage generally and socially might be public copulation, but I don't think that Radio 1 can ever be blamed for contributing to this social trend, if it ever happens! . . .

May I just close by saying that Gary refers to 'Willie on the Plonker', he does not refer to 'Willie and the Plonker', nor 'Willie and his Plonker'. Willy has always been a nickname not only for male private parts but also for people with the surname of Williams, and I believe that if you start examining every common or garden nickname and look for further implications, the fun would really go from One . . .

It might further interest you to know that at the end of this month Gary Davies's producer is going on to another commitment, and Gary Davies's new producer's name is Martin Cox, and his name does not lend itself to any fun phrase, nor does Martin Cox play the piano, so in fact the 'Willie on the Plonker' spot will not be happening in the future.

Nicky Campbell (Disc Jockey): Doreen Davies brought me in from Capital, not really my ideal home. One day there I was told, 'Cut out the satire, do a link like "I was walking along Oxford Street today and all you girls are looking really sexy."' In those days, Doreen Davies was the head of music at Radio 1, an apparatchik who'd come up the ranks from being a secretary on the light programme, a chain-smoking wise old bird with a wig. When she took me on she said, 'I like your voice and I like what you say with it,' which I thought was a curious turn of phrase. In those days it was also important what I looked like, because I was quite sort of pretty, sort of boyish, and so I fitted the bill on all levels probably, with the extra added bonus of having a university degree, which they were beginning to find quite interesting. I think they were impressed with that.

My accent has never been exactly hard Gorbals – 'See you Jimmy!' – just sort of light Edinburgh, sort of Edinburgh Academy, same school as Magnus Magnusson. That sort of Celtic lilt is always seen as quite attractive. But I remember quite early on doing a covering stint on the breakfast show and the feedback I got back from management was that people in the North of England wouldn't understand what I was talking about, which is so offensive not only to me but also to the listeners, and also it showed you the kind of lowest common denominator that they believed was the way ahead. Every time DLT saw me, and Mike Read was the same, they used to say, 'Och aye the noo, it's a braw, moonlich nich the noo!' – extraordinary to have to deal with it.

I always thought Beerling was a bit like a second-hand car salesman. He never inspired me, I always felt quite uncomfortable in his presence. And I just think the whole way it was run in those days – with this power axis of Bates and whatever – it was bad and it was drifting, and the music policy was all over the place. Beerling used to have this thing in the studio – I don't think he really understood subtlety – it was 'One thought, one link', a big poster with this on. That was Beerling's philosophy – one thought, one link. 'Don't over-burden your links with too much thought' – it was like something out of the cultural revolution. Absolute bollocks. For some of the DJs in those days it was an intellectual challenge of Einsteinian proportions just to come up with one thought every link, but not for some of us.

Andy Kershaw: This Nelson Mandela memo from Johnny Beerling – isn't that remarkable? [*Reads*:] 'The official title of this event is Nelson Mandela – An International Tribute for a Free South Africa, but after discussions with John Wilson, Controller Editorial Policy, we have agreed that on air we will refer to it not by this title but under a variety of names, i.e. the international tribute to Nelson Mandela, the Nelson Mandela concert, a musical celebration for Nelson Mandela . . . I do not want any confusion between the rock'n'roll show business elements and the political nature of it.'

You've got a whole day's broadcasting and you can't once mention the fact or refer to the fact that he's been incarcerated for twenty years, and you can't make any reference to the fact that he's now free and what this means for South Africa.

The thing about Radio 1 then was that it was end-of-the-pier show and people knew that it was end-of-the-pier show. Now they think they're smart.

John Birt (Director-General): I took the main burden of talking to Britain's politicians, left and right. And it was commonplace at the time [1993] for a lot of people to have a different vision of the BBC, which was one of just having one television channel and two national radio networks – Radio 3 and Radio 4. At the time people were paying a £40 licence fee.

That was a sort of pure market failure version of the BBC. There were some powerful people in the Conservative Party who thought that the BBC was just too big, should be smaller, should leave most of these things to the market place, including Radio 1 and Radio 2.

Simon Bates: The idea of privatizing Radio 1 was always a myth, but you needed an excuse to change things. People believed it, and people were worried. Under Thatcher, people's backs at the BBC were against the wall constantly.

Realistically, how could it be privatized? The commercial stations wouldn't tolerate it because it would destroy the ethos of commercial broadcasting. A few people in the Tory Party might have thought about it as being a way of slapping the BBC around the back of the head, but what reason would there be for it logically? There isn't one. The only reason would be if Norman Tebbit felt like slapping the BBC across the face.

Secondly, how do you do it? You're talking about an act of parliament. And the furore it would cause . . . Most of the time, Thatcher attacking the BBC consisted of rattling cages.

But I could understand at the time why people were worried about it.

Johnny Beerling: I suppose I miss the team. Despite all the internal bickering we were a great team, we used to have an awful lot of fun, and it was fun to head a successful team. Now I believe that's gone, that today they're a sort of team of individuals all working on their separate programmes.

I've had very few dealings with Matthew Bannister, even in my last days. It's interesting that there's a new style of management that doesn't really want to owe anything to the past. If anything, it almost seems the past doesn't exist for them. I don't mind but . . . I think since I left, the number of conversations Matthew and I have had could be counted on the fingers of one hand.

Matthew Bannister: All I know is that Johnny decided to leave. He went to work at Unique Broadcasting, the independent production company co-founded by Noel Edmonds.

I didn't feel part of his world at all. Johnny was very helpful, and gave me all the files on people who worked there, and talked to me about the strengths and weaknesses of the team, but it was clear that my style was very different from his, and my views were extremely different. So there was a certain sense of, 'Well, thanks very much indeed, but I need to think about the future.'

Johnny Beerling was a man who had worked at Radio 1 for twenty-six years, ever since it began. An absolute fanatic about gadgets and technology, and lots of Psion organizers on his desk going off all the time. He came from an engineering background in the BBC, and you could see that this was a man who had pioneered major technical feats – the Simon Bates Round the World Challenge with satellite links from the Kalahari Desert, live shows from all over the world. One of his great things was the invention of the roadshow. He wore a blazer and slacks and a tie, and had his hair very neatly combed. He had a pink leather swivel-chair.

Johnny Beerling: I left on very happy terms with the BBC, no animosity at all, and I handed over to Matthew on 1 November 1993. It was the BPI Man of the Year dinner, I can't remember who was being honoured, but as it got to midnight I ceremoniously handed over the badge of office to Matthew, it was a bit of fun on the stage that night.

But my official send-off was at the Café Royal. I was on the fund-raising committee for Music Therapy and so they decided to take the opportunity of my leaving to organize a music business farewell, which was an excuse to raise more funds for Music Therapy and the Brit school, and I'm still a governor of the Brit school now. So they had sold tickets for this function which was a great night, all sorts of people turned up, it was a fairly alcoholic evening for me, as you can imagine. I mean, it was great to be honoured by so many people who turned up. It was just a hall full of people, and various acts came up and performed on stage. That was the night.

Simon Garfield: There was a special programme printed for the evening, with adverts and congratulations, reflecting his illustrious career at Radio 1. The programme mentioned how he produced the very first show, Tony Blackburn, on the new network – and had introduced a new style of documentary with his Beatles history, and had dreamt up the roadshow. There were personal tributes from those he had worked with, many of which talked about how he liked to go fishing. Tim Blackmore, a one-time colleague, spoke of how Beerling had helped guide Radio 1 'from the first jingle through to its position as the most comprehensive new music outlet in Britain'. John Peel also contributed a brief tribute: 'Well, I've always found him a good fuck.'

Several years later Beerling gave me a guided tour around the mementoes in his house in Rotherhithe.

Johnny Beerling: Being very promotional minded, we had had a relationship with the Red Arrows who'd done several displays at the Radio 1 Roadshow, so in this photograph we see the Red Arrows flying in a '1' formation, and they flew the length of the country from somewhere down near Bourne-mouth to up near Scotland on the day of Radio 1's twenty-fifth anniversary. Noel Edmonds flew in the lead aircraft and did excerpts into the breakfast show as he flew up. Noel loves flying anyway. So that's a really nice one, that was actually taken on the rehearsal which was a much better day than the day of the actual flight, which was one of those days when it was very foggy and low cloud. They came over here at Tower Bridge.

These here are all significant *Radio Times* covers of programmes that were commissioned during the time I was controller. Lennon, obviously. Abba. This was the Summer of '84 which was the precursor to Elton at Wembley, and the idea was that Noel Bush and John Reid put on a concert in the summer of '84 which was the year before Live Aid, and it was the first of the major concerts where we did the sound, and it went on all afternoon and we took it on radio, and Reid's company kept the TV rights to it and subsequently issued it as a video. This was the first tie-in we did on a major concert, there was a very good line-up. Somebody went sick at the last minute, maybe Paul Young, I can't remember. Good concert, though, great day, day like today with sunshine. Here are other interesting ones. Well, the Global Juke Box – Live Aid would be one of the highlights, where Radio 1 did the sound for the world, it was just an amazing experience.

This was a good one, Barry Humphries as a Radio 1 DJ, again I think that was part of the twenty-fifth anniversary. I talked Dame Edna into doing a special for us. This one's a spoof that was done when I left Radio 1. That's me. There's another one – Clapton, we took a number of the Clapton concerts in the Albert Hall, and we made a documentary about him.

This is what I call the BBC Memorial Bathroom. On the door of the toilet we have the first record ever played on Radio 1, presented by Radio and Record News on behalf of the record industry to mark ten years of Radio 1, 30 September 1977, and there it is – 'Flowers in the Rain' by the Move.

That's from 30 June 1990: Knebworth, the poster. This is an interesting one, from the *Star*: George Michael made the famous record 'I Want Your Sex', that was before 'Relax', no it was probably after 'Relax'. Because George Michael had a lot of pre-pubescent fans, the idea of little girls of ten and eleven singing 'I want your sex' over breakfast wasn't a particularly good idea, so I decided the record should only be played after 9 p.m., which attracted enormous fervour.

A photograph of Noel Edmonds and Harry Chapin – he was a huge supporter of world hunger and deprived children, and he would have been immensely proud of Live Aid had he lived. He was a great personal friend and I was really sad when he died, his records were played a lot, I suppose 'W.O.L.D.' was the best-known one.

Here's a cartoon which depicts Tony Blackburn in a box being exported to America outside the door of Radio 1. I inherited this. The caption underneath says, 'Stop struggling, Mr Blackburn, and think of this as helping your country's export drive.'

I did start the Radio 1 Roadshow with the idea that being a national station one of the problems of competition was always that the local stations were just that, local, and we were perceived as that station down there or up there in London, but the notion was to get the DJs out and about to meet their audience. Alan Coren got hold of this picture from *Punch* for me, it was the original artwork, in which he put the Pope on stage at the Radio 1 Roadshow, and changed our logo into a cross.

This is the 1988 album, Radio 1's twenty-fifth birthday album, and there's a gold disc commemorating that. A poster for another concert that we did. That's an interesting picture at the top – it's Leo Sayer with Terry Ellis and Chris Stone and Leo's wife, and that's at the Bottom Line in New York when he had a hit with . . . well, he hadn't got a hit then, it was 'When I Need Love' was out, that was a fantastic evening, I was there with Jonathan King, Bette Midler, Leo Sayer and Chris Ellis and we all went to the concert.

The one next to it is when I got an award for outstanding services to the music industry. Fluff and Nicky Horne, Tommy Vance, Jakki Brambles, Simon Bates, various other people and Status Quo who won't get played on Radio 1 now. I think they were a great band – they survived as long as I did, and they played on our twenty-fifth anniversary.

Some little toy cars . . . little roadshow trucks . . . a Trabant from Berlin, a U2 thing. A rather risqué poster there – 'Make sure you've got One on tonight' – meaning Radio 1, but also a condom. That miners photograph, well we used to do a series of promotional tours, by some coincidence about the time when a new commercial station was opening in order to take off some of the gloss and promote our network, and that was a week we did in the Leeds area, and we would do OBs from around the area but also play a charity football match or do some charity discos or fundraise for the Variety Club. So John Peel, Simon Bates and myself went down the Prince of Wales quarry.

And here we've got a montage done for my departure – 'Thirty-six years in the BBC' – a very young David Cassidy who I last saw on stage in New York in *Blood Brothers*, playing a Liverpudlian which is quite a change for him. I can't begin to recognize half of these people. There's Bates going off around the world, there's Fluff, and Mike Smith – that was probably on one of the royal weddings when we broadcast from the Mall. There's Peel when we went to Moscow and broadcast from Russia for the week, Moscow and Leningrad. That's Bates again, off on round the world. And there we are. And is that Michael Jackson? Yes it is.

These passes are all from gigs and forums and backstage passes and original logos. That's Jonathan Ross – he did a series of evening programmes for us.

We had our own thirty-year reunion in Bromley. Doreen Davies organized it. A very pleasant evening, no back-biting or anything. It was just nice to see some of the old guys. Travis turned up, Johnnie Walker, Paul Burnett, Mike Read. Bates unfortunately couldn't make it. A very pleasant evening.

Simon Mayo (Disc Jockey): I was invited but I didn't go, because I thought it would all become very sad and bitter. It would be an evening of 'Isn't it all shite now, look at the figures, I remember the old days . . . *Housewives' Choice, Our Tune* . . .'

Just as the Trotskyists like to rewrite history, the history of Radio 1 is rewritten according to who's telling it. The old stuff did need changing, but it wasn't all bad. If you watch old editions of *Fawlty Towers* they make jokes about black people – like the episode 'The Germans', when Sybil's in bed and Basil opens the door in her room and there's a big black doctor, and he recoils in horror. In the seventies that's what people did, that was acceptable, and Radio 1 was part of that. It's no use looking back now and saying, 'Isn't that terrible?' That's the way it was, you know. They did some great stuff. I don't like this idea of 'everything used to be terrible, and now it's all fine and on the button'. Radio 1 was always on the button. Traditionally it has always been part of youth culture. Yes, it did go off the boil and become Smashie and Nicey, but . . . beware the revisionists.

John Peel: The most appalling event in the Radio 1 year – and it required something pretty special to take that particular accolade – was always the Radio 1 DJ Christmas party, and in the way of these things it would take place in October. You'd have to go to one of the Broadcasting House council chambers. It would go on for hours, because they would record the entire thing, and because I was married and had children I would be asked the same question each year by Mike Read. It was, 'You've got a family, and how are you going to spend your Christmas?' I told him what we were going to do, and then they'd play 'Teenage Kicks', and then I'd go and get drunk.

Always the first thing that people did when they came into the room was look anxiously at the seating plan, and you could tell by the look on their faces whether they had found themselves anywhere in the vicinity of Simon Bates. General rejoicing, quite clearly, if they found that they were not.

On one occasion Kid Jensen, Paul Burnett and myself – not a carefully honed fighting team, but nevertheless filled with drink – we went down and waited in the underground carpark at the BBC for the opportunity to beat up Simon Bates. Fortunately he didn't turn up, or we might have suffered an embarrassing reverse, as he's probably stronger than us.

Chapter 2

The Weeping Truckdrivers

DLT: 'Radio is better than any drugs'

Steven Armstrong (Broadcasting Journalist): I remember a character in what I think was a Douglas Adams book, an American woman who comes to London, and the two things she notices most of all are that pizzas don't deliver – this was in the mid-eighties, before Domino's – and how bad the radio is here. She's listening to Radio 1 in her hotel room, and she's waiting for this comedy voice to stop talking and the DJ to return. But gradually it dawns on her – that was the DJ's normal voice.

I first listened to Radio 1 with my brother, taping the charts on Sunday evening. Recently I discovered a tape that I'd made at the time – Paul Nicholas's 'Grandma's Party' was in the charts. I have a mental picture of me and my brother crouching down holding a microphone to the radio speaker. We listened, of course, but Radio 1 in the eighties was just ridiculous. One incident that stands out was when there was all this tabloid furore about the Beastie Boys, and Simon Bates played a Run DMC track and then 'No Sleep 'til Brooklyn'. The impression he gave you was that he had done something that was so dangerous and so frightening, that it was tantamount to punching the prime minister.

All the daytime people were laughable characters, even Simon Mayo on the breakfast show. Gary Davies with all these terrible single-entendres about his boxer shorts and his bit in the middle . . . It was as if the radio had been taken over by the people who were the guides on Club 18–30. Dave Lee Travis – the self-named Hairy Cornflake – he physically made me choke when I heard his voice. He had this stupid snooker game – I can't find the words to describe it. In the early nineties I had a long argument with the programme controller at Piccadilly Radio in Manchester, who was convinced that Dave Lee Travis was the greatest presenter in British radio. I was stunned into silence.

Dave Lee Travis (Disc Jockey – on air, 23 August 1986): Today we have the final of the current tournament of *Give Us* *a Break*, snooker on the radio. Contestants from Bath, Romford, Sheffield and Droitwich Spa. We'll have the tranogram, the dreaded cringe of course at twelve o'clock, and two featured albums, the new one from Daryl Hall, and the recent classic from Kid Creole and de Coconuts. So keep it here, as somebody once said. We have three hours of mayhem for you! [*Plays Kid Creole.*]

['*Annie, I'm Not Your Daddy*' fades out.] Methinks he doth protest too much! To get it out the way, I've been away. Between last week's show and this week's show I thought I'd take the only opportunity I had for a break, and I went over to Corfu, which is a bad place to go in the middle of August when it's extremely hot and the hotels don't have air-conditioning. So for some reason I've got a bit of laryngitis and I do apologize for that. [*Plays a Eurythmics record.*] That's the Eurythmics. Even after all these years I can't help being amused by the name. The Eurythmics! Wonderful.

Now then, last week you may recall that we set you up with a special clue for a two-word tranogram, and we referred to the behaviour of one Bruno Brookes at Alton Towers, saying he was having a go on all the dodgy rides and everything, and that this could well be a good description of him. Two words. We played 'Rip It Up', 'It's Over', 'Sundown', 'Killer Queen', 'Johnny Be Good', 'Our House', 'Call Me', 'Kissing With Confidence', 'Eyes Without a Face' and 'You Might Need Somebody'. Put that all together, perfect description of Bruno Brookes – Risk Jockey. A Risk Jockey! Wasn't that brilliant? We loved it. The first three out the bag were Pat Butler from Alton in Hampshire – oh dear, I don't like the name of your road, Spittlehatch, you've got to move, Pat, you've got to move out of there! David Walsh from South Shore, Blackpool, that's a big address. And Sue Coe, from Leamington Spa. Prizes on the way to you.

Harry Enfield (Comedian): Smashie and Nicey are in my opinion the best characters Paul and I have done together . . .

It seemed odd to me that, although millions of people listened to Radio 1 every day, no comedian had ever taken off their DJs before us. It had always struck Paul and me that there were two main types of DJs – those who loved music like John Peel and Alan Freeman, and those who loved the sound of their own voices, like DLT.

Radio 1 also struck us as a funny old place because, in 1990, when we started doing the DJs, the whole youth culture was ultra-modern, with the take-off of dance music and fashion-conscious, music-based magazines like *Q*, but Radio 1 was still dominated by DJs with seventies haircuts and cuddly cardigans, whose idea of a good record was Rolf Harris's 'Tie Me Kangaroo Down'.

Steven Armstrong: The problem was that the majority of the country didn't have an alternative if you wanted to hear pop music. If you lived in London you were spoilt with Capital, but most people had the equivalent of what I had at college – the choice of Radio 1 or Red Dragon Radio. On the Red Dragon breakfast show they had a presenter who had a side-kick with a speeded-up voice which was supposed to be a dragon. Every twenty minutes there would be classified adverts, which meant people would call in on the phone and say, on air, 'I've got this chopper bike for sale for £100.'

Dave Lee Travis (1998): We're in such a ludicrous business. Show business is so stupid, it's full of people who are by definition pretty full of themselves. And that's the way I look at it sometimes, and I think, What is this, you know, why aren't I doing a more sensible job? I have to say this at the top of this interview because I just need to make clear my feelings about our business.

I've often thought, when I've got a bit depressed about it – everybody gets a bit depressed and they think, Oh God, it's been a bad week, or a friend has died and at the side of all this, what is radio? And the times I've questioned it and I've said, 'It is one of the most pathetic things in the world, to be on a radio, talking to people and making nonsensical jokes and playing music for a living.' And then I counterbalance that by having chatted to members of the public that I meet on the street and meeting people that have had a pretty ropey time, maybe been in hospital for long periods and things like that.

And I know it sounds very trite to say it, but you do actually get a feedback that in somebody's life who has got all bad news, radio actually is very important and it is better than any drugs from the chemist to make you feel better.

Smashie: Fab-four-tastic! That was the, err, Beatles, err – I love the Beatles, don't you? – with 'Eight Days a Week'.

Nicey: There's only seven days in a week, mate.

Smashie: Right, thanks, mate.

Nicey: Don't mention it.

Smashie: Erm, but I think you'll find that what the Beatles – I love the Beatles, don't you? – were saying –

Nicey: I don't care what the Beatles – I love the Beatles, don't you? – were saying, mate, there's only seven days in a week, never longer, never shorter. It's the law!

Smashie: Right!

Nicey: Right, starts on a Monday, goes through to a Sunday, with a Wednesday, Friday-type stuff in the middle, and the weekend on the end.

Smashie: I love the weekend, don't you, mate?

Nicey: Me too, mate.

Smashie: Right, well one thing I do know, is that err, today, is err, Tuesday which is quite literally, err – Tuesday.

Nicey: I love Tuesdays, don't you, mate?

Smashie: Certainly do, mate. It's one of the best between Monday- and Wednesday-type days we've got.

Nicey: It's the only between Monday- and Wednesday-type day we've got, mate. It may not have the glamour and excitement of a Saturday, or the mournfulness of a Monday morn, but it's our Tuesday, the good, old-fashioned, honest to goodness, down to earth, great British Tuesday, and if those Eurocrats, Bureaucrats and other Bonkerscrats try and take our Tuesday away from us, they'll have to get past me first. And if they think I'm gonna start me show by saying 'Bonjourno doodle-doo', and 'Guten Morgen, mongous', they've got another thing coming.

Smashie: I don't think they are gonna do that, mate. It'd be frogadobadabulously bonkers, mate. Because what makes a nation is not its borders or its monetary system, no, it's its radio stations, such as Radio Fab FM, and the people who work therein. Such as you, Nicey. You are what makes Britain great.

Dave Lee Travis: Well first of all, I had been doing, before the snooker, lots of mad games on the radio which didn't seem to fit, and perhaps that's why they were successful.

The snooker on the radio was the result of my producer at the time knowing that we both loved snooker, and he literally said to me one day, 'Why don't you play snooker on the radio?'

And I said, 'Oh yeah,' and I immediately . . . I didn't even have to think about that. I immediately had the sound effects of the balls dropping in the hole and clashing against each other and the ludicrousness of the whole situation so appealed to me that I sat down immediately and started to create the game.

The easy questions for one point for a red and . . . depending what colour you want, the questions got harder and harder. And it was just a stupid, stupid idea. And looking at it now, people always remember it, which is great.

Simon Garfield: I met him in his studio at Chiltern FM, in Dunstable. A huge, affable man in jeans and jumper, he said he was still getting over the laryngitis that had recently kept him off the air. He didn't work for Chiltern FM, he explained, but used their studio as it was a short drive from his house. He was now the mid-morning jockey for Classic Gold, an all-hits station that reached all over the home counties, and beyond.

On the way to his studio he chatted to producers and assistants who treated him with respect. He passed a woman eating lunch at her desk, and reached over her shoulder to put one of his large hands in her crisp packet. They were beef flavour. 'Not ideal for a vegetarian,' he remarked.

Simon Bates: I have to say, whatever Dave had in comparison with me, bottle it, because he was immensely popular. He was the most popular breakfast show, far more popular than Chris Evans ever was. Beerling came in on one Monday morning and said, 'I don't fucking believe this – yesterday Travis talked about his local fire brigade for half an hour without playing a record.' I said, 'What are you going to do?' He said, 'Nothing. He's popular.'

Beerling was not a slave to figures, but he was aware of the power of them, especially when he got up in front of the board of governors. He was able to offer the figures as a panacea, just as now the music and the attitude is offered as a panacea.

With a few notable exceptions – Blackburn, Travis, Noel Edmonds on a Sunday morning – the rest of us were B-grade. But we worked very hard to bring stuff in that made up for our lack of whatever we were.

Dave Lee Travis (on air, 23 August 1986): Thirteen and a half minutes after ten, and if you've just joined us, you're in time to settle back in a favourite chair and listen to some other poor so-and-so being put through it, through the grinder. Today is the grand final of the current tournament of *Give Us a Break*.

DLT: Hello, Linda?

Linda: Hello?

DLT: Helloooo! How are you?

Linda: Fine thanks. And you?

DLT: Hey . . . not so bad.

Linda: Good.

DLT: Not so bad. Now Linda, you're from Lower Weston in Bath.

Linda: That's right.

DLT: Your last break was nineteen.

Linda: Uh-huh.

DLT: It's come to me on the grapevine that, you know, every now and then there's a hero?

Linda: Yuh.

DLT: You know, whether it's some film star or something like that? The hero of the moment it seems that everyone's worried about is the contestant who's on last, Elaine Harding the teacher, because she got forty-eight last week.

Linda: Yuh. Huh-huh.

DLT: And it seems that everybody at the moment is trying to get on the next bus to Droitwich Spa in Worcestershire to sort her out. And pay her off or something. However, as you know, on the day the bottle can go, and a person who's previously had incredible scores could only have one. Mentioning no teachers and no accountants, of course.

Linda: That's right.

DLT: Linda, are you ready to do battle?

Linda: Yes.

DLT: Okay, darling. Now this is the final, and it's no different from any other game, except that if you lose you lose a fantastic prize and go home shamefaced – no, I'm teasing. I'm teasing. Just treat it like a normal game. I'll always give you some extra time. The first answer's the only one I can accept, so please think. All right?

Linda: Right.

DLT: Are you sitting down?

Linda: Yeah.

DLT: All right, here we go. Which singer wrote the song 'Happy Birthday' as a tribute to Martin Luther King?

Linda: Stevie Wonder.

DLT [*after sound-effect of snooker ball being hit into a pocket*]: Stevie Wonder is right for one point, and it's your choice of colour.

Linda: Brown, please.

DLT: Brown. Good starting-point for a final. Worth four points. What is measured on the Beaufort scale? The Beaufort scale. What is measured . . . on that?

Linda: Is it wind?

DLT: It could be [*ball hits pocket*]. See? No jokes from me. Keeping it clean. Right, which guitarist co-wrote the award-winning music for the recent BBC thriller *The Edge of Darkness*?

Linda: Eric Clapton.

DLT: [*Crack!*] Eric Clapton is right. And a colour, please, Linda.

Linda: Brown again, please.

DLT: Another brown. Who was Jon Voight's co-star in the film *Midnight Cowboy*?

Linda: Oh . . . *Midnight Cowboy*. Err . . .

DLT: Think carefully. You've probably seen the film as well, haven't you?

Linda: Yeah, it was the same one as in the other film – Dustin Hoffman.

DLT: [*Crack!*] I had terrible, terrible visions of you saying, 'Oh, wasn't he the guy who got dressed up as woman, I know his name . . .' Oh, I couldn't have handled that . . . Which group had hits in the sixties with 'Daydream Believer' and 'Last Train to Clarksville'?

Linda: The Monkees.

DLT: Yeah, I believe they're back together again, aren't they, or something?

Linda: Yeah, they're supposed to be.

DLT: Oh gawd. I don't think I could handle the Monkees again. Nice as they are, and I love Davy Jones, an old mate from Manchester . . .

[*The quiz continues for several minutes, as Linda answers correctly many more times. Finally, she is stumped by which two oceans meet near the Cape of Good Hope?*]

DLT: I need an answer from you, darling. This is the final. Name me two oceans!

Linda: Is it the Atlantic?

DLT: That's one correct. The next one better be right.

Linda: . . . and the Pacific.

DLT: [*Sound effect goes Whack Whack Oops.*] No, it's the Indian. Are you still with us? You did very well . . . 5, 10, 16, 17, 22, 23, 28, 33, yuh, that's a good score – are you fairly happy with that?

Linda: Not really.

DLT: How many did you want, then?

Linda: Sixty-seven.

Trevor Dann (Former Producer, now Head of BBC Music Entertainment): Travis did the breakfast show for four years, taking over from Noel. The Hairy Cornflake and all that bollocks. They took him off in the early eighties and put Mike Read on, and they put DLT on the *Afternoon Show*. I found myself producing him for about nine months. DLT was very much Jimmy Savile's era – old school, the music very secondary. Quite hard work, really. He needed to reposition himself, because in those days if you'd done *Breakfast* and you got taken off it, you were on the way out big-time.

I thought that the one thing we could do was to make him into somebody who had some choice in music. My greatest achievement with Travis was making a hit out of 'Once in a Lifetime' by Talking Heads, originally only an album track. In those days you could play what you liked, because for eighteen months there was no playlist at all. So my thing was playing lots of Tom Petty and the other hip people of the day, and saying, 'Let's not play Shakin' Stevens doing "Green Door".' Our other hit was Tony Capstick doing the Hovis advert – you know, 'T'lads had diphtheria . . .'

So we kind of bonded, and he put me on the air – early zoo bollocks. I was billed as Captain Audio, and I had to stand behind him a lot and talk shit and go 'Whooosh!'

After that, I'm not sure it ever really worked for him again. I think he just felt the world overtaking him. That final speech when he left was classic DLT. One of the reasons he got taken off the breakfast show was because he did this great rant about whaling. He had a very high idea of what he could achieve because he was Dave Lee Travis. He was used to having been a very big star. It became like a footballer going downhill. He knew what it was like playing at Wembley, and now he's lucky to turn out for Stevenage.

Did you see him turn up on *House Party* recently? That would have taken a lot of courage. He was really down on

Noel – they used to josh about, but they really didn't like each other. He always felt that Noel got better treatment than he did. And DLT and Simon Bates . . . these were clashes of absolutely monstrous egos.

Dave Lee Travis: There was one morning when I got a severe bollocking from the boss because I'd spent a considerable amount of time on the breakfast show talking about seal culling. I was so incensed about it that day, and there happened to be a page advert in every single daily newspaper. I just said, 'Most of you are having your breakfast now, and if you feel you might be put off by what I'm about to say, please turn the radio down for a few minutes . . .'

I was talking about the fact that these seals were being culled and then having their skin ripped off them and some of them were still alive when it happened and all . . . And I got so mad about this and I said, 'Instead of just getting annoyed now and, like a traffic accident, feeling strongly about it, slowing down, and then ten minutes later you've forgotten about it and you're getting on with your life, well I don't want you to forget about it. If you have any newspaper in your house, there's a piece of paper looking for your signature, saying, "We don't want to do this any more." Now don't think about it, just do it.' I got severely taken to task about that, and I remember being told that I was nearly taken off the air.

You had to use your powers wisely. If a DJ who you identify with says the same thing as a newsreader, from a DJ it means a little more. That item has come from a disc jockey, a friend in the home who plays your kind of music, so you sit up and take a bit more notice. Anybody who'd listen to me at Radio 1 would probably laugh their heads off and say, 'Oh he got on his soap box a few times.' Yes I did, but we're only talking three or four occasions in the entire time I was there.

There was the seals, and then there was nurses. I came out and saw nurses on strike and I was really pissed off that nurses had to be put in the position where they actually had to walk around with placards. And I got on my high horse about that. I always remember, I saw a wonderful sign one of the nurses was holding up and it was almost the centrepiece of what I was saying that day. She was outside a hospital with a big sign above her which said, 'If we don't work, you don't work.' And I thought that was a great thing, like the standard-bearing slogan for all nurses.

Johnny Beerling: He already knew that if he talked to the press about how he really felt about the BBC I would have no alternative but to fire him, and he did. He came in one day and said, 'I've done it now,' and I said, 'What have you done?' and he said, 'I've given an interview to the *Sun* in which I've told them what I think about the changes here.' I said, 'Well, you know in that case I've got no alternative but to take you off,' and Dave and I never fell out about it, he could understand I was doing my job, and he did what he had to do.

He'd been to see John Birt and he'd been to see Frances Line, who was then the controller of Radio 2, and he knew full well that the sort of music he was playing and the style of presentation he was doing didn't really fit with the way in which Radio 1 was changing, albeit gradually. He would have happily gone to Radio 2 but the controller of Radio 2 didn't want him, and that sort of led to the outburst and all the rest of it, and I think it's all very sad.

Dave Lee Travis: The fault that Radio 1 had running through it was that as it got older it was bringing the audience with it. Now I say that's a fault, but if you put as much money as you want into a station now to make it do what Radio 1 did almost by accident, it could not be achieved.

The mid-sixties was the right time for a national radio station with big name people to develop. The problem came twenty years after that when the same people are still there. The same people were doing a good job, they hadn't lost touch with anybody, but the problem was that they dragged these listeners, who were then sixteen, with them, and they were now thirty-six.

And this is not done, you don't do this in radio these days – you either go for the kids or you go for the old folks, and you can't possibly entertain all of them. But that was the uniqueness of Radio 1.

I and many other people at the BBC were of the opinion that this couldn't go on. You know, you'd have to draw the line somewhere. I was always in agreement with the fact that Radio 1 eventually would become a teeny-bop station, but that somewhere along the line the people on it would, like the Simon Bates and the Mike Reads and the Paul Burnetts and myself, would actually just move a notch into almost Radio 1-and-a-half.

And remember that I had this from the horse's mouth. I'd been in to see John Birt and other people and asked them what the plan was for Radio 1, where was it going to go. And I was told, in no uncertain terms, that Radio 1 was going to go for the audience up to twenty-five. And that Radio 2 would go for, I think it was forty-fives upwards.

And I said, 'What about the audience in between twenty-five and forty-five, which is actually the biggest core audience of any radio network? This was at the time when Virgin Radio came in and started aiming for that crowd.

And I just felt that the BBC policy was the biggest nonsensical attitude, having built up this incredible reputation . . . just to throw it away . . . to actually say to your audience, 'We don't want you.'

John Birt: The thing that most struck me was to learn that the average age of the Radio 1 audience was thirty-one years old. And the vision was of a network which had been under very effective management over a long period of time, with a very strong culture of its own, but it was a group of people that had grown old together. And I remember at the time, I think it was just after George Carey had been appointed Archbishop of

Canterbury, joking that we need more DJs on Radio 1 who are younger than the Prime Minister, the Archbishop of Canterbury and the Director-General of the BBC. I was forty-seven at the time. Smashie and Nicey undoubtedly overstated the problem, but there was more than a grain of truth in it. So it wasn't a question of changing the tradition, it was reinterpreting it and being clearer what our target audience was.

Dave Lee Travis: I didn't think I was going to resign on air. I thought, My time has come, I've got to go, I can't take any more of this. I would have done it the normal route, but one day I snapped on air and thought, No, tell the listeners before I tell anybody else, then at least they'll remember it was me that told them and they won't get any false reports from the papers.

But only this week I read a piece about Matthew Bannister who was responsible for firing Dave Lee Travis . . . Five million people heard me resign live on the radio, and they still think I was fired. I was out of that building before Matthew ever got near it.

What happened was, Johnny did say, 'Oh that was a bit dicey, that, but you know what, with a bit of damage limitation . . . we'd better leave it alone, don't say any more, don't go public with it any more and we'll be all right.' And I said, 'You'll be lucky.'

On air I kept it down to approximately one minute. But then the whole thing just exploded and the press all piled up outside Egton House that day. Having done what I did on air I thought, Well, what the hell, let's get to the press and talk it through. Because everybody was hounding me every day.

At that point, though, I was assuming that I might have carried on to the end of my contract, but I didn't. I came off air straight away. So sad really, after twenty-seven years there, I didn't even have a chance to say goodbye properly on the radio. That is probably one regret I have. Just for the listeners.

Matthew Bannister: I was in Minorca in August, the summer of 1993, and I went to the paper shop in this little town, and on the front of the *Sun* it says, 'DLT quits Radio 1 on air.' There was a double-page spread, 'Why I hate the BBC bosses', by DLT. I had been appointed controller, but I hadn't taken over officially yet – Johnny Beerling was still in charge. I felt quite relieved that I didn't have to manage the situation, obviously a difficult one. I had given no hint of what I wanted to do, but of course the debate about Radio 1's future had been going on for quite a long time before I arrived, and clearly that left the station in a state of some flux. The atmosphere was not one of 'Radio 1's in great shape – please take over and carry it on to greater triumphs.' But even though it was clear that change was going to happen, nobody had articulated that the changes would involve DLT, least of all me. To this day I've never met DLT.

Jo Whiley (Disc Jockey): When I joined, the revolution hadn't quite started yet. My producer also used to produce Dave Lee Travis, so when I was practising at the beginning I used to borrow DLT's headphones. I used to go home reeking of Dave Lee Travis's cologne. It was like I had taken Dave to bed with me – horrible, distasteful. After his shock resignation it was very exciting. It was like, who's going to go next?

I'd pass Simon Bates in the corridor, but to him I could have been the cleaner. Once I came in on a Saturday afternoon to practise, and I was thinking, These are the world-famous Radio 1 studios . . . and I looked across from my studio to another, and Fluff Freeman was doing his rock show, and he looked over and said, 'All right, Jo?' I thought, God, he knows who I am. He was the only person there who was vaguely friendly. Everyone seemed terrified their whole world was going to collapse.

Kevin Greening (Disc Jockey): When I arrived at the end of 1993 quite a few of the old guard were still around, and I was regarded with deep suspicion. I had the advantage that I was fairly unknown, not like Danny Baker coming in and facing this hostile reception, but it was still very uncomfortable. It didn't feel like any radio station I had been in. The programme teams were laws unto themselves, to the extent that, because the music was handpicked, producers would deliberately schedule listener-unfriendly records at the end of their shows to dent the inherited audiences of the show that followed. And the only way that some producers talked to their DJs was through their agents.

The turns were artistes. I sat in for Simon Mayo on midmorning for a few days, and whenever I was in his seat, I could feel this record box between my legs with records and papers in it, and I had to kick it out of the way before I could get in my seat and start the show. Then every day at about ten to ten someone I didn't recognize would come into the studio and silently take the record box from the studio and walk out again. I didn't understand what was going on, but then it became clear that it was Bruno Brookes's box, and it was deemed unsuitable for him to carry his own box from the studio – too much of a chore, so an assistant had to do it for him.

Dave Lee Travis: Remember that I was in an office with a bunch of girls, the secretaries for the shows, that worked their nuts off to help the DJs get it right. There were production values there that were very good and the whole team at Radio 1 was a team – yes, of course you get an old family feel when you've been there a long time together. And even prior to the big changes, parts of our family got pruned off. The accountants moved in and said, 'We can do this cheaper.'

If you ask me, you should stick accountants on an island somewhere and let them rot and we'd have had good showbusiness. The ability to juggle figures in the way that accountants do and the ability to be entertaining do not go hand in hand.

There was a growing resentment and anger in lots of people who were not in a position to say anything for fear of losing their jobs. And that is a very, very large part, no matter what anybody else tells you, a very large part of the reason that I said on air that there are, and I quote, 'There are things going on at the BBC that I just cannot agree with,' and I didn't have any option but to leave because I couldn't do anything about it. That staff were being walked over, and they couldn't speak for themselves, and I thought, No, this is fucking ridiculous, this is outrageous, I'm not . . . Everybody just lets these things happen and I'm not the sort of person that can do that, and I will not sit by while somebody quietly chops my hands off.

Andy Parfitt (then Chief Assistant to the Controller): He thought it was very much like that wonderful broadcaster in India, Mark Tully, which I thought was the laugh of the century. You know, he told people, 'I believe, that under John Birt's BBC there is no room for creative talent such as myself, and I'm joining John Tusa and Mark Tully in quitting . . .' The arrogance of the man!

Dave Lee Travis: What a lot of people were desperate to do was to see somebody in the popular music segment of the BBC actually do this and say, 'This is a load of bollocks.' Nobody had said that before. You know that great broadcaster Mark Tully? What had happened was Mark Tully had done this from the far end of the spectrum where nary a Radio 1 listener would dare to tread. 'Who's Mark Tully?' they'd probably say. But there's Mark Tully, this amazing journalist who has stood like a rock for so many years, and he'd done this himself. He was talking about the BBC going mad, and just imploding. And now they have the other end of the spectrum. They've got Mark Tully here and right at the other end is Dave Lee Travis. The press thinks, 'Now there must be a story.'

I do not put myself in anything like the class of someone like Mark Tully. Totally different side of the business. But now there's DLT at one end, Mark Tully at the other, there must be something wrong if both these people who are from totally different backgrounds are saying the same thing.

And I guess that's why it became so big and I only thought about that later, that it must have been the Mark Tully thing.

Simon Bates: After we left, it was a mistake to say about us old turns, 'They were crap.' The simplest message that should have gone out was, 'It was great for the time.' Because actually, that's all it was. A lot of it was very poor, a lot of it was filling in for rather inadequate music, a lot of it was shambolic, but it worked for the time.

Dave enjoyed that classic Radio 1 circus thing – the roadshow, the parties, the Playboy club and all that crap – he enjoyed it, but I was a hundred years old and hated it.

Simon Garfield: Simon Bates told me his main home was in Buckinghamshire, where he had a farm and liked to stud horses. But I saw him in his little flat around the corner from Broadcasting House. 'This place is really a crash pad,' he said. 'I would love to tell you that I take drugs and bring horny young women here on a regular basis, but I never do. I was always too bright to take drugs, and horny young women were never very interested in me, for some reason.'

These days he had a morning show on Liberty, and filed regular pieces for ABC television in America. He took some persuading to talk about his life as a turn, but after a while it was clear he was really quite enjoying it.

Simon Bates: All turns are barking mad. You can't employ larger-than-life people and then be surprised by what they do. So first of all you take the knives away from them before they come in the building. One Radio 1 DJ about two years ago used to carry a gun.

What is the one thing that all performers and all writers are? They're paranoid. Your commitment to your own standards is all you have. You do care that you don't fuck up. So the nicest thing in the world is when someone comes along and says, 'I think you're terrific at what you do.' The nicest thing in the world. You go home and hug yourself with delight. So if you tell a turn that they were terrific, it makes them feel loved.

With Matthew Bannister it was only right that a new controller wants to change things. The old controller is worn out, and the old turns are worn out. Be it Melvyn Bragg or Simon Bates, worn out. But what you mustn't do is forget to tell your audience that you're still going to be there for them.

On my old time slot, nine to twelve, you could have put a coffee cup on that programme and you'd still have an audience. It's basically music-based, just really playing records. But you bugger around with it at your peril.

Simon Garfield: He spoke a little about *Our Tune*, the sappy, raw, compulsive, maudlin true-life letters he read out in the middle of the morning as the love theme from *Romeo and Juliet* jerked tears in the background. Management tended to hate the slot, he said, regarding it as too down-market, but listeners jammed the switchboards whenever it didn't appear. Occasionally he would receive letters from people who were ready to kill themselves, but most had a redemptive quality: coming to terms with a lost love, or a rash decision, or a troubled sexuality. He didn't choose the letters himself, he said – that was his producer's job. But he read them in such a way that made you care about people you never met, and like DLT before him, he hoped he made listeners feel a little less alone.

Other listeners, of course, just saw the item as sentimental hackwork, something that defined the station's condescension and vanity.

Simon Bates: Frankly, I'd been there two or three years too long. I wasn't powerful, but I was very loud. Being loud got you things, an extra bit of budget. I was old even then, and could hardly be considered a hip, groovy thing, so there was a great deal of work to be done to make up for that. I did have a lot of ideas, some of them flamboyantly and extravagantly stupid. We did a programme about World War II bombers. It's a very romantic thing, and I'm a great believer that stories are what radio is all about. We did this, and it went well, won a Sony award or something. The next thing I did with my producer was go over to the Somme, and we came back with all sorts of ideas for programmes that were fantastically unsuit-

Simon Bates:
'Horny young women were
never very interested'

able for Radio 1. We went into Beerling's office moist with excitement trying to sell this idea. It was to be twenty-six parts, huge budget – it was virtually a rerun of the First World War. Beerling did sit there quietly for about twenty minutes while we explained this idea, which for him was a pretty good attention span. Then he looked at me and said, 'You must be fucking out of your mind!'

Running a gossip network? I may have appeared to, but I expect that was just a perception from those who didn't know me at all. The truth is, there were two or three cliques. You need to talk to Lycett about that. There was a lot of jealousy about because it was perceived that I was doing what I wanted, but this wasn't true at all.

Nicky Campbell: In those days a couple of people used to poison the well a bit, just because it was the age of the DJ as sort of huge star and they were raking it in with lucrative supermarket openings and maybe four figures just for an hour in a nightclub. They might do three or four appearances a week and then come in for their shows knackered. They were very bitchy, and I remember being slagged off on air by both Steve Wright and Simon Bates, because they'd got something into their head about me, I can't remember what. In their perception I probably got big for my boots, and I probably did, but everyone sort of goes through a little phase when they become successful when they become a pain in the arse.

They'd slag you off on the air and make jokes, and you go to Johnny Beerling and say, 'Could you do something about this?', and nothing was ever done because these guys had such power bases and they were seen as the be-all and the utter end-all. It doesn't actually rankle me at all – I like Steve Wright, and if I saw Bates in the street I'd chat to him at a superficial level and it would be fine. I suppose it's like a rite of passage, a bit like being in a public school. They were sixth formers and we were like first years. So they'd pick on people, and then it would change and they'd pick on someone else, Mayo or someone. At the time you thought, Well this is what it's like, this is how it should be.

Chris Lycett (Executive Producer): I produced Simon Bates in the early eighties. The point about Bates was that he had so much energy and so much enthusiasm for radio that he was, in that sense, a pleasure to work with. Barely a day would go past without him coming up with some feature we should be doing, generally journalistic. He was always a bit of a frustrated journalist. Of course, the bad side of him was, certainly towards the end and through most of my relationship with him, that he was megalomanic and became totally uncontrollable. I suppose because he succeeded a lot and had a very good reputation within the industry. The point was, Bates did deliver. If you think of some of the major events he got involved in – when he went around the world, even in those days real ground-breaking stuff.

He's a very, very forceful character, and we had our rows, and he was always very headstrong. Latterly, in his last two years, he was in freefall in terms of making decisions, coming up with programme ideas with very little consideration of the network or whether or not he'd got permission to do them. He was literally out on a wire. A shame, because I still think he is a very good broadcaster. But at times he was an absolute monster. He came out of an era in which DJs really were the biggest thing, the nearest I've ever come to working with pop stars.

Simon Bates: About ten years ago I went around the world with a guy called Jonathon Ruffle, my producer. Today technologically you could do it standing on your head, but back then broadcasting from the Kalahari was a bit difficult. There was huge resentment that we were doing this. People realized that the reason I was doing it was because I didn't want to do the roadshow. I would literally go to the far ends of the earth to avoid it. The roadshow then – you ended up doing an hour and a half on air, but you had to do two weeks of slogging around the seaside wearing stupid costumes. And going round the world was good fun – shagging about on BBC time and money. But the trick was maintaining audiences, keeping things running as a soap opera.

I was seventeen years at Radio 1. I have no interest in looking back on those days – what on earth for? The advantage of populist radio is that it's gone the next minute.

Matthew Bannister: We'd been getting our plans together in which Bates didn't feature, but we hadn't spoken to him about it. I think it was Beerling's plan to move him to weekends, but I didn't want that.

I suddenly got a phonecall from the press office saying, 'It's running on this news agency that Simon Bates is leaving.' So I went into his studio, something he described in his book, painting me as a 'florid red-faced fat bloke' or something, so I went into his studio and said, 'Could you come and see me after the show to talk about this story that's running on the news agency?' So he came in after the show, and I said, 'Look, I'm happy for you to go, and you don't feature in my plans for the future, but can we manage this sensibly?'

He said, 'Don't tell me that, luvvy, I've got to go out there and talk to the press. There's already a story running. You don't know how to deal with these things.'

I said, 'What we could do is get a cab from the other exit from Egton House, where the press are not gathered, and then you won't have to talk to them, and you can go home and think about this.'

'Don't be so silly, luvvy. I've got to talk to my public. I am a journalist – I know how to handle these things.'

So I said, 'Well, off you go, but I do think it would be better for the BBC and all of us if this was an amicable parting. I'm very happy to say that you're leaving to pursue your other interests, providing you're happy to say that this is an amicable split.' I think he broadly did, in the end, but he wouldn't exit without talking to the press, and he was then pursued by them down the street to his flat around the corner, which of course is what he wanted.

So that was my first taste of press manipulation. The news agency had been given the story in order to precipitate the press interest so that he could go out with a bang and a lot of glory. He wanted to leave before he was pushed, and in a very public way, but without telling me in case I stopped him.

I also then said, 'Okay, if you talk to the press briefly in the street will you then please not do any other interviews?' only to then find that he was on breakfast television the next morning.

So that was my first taste of the behaviour of these people, as people who did not keep to their word and deal with things in a mutually agreed way, but as people who pursued their own interests, and made sure that they used the press to come out of it with as much of their career intact as possible. This was quite hard to deal with.

You see, I couldn't say anything. If I had said, 'Well, he was never in my plans anyway,' I would have got into a very public row with him. And since he was far more famous than me, and far more manipulative with the press than I was prepared to be, I didn't see any mileage in that.

John Peel: You have to say he was a remarkable man. I was always given to understand that when Bates launched into *Our Tune* it was when the station had its biggest audience of the day. At eleven in the morning every layby on every major road in the country was full of weeping truckdrivers.

Chapter 3

Round at Chris's and his Missus

Matthew Bannister: 'He was an actor, that was his thing'

Matthew Bannister: You could say my Radio 1 career began with *Newsbeat*. I read the news on most of the DJ's shows – on DLT's show, on Simon Bates's show, on Gary Davies's show, breakfast show, late nights, weekends. When I began, which was 1983, Mike Smith kindly took me round and introduced me to the other DJs, but I had very little contact with the big names. *Newsbeat* was very much a sub-editor's programme, taking material from BBC correspondents around the world and taking stories out of the papers and turning them into audio that would fit the style of the station, as opposed to in the style of *Today* or *PM*. I made something of a fool of myself by doing the funny stories at the end – forced puns and that nonsense.

I did some budget stuff live with Steve Wright on his show, and I did a piece live into the Simon Bates show when Michael Jackson came to unveil his waxwork at Madame Tussaud's. I was doing live inserts as Michael drove up in his limo, and talking to the great crowds of people in Marylebone Road. As he arrived I was live on air, and I went in the wake of him and his bodyguard, and carried on talking, and suddenly found myself in the lift with them as the doors were closing. Very quietly I said, 'Simon, I'm in the lift with Michael Jackson, I better hand back to you,' because this guard was looking at me in a very menacing way. Michael Jackson was then shown around backstage, where there was a waxwork of Paul McCartney. They had only just done 'Ebony and Ivory' together. I said to him, 'Michael, what do you think of the bust of Paul?' He said, 'Well I . . .', and then two guys picked me up and threw me out into the street.

I went through Heathrow with Duran Duran at the height of their fame and got into their limo with them with the fans banging on the sides. I did a lot of pop interviews – Limahl, a very long interview with Paddy McAloon.

I was born in Sheffield. My parents were middle-class. My father was a research chemist in British Steel, and my mother was a physiotherapist. I'm the eldest of three brothers. I grew up entirely in Sheffield, I lived there for eighteen years until I went off to university in Nottingham. The first memories of music I have are two. My father is a real music fan, principally classical but also jazz, so in the house there was always music being played. He was a great fan of Frank Sinatra, Ella Fitzgerald, Cole Porter. He used to take me to see the Hallé Orchestra on Friday night at Sheffield City Hall. He had a season ticket.

I quite enjoyed it. I was a choirboy, and I had been selected by my school to join the Sheffield Cathedral Choir when I was still at primary school, and I used to go five times a week. It was very important to me. I also learned the violin, which I didn't enjoy very much, but I got to enjoy later in life. There was always radio around as well, as my father was an enormous fan of radio comedy which he used to tape on a reel-to-reel – the Goons and Hancock, the *Navy Lark*, Jimmy Clitheroe. I adored them, and I associate them very warmly with my childhood. He was a big speech radio fan – listened to the light programme, and then what became Radio 4, before the big revolution in broadcasting occurred in 1967, when Radio 1 was launched, and each station had a new identity and number.

I was later getting into pop music than most, I think because I was the eldest, so there wasn't anyone bringing it into the house. I was ten when Radio 1 was launched, but it made little impact in my life until I was fourteen or fifteen. I missed the Beatles entirely, first time round. My first concert was Jethro Tull doing *Thick as a Brick*, the concept album, all the way through. Lindisfarne were very important to me. I saw them at Sheffield city hall supported by Genesis, with Peter Gabriel dressed as a fox in a dress, being booed off. I roadied for some friends in a band, and very quickly my interests switched to David Bowie, the Velvet Underground and Roxy Music. I was asked recently what was the best rock single of the last thirty years, and it took me some time to come to an answer, but now I think I would say 'Virginia Plain', one of the most perfect and inventive singles, and it never was on the album, but it was later on the CD.

Then I began to enjoy playing the violin, and putting a pick-up on it, and getting into a folk-rock band which was much influenced by Dave Swarbrick and Fairport Convention and Richard Thompson. We used to play various local folk clubs, and we had terrible rows with the purists who were finger-in-the-ear types, and they hated us using amplification. We were called Hobb, I've no idea why. Radio Sheffield invited us to do three tracks for their folk programme. Quite a big thing in our lives, at seventeen, and it was produced by John Leonard, who later went on to produce Mark Radcliffe. I also played in an electric string quartet. We used to have a drummer, and our songs used to begin with a few bars of Bach, and then go into 'Honky Tonk Women' by the Rolling Stones. You can make quite a lot of noise. It was run by a man who was a park keeper in his spare time.

With radio my obsession was mostly speech, and I remember an Apollo moon mission, the one that got into trouble, and I used my father's tape recorder to tape news bulletins, getting up at seven o'clock to track the progress of this mission, and then put together a sort of programme.

I went to read law at Nottingham. I thought I should do something useful, where you'd get a job at the end of it. I think I was drawn towards the drama of law – the barristers I'd seen on television. I had interviews at Oxford and Cambridge, but failed to get a place there, but Nottingham turned out to be a wonderful campus and an exciting time. There was a very thriving dramatic society. It quickly became apparent that law was not for me. I spent an awful lot of time in the theatre, directing in my second year, which I was better at than acting. My productions were always very populist, compared to my colleagues who were doing Brecht. I did *The Importance of Being Earnest* and *My Fair Lady* with a cast of seven.

I used to listen to Radio Trent, which had Kid Jensen on it, and friends of mine in London brought up tapes of *Your*

Mother Wouldn't Like It with the DJ Nicky Horne on Capital. He played the kinds of records that I liked, album tracks, Van Morrison. Punk really passed me by, and passed Nottingham by, although there was this court case which involved Richard Branson being sued for displaying the *Never Mind the Bollocks* album in the Virgin store in Nottingham. He was defended by John Mortimer, and one of the professors at the university gave evidence in support of Richard, and we were all excited about that.

The show that really engaged me at Radio 1 was the Noel Edmonds Sunday morning show, which was very inventive and created an imaginary world, wind-up phonecalls, like nothing I'd ever heard before. It was clearly highly produced, although I didn't know what that meant at the time. It had things like John Gielgud reading *The Railway Children* and Brian Perkins reading the news.

But Radio 1 was not highly regarded, not an integral part of a student's life. You would tune in to John Peel from time to time, but mostly it was the station of Gary Glitter and Bay City Rollers, not what you listened to when you went back to your student bedsit.

I applied for a course in theatre directing at Cardiff, but before I'd got a grant I had a drink with a friend who'd gone on to be a sports reporter at Radio Nottingham. He said he was really enjoying it, so I wrote to Radio Nottingham saying, 'I'm a bright lad and I'm really interested in you.' I read them up in the *Radio Times*. I had an interview, and then in one week I received a letter from the local authority offering me a grant of £985 a year to study theatre directing in Cardiff, and a letter from Radio Nottingham offering me a contract at £3,000 a year to work as a kind of freelance reporter/dogsbody. The filthy lucre won out. Also, I could see something exciting about receiving a letter with the BBC logo on it. That was a proper job. That was an institution.

I was taking over the job previously done by a guy called Trevor Dann, who was promoted to become a full-time producer. The first interview I did was with a woman from Alaska who had come to see the mayor. I had to ask her what she thought of Nottingham. In the evenings I helped out on Trevor Dann's rock show, filling out forms for him, showing guests up from reception. Strangely exciting.

Trevor Dann: I taught him how to work the Uher, the little portable tape machine, and one of the first things he did was help me make a documentary about Trowell service station on the M1. It's the one in Nottinghamshire near Junction 27, and we were doing 'A day in the life of a motorway service station', a classic, and he came out and helped, very much the new boy. He was an actor, that was his thing. I think that the key to Matthew is that he is an actor and a lawyer, and he doesn't like me saying that he's the new Rumpole of the Bailey but he's got that kind of John Mortimer thing about him. He read law but he spent most of his time working for the drama society. When I met him he lived in a student flat with a gay actor called Crispin – I don't think he lived *with* him, but they lived in the same property – and so Matthew was a kind of, as he is now, fantastically articulate advocate who also loved getting pissed and behaving like an actor, and it's those two sides of him that you can still see in him now. He's a creative bloke, but he's also a corporate politician and a lawyer, and those two ingredients have come together to form a pretty potent mixture.

For a long time we were chums, seriously good friends. I was older than him and I think he kind of looked up to me a bit, because by this time I was on the air doing a daily show, and was a bit of a local cheese. I liked him – he was so funny and he was really good company, and frankly in a local radio station in the seventies, you didn't meet a lot of people who liked Frank Zappa and had ever read a book, and so we had a lot in common. We saw a bit less of each other when he became a news man. He never had any journalistic training but he just went from being this general reporter figure to doing more news interviews, and then became the presenter of the breakfast show, which he was well qualified to do as he had a really good voice.

Matthew Bannister: I was the main presenter on an all-speech programme, linking the tapes and the interviews, pretty young at twenty-two. Up at five in the morning, and then sleeping in the afternoons.

I got a job at Capital, as a reporter. On my first day a bomb went off in Oxford Street, killing a bomb disposal expert, and everyone else in the office was out on other assignments so they sent me. I didn't know where Oxford Street was. I managed to get some eyewitnesses on tape and interviewed a police chief, and then I couldn't find my way back to Euston Tower. I fell on the air, breathless. I'm sure it was a dreadful piece of broadcasting.

I began to see the possibilities of using sound. I've never been a great writer, I've done sketches, but not much prose. Capital was a rude awakening – pop radio, fast, brash, London, and the editor throws things at you and says, 'That's shit, do it again.' All very exhilarating – about being taught to write a very complex story in four sentences, like tabloid journalism.

It was on Capital that I was heard by the editor of *Newsbeat* who asked me in to do a voice test.

Everything seemed to happen in three-year cycles, so I began *Newsbeat* in 1983, and three years later I found myself back at Capital, where a friend was made head of news and talks and I became his deputy, and I became the presenter on *The Way It Is*. We wanted to change all the rules – not to lead on items because we thought they were important, but to lead with things that we thought the audience would be interested in – a different policy from the BBC. We did serious things, like gun control in London after the Tottenham riots, but also things about how many willies there were on London statues. It had very terrible puns, and big jingles blasting off all over the place, and it was perhaps the greatest fun I've had in my life.

I like changing things, and I like having new ideas. What I find more difficult is maintaining it once you've got the thing running. The reason my career moved in three-year cycles – because I suspect that's how long it takes to go in, change something and get it established. Then you get a bit bored and start to look around for something else. So I saw a job in the paper for Managing Editor, Radio London, which then became GLR. Radio London was not particularly good, in a bit of a mess.

Trevor Dann: When he first came to London, Matthew needed somewhere to stay. At the time I was working with Richard Skinner, because Skinner was presenting *Round Table* and I was producing it, and Skinner had bought a house in Shepherd's Bush and he needed someone to house-share, so I put him in touch with Matthew, and Matthew and Skinner shared this place in Shepherd's Bush for a while. There were legendary young-men-on-the-raz stories, none of which you'll drag out of me while the machine's on. When he went back to Capital I went to television, at which point he then got married, and we didn't see each other for an assortment of reasons. And then the next time I saw him was about '87, I literally bumped into him in Stoke Newington when I was buying

Trevor Dann:
'Matthew's career and mine prove that losing audience is no bar to progress'

a car and he was going to the bank. At that point he had a beard. We had a cup of tea and forgot all about it until, at the beginning of 1988, the twentieth anniversary of Radio Nottingham, we were both separately invited to a party.

There were two parties, one in Nottingham, one in the upstairs room of the Yorkshire Grey down here, and he and I went up to Nottingham on the train together, and I'm sure at that point I was saying, 'I'm having a bloody rotten time working in television because Janet Street Porter wants to get rid of us all.' When we met again at the Yorkshire Grey do, he took me on one side and said, 'Look, I've got an idea: you know Radio London is being revamped and they want to change it and they're looking for a new manager . . .' And I said, 'No.' He said, 'Well, I've had a word and I think I might be in for it. I know you're a bit fed up with telly, why don't you and I do this together? I'll wear the suits, you pick the records.' We just spent the evening cooking up this idea. Now, of course, I'm tempted to feel I was rowed into the frame because he needed me, but at that point I thought, Oh this is nice, this is us as old chums, kind of putting the show back on the road.

We launched in October '88. We were going up against the big budgets of Capital and Radio 1, and all we really had was ingenuity. Now, of course, when you look back on it you think, We didn't do too badly, really. On the weekends we had Danny Baker, Chris Morris and Chris Evans – you wouldn't be able to put that together now for less than several million pounds, and we had them all for £25K a year, each of them. I think Danny was a bit more than that, but none of them got any serious money, they were all £100 a show maximum.

The first person we hired was Emma Freud, Matthew's idea. At the time she'd got a bit of press because she was doing interviews in bed with people on some late night show. This was before Paula Yates started doing interviews in bed with people at breakfast. Matthew thought she represented the sort of person that we needed, and he and I had lunch with her in the canteen at LWT, and offered her a show. She said, 'I'd have no idea how to do it.' But we talked her into it – a real risk.

We put an advert in the paper for producers. One applicant was a guy called John Revell who'd come from Virgin Retail – he'd set up Virgin's in-store radio. And the other one was a guy who used to work on Piccadilly in Manchester, and then produced Jonathan Ross on Radio Radio, Richard Branson's evening sustaining service for independent local radio, a guy called Chris Evans. So Revell came in for an interview and did his turn, and two or three candidates later Evans arrived, and at the end of the interview Matthew said to Chris, 'I've seen that tie somewhere before, haven't I?' Evans said, 'Yes, it's Revell's tie, I borrowed it. I didn't realize you had to wear a tie for the BBC.' His application form had all the standard things on the front, and then on the back you flip it over and it has a little space which says, 'Please add any other personal information you consider relevant.' He wrote something like, 'I know I'm the ideal person for this job for the following reasons: 1 I have Neil Ferris's home phone number [a leading record industry promotions man]' . . . and I can't remember what 2 was, but 3 was 'Pressure is my middle name – see over.' And you turned it back again and he'd written his full name out as Christopher Pressure Evans. And that was his thing, a very likeable young man. Evans went on to produce Emma. Emma had a really natural ability, but the show definitely benefited by being produced by Evans. One reason he's a great presenter is because he understands producing. Nobody actually produces Chris, he does it himself. In those days he wouldn't go on the air. He used to say, 'I'm not ready yet.'

Matthew Bannister: Chris and Emma had very stupid ideas. They had a character called Tone, that was simply a piece of tone that spoke to the listeners, and a competition called 'Name That Pope', where they had got out a history book and read out facts about a pope and you had to ring in to say if it was Pius V or John III, or whatever, and nobody ever got it right.

Then he went on to produce Danny Baker when Danny started on the weekend breakfast show, and that combination was electric. They were in love with Michaela Strachan on a Saturday morning children's show, and they used to watch it when they were on the radio. There was one warm morning when the show was coming from outside Camden Lock, and Danny said, 'Wow, get your televisions on, Michaela's looking fantastic this morning. Wouldn't it be great if someone walked up behind Michaela with a big sign saying "Listen to Danny Baker on GLR", so ring up now and volunteer.' I actually got out of bed and turned on my television to watch this happen. They found a volunteer, and on the air Danny said, 'Nothing's happened yet, nothing's happened yet . . . but there he is!' And someone walked by with a huge sign – absolutely wonderful.

Trevor Dann: Chris felt it was time to go on the air in 1990. He did Saturday afternoons in the summer for a short run, and once he'd started he was keen to keep going. We then put him on weekday evenings to do a show called *The Greenhouse*, which was meant to have some kind of environmental vibe to it. He'd surround himself with plants in the studio, and send all the eco issues up terribly. He then moved to weekends and did Saturday mornings, and for a while he did Sunday mornings as well, before he finally departed altogether and went to the *Big Breakfast*. I think he was great from the off. I count myself really fortunate to have been around him at that point, he was just brilliant, he was George Best, he was . . . every idea he had . . . well, it wasn't that every idea was good, it was that he had so many brilliant ideas that you could choose from such a huge range. The fact that he was unknown was a very potent thing: he could ring up Michael Parkinson or Ernie Wise or the Chancellor of the Exchequer and be a cheeky young man with them, which was very endearing. He could also talk about himself, a bloke who lived in a flat whose plumbing didn't work and whose car broke down.

Matthew Bannister: *The Greenhouse* was a kids' show which always got us into trouble because he used to encourage kids to come on and say who the worst teacher in their school was, and why. People still talk of the weekend shows with great affection. He had *Round at Chris's and his Missus,* and this thing where he would just encourage everyone to shout 'Billy!' at each other in the car.

This was some contrast to how things had been. When I took over it had an all-speech breakfast show, like the *Today* programme but with no resources, followed by Tony Blackburn playing soul music and talking about his Big Twelve Incher and talking dirty to women on the air. Followed by a woman who was playing sort of soul music but was very very very sub-Radio 2. Followed by Mike Sparrow doing *Sparrow over London.* Followed every night by *Black Londoners.* On Friday nights there was *Charlie's Rural Rides,* in which a man with a beard talked to you about the countryside and boy scouts.

Initially with Tony Blackburn I thought, Well, we've only got one star on this station, maybe for a short time he could still be something. But shortly after my appointment had been announced he said that he was off to Capital Gold, which was just being set up. He had a three-month notice period.

On my first day he made some comment about the news bulletin, and I went to see him and I warned him about this. I checked his contract and the previous managing editor had put a really bizarre clause in there which said something like, 'You shall not use your programme as a platform for your personal views on foxhunting or plugging your appearance as a pantomime dame or any other matter of this kind.'

So we said, 'Well, if he does this again, this will be in breach of his contract.' The very next day there was a news item about Sam McClusky, the seamen's union leader who was involved in an industrial dispute on the south coast on the ferries, and Blackburn said something to the effect of, 'Isn't it amazing how all trade union leaders are fat Scottish gits.'

So I just called him in after the programme and said, 'I'm terribly sorry, you've done your last programme now, you must clear your desk and go now because this is getting beyond a joke and it's going to get us into trouble.' Tony went off in high dudgeon.

Within a year we had an entirely new staff. The idea was to do a fifty-fifty speech and music mix for twenty-five to forty-five year olds. But we had to do it on a shoestring – a total budget annually of £1.8 million for eighteen hours a day broadcasting, perhaps the size of Capital's marketing budget. With our marketing budget we could afford a car sticker.

The plan was to fill a hole in the provision for people in London by targeting twenty-five to forty-five year olds, with a fifty-fifty music to speech ratio. We played a lot of music that never gets heard on the radio. One of the great moments was bumping into Richard Thompson in the corridor when he'd come in to play live in the mid-morning show.

And the speech conveyed the excitement of living in London and would reflect alternative comedy, restaurants, theatres, clubs. The whole thing was to be a three-year experiment, and it would be reviewed by the BBC governors to see if it had worked. Shortly before the review was due, I tried to influence the outcome by inviting members of the board of governors round to see the station. When Baroness James visited I had to tell Chris Evans not to skateboard down the corridor with only his underpants on, which was something that he liked to do.

But we passed the test, the governors approved. I'd been there about three years, and I began to think, Well, I ought to do something else now, we've done this.

Wherever two or three people are gathered together who were at GLR during that period, they reminisce through rose-tinted spectacles about how wonderful it was because there was this sense of a lot of young talented people against the world. And the audience was fanatical. When Trevor and I used to go on air and receive calls from the listeners in one of the BBC's accountability drives, everyone used to think we'd fixed it because it was like a love-in.

Trevor Dann: I always say in speeches that we took over Radio London's pathetic 10 per cent and turned it into an enormous 6 per cent – a triumph. Frankly, Matthew's career and mine prove that losing audience is no bar to progress. GLR is highly thought of by the people who like it, and is respected and pretty well thought of by the BBC, but it was not a popular idea and we were quite simply wrong – we thought if you put together a kind of slightly more mature, grown-up version of Capital with a music policy that assumes that people don't want disposable pop, they want Bruce Springsteen and the Rolling Stones and Van Morrison, because that's what all the audience research always says, you'd then clean up. But actually you end up falling down a bit of a hole between the two, and gradually as more niche stations emerged that were either all music or all speech, we didn't quite hit it right.

If there's a point at which he and I began to fall out, it would be because after he left in 1991 it very much became 'Trevor's radio station', because insofar as there was any credit in the industry it became mine. He once sat with me in the back of a car and said something like, 'It's hard for me to say this, but actually it's better now I've left.' And it was actually, it was better. I think I'm a better scheduler than he is, but what I couldn't do was fight the BBC, and Matthew had kept the BBC at bay.

Matthew Bannister: After about three years, I saw this advert for a job charmingly entitled Chief Assistant to the Director of Corporate Affairs. It said the BBC was about to undertake a thorough review of all its activities in preparation for the debate about the renewal of its charter, and they wanted somebody to co-ordinate that review.

It emerged that this was going to be a radical, nothing ruled in, nothing ruled out, blue-skies review of the BBC. They wanted somebody with a completely open mind who was not saying, 'Under no circumstances must you touch X or Y or Z,' and I made it clear that when I've gone anywhere I've always wanted to change it. And improve it, I hope.

We set up fifteen groups who were largely looking at areas they didn't work in, again to help the sense of radicalism. And it was my job to organize the timetable, working with McKinsey consultants to be the interface between the BBC culture and the consultants' culture. It ended up with the publication of *Extending Choice*, the document we wrote to begin the debate with the government about the renewal of the BBC's charter: what was the role of the BBC in the next ten years? Do we still need a BBC? If so, what should it do?

We discussed everything, including the role of Radio 1, although one of the frustrating things about being a chief assistant in the BBC is that you're party to an enormous number of very high-powered conversations, but your contribution is pretty low key.

This was followed by the programme strategy review led by Alan Yentob and Liz Forgan, and again I was the co-ordinator.

John Birt: I'd noted GLR as a great programming success – obviously a real entrepreneur at work there, spotting talent. You always noticed that. Then he came to the centre . . . I worked closely with him on the *Extending Choice*, he was a masterful strategist, and a very accomplished manager of a large project. So you note that down.

Matthew Bannister: Getting my job at Radio 1 was an attempt to turn the philosophical argument into reality, into real, creative discussions with programme makers. And ultimately change the station dramatically. Of course, I would have liked to have believed that it would have been a smoother ride, rather than the true nature of the change, which soon turned into a bit of a nightmare.

John Birt: When we came to appoint Matthew, we never said, 'You've got to improve the number of people listening.'

Chapter 4

Bruno Brookes Was Feeling Very Tempted

Johnny Beerling and Bruno Brookes:
'The *News of the World* are pushing cheques through his letterbox'

Kevin Greening: Prior to Matthew's arrival it's wrong to say that the station had run out of steam – it was still doing 19 million listeners' worth of business. There was Smashie and Nicey and other detractors, but after dark it also had the *Evening Session* and John Peel and was experimenting with new comedy. If you wanted to listen to cutting edge music in this country, where else could you turn in the early nineties? – certainly not Capital Radio, and there was no Kiss yet. Pasture FM in Countryshire would play a U2 record and regard it as the outer edge of their playlist envelope. Very few people were going round thinking, Radio 1 is a big fat dinosaur and needs to be changed. It used to be the BBC's job to be everything, and Radio 1 was like BBC1 – popular mass entertainment. At the time you didn't open the *Sun* and see Gary Bushell writing 'Radio 1 has had its day.' In fact the opposite happened – as soon as Matthew came it was 'Bannister is tearing up our well-loved radio station.'

Annie Nightingale: It was a terrifying and painful time, everyone frightened for their jobs, producers as well as DJs. No one was talking to each other. I'd survived a few shake-ups before, but this was on a very different level, approaching hysteria.

John Peel: Matthew has always been very kind to me, and said that as long as he's controller there will always be a John Peel programme to delight the nation's youth. Unfortunately, he said the same thing to Johnnie Walker, and he departed Radio 1 only a few months afterwards.

Matthew Bannister: The important thing was to consolidate a management team, and to separate commissioning from production. The team I started with was Chris Lycett, Paul Robinson, who now runs Talk Radio and was doing the music policy, and Andy Parfitt, who I made into editor. He endeared himself to me the first time I had lunch with him by getting a piece of paper and saying, 'I want to show you how Radio 1 is really organized – here's the organizational chart.'

He just drew a huge mass of squiggles on a sheet of paper, like a plate of spaghetti. So we set about trying to sort it out.

Andy Parfitt: I came to Radio 1 in order to make a career change for myself, to learn about administration and management, and I was going to leave it relatively quickly after I joined, because I didn't feel there was any appetite for change at all.

Under Johnny Beerling I was asked to look at the budget and make cuts. There was a contingency fund for keeping DJs when Virgin launched – if any of our DJs were approached by Virgin offering big money we would be able to counter them. But this money was just sloshing around. Any attempt to put sums of money to better use was . . . I was just ignored. The place was atrophied. I remember in my first week getting an e-mail saying, 'Why don't you fuck off to Radio 4 where you belong?', signed Anonymous. That came from the shop floor, because of the way I spoke, because of my background, because it was well known that those people who came to work as chief assistant were ponces from the BBC who didn't understand anything about music.

There were some good people at Radio 1, but until Matthew arrived no one had combined such a voracious appetite for change and the ability to bring it about.

Matthew Bannister: We decided to talk to people away from the station, either in my old office in Broadcasting House, or the White House Hotel up at Regent's Park, where we hired a small room. I then called in all these people to 'discuss their futures'. Clearly some people were capable of making the change, and some clearly needed to move on. It would have been lovely to have had more time, but we had to do something about the weekends now that DLT had gone, and that meant moving several people around almost immediately. We also had a hell of a lot of people's contracts coming up for renewal. Or not.

Annie Nightingale: I was given a stand-in job for two weeks, the old Mark Radcliffe slot between ten and midnight. I knew Matthew was taking over, and I thought that he'd be listening, so I stayed in the office until four in the morning programming next day's show. I'd make sure that the people I interviewed would be damn interesting – I had the editor of the *Big Issue* on and Robert Rodriguez, the director of *El Mariachi*.

I had worked with Matthew at GLR. We used to go down the pub, but when he left he became a more distant figure. I had to go to this room in Broadcasting House to see him, I was sworn to secrecy, not allowed to tell anyone where I was going, everyone very nervous of leaks. He said, 'I've been listening to what you've been doing over the last two weeks and I loved it. I'd like you to do . . .'

Then shortly afterwards someone called up to say, 'I've just seen your face on breakfast TV with a great red cross over it,' running with a story that I was one of the people who was being sacked. Matthew apologized to us all afterwards: 'I'm sorry I put you all through this.'

Matthew Bannister: We would either have had to sign DJs up for at least twelve months because of the stature of some of these people, or let them go. And some of the big names were demanding a deal for two years.

Any schedule reshuffle at Radio 1 is a matter of playing three-dimensional chess in the dark with your hands tied behind your back, because you move one bit, and then everything falls over. One person comes out of my office and tells someone that they've got a new slot, but the person they're telling is in that slot at the moment and doesn't know if they've also got a new slot or are being fired. So you have to do the whole thing really fast, and you have to plan even the smallest schedule change in absolutely the right sequence, so that hermetically sealed pockets of it can be concluded without upsetting people. People who are being promoted come in first, then people who are being demoted come in afterwards. But even then you have to see the promoted ones in the right order, because they're the ones who are most likely to spread rumours.

Also, if someone says no to a move, it upsets everything.

Nicky Campbell: I was reasonably confident myself because everything that Bannister was saying Radio 1 had to be and all the noises being made about the future direction of the station seemed to be in line with what I was already doing. But Matthew is a man who keeps his cards close to his chest, he can say a lot without saying anything, a very skilful politician.

Matthew Bannister: It was an extremely stressful and difficult few days. I met so much resistance early on that I became quite adrift from most of the staff. Given my time again, I would have changed the production people before I changed the front of house. Given a year, I would have liked to have got in some new production people with fresh ideas – people who could support the new DJs we were going to bring in. As it happened, we had to get rid of the DJs because they were all about to explode anyway.

But there were also some wonderful moments, like telling Steve Lamacq and Jo Whiley that I wanted them to present the *Evening Session*, because they'd only been on a few weeks' trial. But some terrible moments too – breaking the news to Bob Harris and others that they were no longer going to be in.

People were upset, of course, and you would expect that. Nicky Campbell in particular was not pleased and didn't want to move to where I wanted him. I wanted to offer him the weekend breakfast show, because he was good, and I didn't want to lose him.

Nicky Campbell: I told him I wasn't available. I was doing a current affairs show for Central Television, and I didn't fancy getting back in the early hours and getting up in the early hours. Also, at the time my now ex-wife was ill, so I was spending a lot of time with her. I had to be with her at home at night, because she had trouble sleeping. Matthew was then backed into a corner, because he had got everything else worked out and I was ruining his jigsaw puzzle.

I rang Gary Davies and said, 'I've been offered your job.' Gary's not a very exciting individual but a perfectly well-meaning chap. He then went to Matthew and said, 'I've heard rumours that my job has been offered to someone else.'

I wanted to do something later on a Saturday and Sunday – the ten to one slot, DLT's old show and potentially a huge audience. What I do would have been good there.

Matthew was holding out for Danny Baker to do that show, but there was a glitch, so Matthew then called me up and offered it to me on a three-month contract. I said, 'Oh yeah – just until you get a contract with someone else sorted out. Go fuck yourself.' And I put the phone down.

And then Danny Baker did it, an unqualified disaster.

Matthew makes mistakes but it's good that he's able to recognize them. Very quickly, to his credit, he saw that I was probably a loss to the station in some way, so within a couple of weeks he said, 'I want you to come back and do drivetime in a few months.' He said that there had been a right fuck-up and he had made a mistake. Maybe it was a case of so many people saying, 'What's Nicky Campbell not there for? We can understand Gary Davies not being there or Bruno Brookes not being there, but Nicky Campbell is surely what we should be about.'

Rhys Hughes (Producer): When I was told that my first job would be producing Campbell, my initial reaction was, 'Oh shit.' The problem with Nicky's image was doing the bloody *Wheel of Fortune* – a lot of people thought, Oh yeah – that bloke who does that quiz show on the telly. There was a problem in that people said they didn't like him, but they'd never listen to him – an element of him being old school, but we did try to reinvent him a little bit. He can be very funny with his one-liners, but would then sometimes ruin them by ramming the point home for another thirty seconds. We worked reasonably hard on the interviews as well. He thinks he's the world's greatest interviewer, but he can go on for half an hour, so he needed to be tighter, and to be told when he had to shut up, and that the interview was about the person he was interviewing and not necessarily about Campbell.

Matthew Bannister: All the DJs were manoeuvring themselves, and whispering, 'What I'd really like to do is da da da.' And I got a bit paranoid – I was pretty nervous of everybody.

I met Danny Baker secretly in a health club at the Meridian Hotel one morning while he was still on Radio 5, and asked him to join me. With presenters I knew I would go to them direct, and then they'd hand you over to the agent who would then play hardball about the amount of money and holidays. You have to get DJs excited about the creative proposition first.

I took Steve Wright to breakfast at the Savoy Hotel, because I was told that this was what he liked to do. It had always been my ambition to get Steve Wright on the breakfast show. Simon Mayo had done it for nearly five years, and he was getting really knackered and saying, 'You've got to get me off, you've got to get me off.'

So at the Savoy I asked Steve to do the breakfast show, and fortunately he wanted to do it. But he didn't want to do it immediately, so we put Mark Goodier on the breakfast show for three months until he was ready. That seemed like the logical thing to do, because Steve had the highest audience share of anybody on the network, and he was a highly respected and loved Radio 1 broadcaster of invention. And normally in a radio station you put your most inventive, most loved broadcaster on at breakfast.

I announced the first changes at a news conference in the council chamber of Broadcasting House, in front of a large number of very hungry journalists. I had to be very careful how we phrased most of it, as at this stage people like Gary Davies were still on and Bruno Brookes was still on and Jakki Brambles was still on, and I was reluctant to give any guarantees to anyone. You could see the journalists going, 'Great story – night of the long knives at Radio 1 . . .', but at that stage I wasn't seen as anything other than this new bloke getting a grip on the station and it was mostly neutral coverage, with big pictures of the new DJs gathered at the famous steps of All Saints Church like all their predecessors had done. The hostility towards me hadn't really gathered pace.

We made a lot of mistakes because we were establishing too many new shows, and I was terribly aware of the pressure to emphasize Radio 1's distinctiveness from commercial radio. The charter renewal discussions with the government were at a crucial stage, and the political agenda encroached into what should have been entirely creative decisions. We allowed far too much speech, and we allowed far too much indiscipline because we didn't have production teams which were behind us to keep these DJs under control. Danny Baker's music policy was never under control, and Danny was very headstrong about what he wanted to play.

That was the biggest culture shock for the audience – to go from DLT and snooker and darts on the radio and the Top Twenty, to Danny Baker and Danny Kelly talking about weird trivia and playing very esoteric album tracks. I remember going to do an interview on *Live and Kicking* on the first Saturday that Danny was on, and sitting in the dressing room at Television Centre waiting to go on to be quizzed by a lot of ten-year-olds, and listening to Danny doing something completely extraordinary on the air which Radio 1 listeners had never heard the like of, and which I thought was very interesting, and very GLR. Sadly, it clearly also had GLR's limited appeal. I persevered with it for a long time, because I thought it was a piece of broadcasting that the BBC ought to be doing, but it was certainly not the kind of broadcasting that was going to appeal to the middle-of-the-road Radio 1 millions who had grown up with the Hairy Cornflake.

Simon Garfield: The listening figures were catastrophic. Every month Bannister and his team would receive a detailed break-down of the audience figures for each show from Radio Joint Audience Research Ltd (Rajar), the body that analysed audience trends for both BBC and commercial radio from a survey of about 20,000 listeners. Before Bannister took over there was already evidence of a slight drop in numbers, caused by the launch of Virgin Radio and other, local, competitors. But what happened now alarmed everyone at the station.

In June 1993, two months before Dave Lee Travis left, Radio 1 had 19.23 million listeners. In November 1993, one month after Bannister introduced his first schedule changes, the figure was 16.86 million. The following month it was 16.06 million. One month later it was 14.84, a loss of almost 4.5 million listeners in seven months. (These figures reflected Radio 1's average weekly reach for listeners aged four and over, where listening implies being in the audience for at least fifteen minutes. The figures for its audience aged fifteen plus were almost as devastating, falling from 16.42 million in June 1993 to 12.87 million seven months later.)

The newspapers didn't see the monthly breakdowns, but they did receive quarterly figures, and they enjoyed them.

Matthew Wright (Showbusiness Reporter for the *Sun, Today* and now the *Mirror*): The strange thing about fading DJs is that the stardom seems to stay in their heads and egos for longer than it may do in other areas of the entertainment profession. In some senses the same was true of the press. I was on the *Sun* when the big purge happened, and we regarded it as an absolute outrage. All the recognizable faces, with their cuddly image, were being swept away. The attitude was: Matthew Bannister is axing the greatest DJs the country has ever known. It seems ludicrous looking back on it now, because people like DLT were so obviously dinosaurs, but at the time it seemed that Radio 1 was signing everybody that Matthew Bannister had met in the Groucho Club.

And that went on to become 'Sliding Down the Bannister', which was the *Sun*'s story, almost a campaign, about how bad the figures were since Matthew took over, and about how many mistakes he'd made. [The accompanying cartoon superimposed the controller's head on a figure heading for a painful collision at the foot of a staircase.] I think it came a bit late. Most of the bloodletting had been done by then.

There was resentment that someone was deliberately trendifying and Sohoizing Radio 1 rather than actually making it the people's station. It's easy to forget that there's millions of people up North in factories who listen to it from the moment they get to work all the way through the day. How are they going relate to Ms Freud? Not very well, judging from the length of time she lasted.

Matthew Bannister: It takes about a year to establish a new radio show, and to establish a new radio show under the press spotlight that we were under, and with production teams who had no idea what I was trying to do and were resistant to it, was extraordinarily difficult. I was certainly prepared to stick to my guns for six months, to see whether this was going to work, and there needed to be an enormous amount of constant badgering and cajoling to get my opinions across, but I did come to the view after a few months that some of these things were not going to work.

Emma Freud was particularly unhappy. I brought her in because she worked well on GLR, she was intelligent, young, funny and I thought she had things to offer. But she was treated very badly by some people at the station, especially other women. She had only come after some persuasion by me, and she stuck her neck out only to be harangued by people who seemed to be jealous of her. Danny had had the foresight to bring his producers with him from Radio 5, to much controversy internally, which meant that he was at least protected by people who knew his world. Whereas Emma was working with people who resented her, and she's a person who likes to work in the radio station nine to five, doing research, talking to others, unlike many DJs who are what they call 'show and go'. She had to sit in this office with this ghastly atmosphere around her. Eventually she decided to leave, partly because of the fact that she'd become pregnant, but I think really because she couldn't stand the heat. And I don't blame her at all, I have a great deal of sympathy for her.

In those days I'd listen to a hell of a lot of the output, from the moment I'd wake up, then in the car, then in the office for most of the day, in the car going home. In the early days I would listen to Radio 4 for fun and Radio 1 for work. And I winced a lot, because I was still listening to a hell of a lot of things I didn't agree with.

Trevor Dann: Emma didn't work because Emma's appeal is quite up-market and intellectual, and the unpalatable truth for Matthew and Andy is that the public largely consists of people who have not read any P.G. Wodehouse, and they just want to be entertained, they don't want to be challenged, they want to have a laugh, and Emma was a bit too up-market, and a bit too stimulating. It's a very difficult line for the BBC to draw, it's very hard to go out to the government and to the politicians in particular when it was the old Tory government, and say, 'We believe that Radio 1 is there simply to be entertaining and get shitloads of listeners.' You can't do that, so you have to talk about other things, about sponsoring live music and nurturing new talent, all those things that Matthew talks about so eloquently and so effectively, but then I think you have to bring those ideas home, and work out how you put them on the air.

Simon Bates: Why did Bannister lose so many listeners? Because the management didn't tell the audience that it was going to be okay. The trick is to tell your listeners, 'You are the most intelligent and perceptive people, and you may not agree with everything we're doing, but stick with us because we're in this together.' But management forgot to communicate. They forgot to say to the listeners, 'Yes, there will be changes, but don't worry, you're still going to love it and we still adore you.'

Johnny Beerling: Listeners are very slow to forgive. If you change one of their friends they might forgive you. If you change, as Matthew Bannister did, all their friends in three months . . . Within three months of my leaving and his taking over, either every DJ was in a new time slot or had been dumped or had left – that's what the audience didn't forgive and that's why it dropped so quickly.

Every controller comes in and makes changes. I made changes. When I came in I thought Jimmy Savile was old hat for the sort of Radio 1 that I'd inherited. He was doing a programme called *Savile's Travels*, Sunday afternoon, and Jimmy and I had a conversation and he quite understood, and we agreed that he would make way for a younger person, which was going to be Mike Read. The audience went down by 2 or 3 million, and I stuck it out for six months, and then went back and brought Alan Freeman back from Capital Radio to take over the slot. But it never really recovered. It pulled the figures back up, but it didn't pull them back up to what Savile had. That's just changing one programme, so you can see the result if you change the whole lot.

If I had changed Radio 1 in the way that Matthew subsequently changed it, the result would have been disastrous. It seemed to me that the BBC needed to rethink the positioning of all of those popular networks, because it wasn't for me as one individual running one network to make a unilateral change. I could foresee that, and I remember a meeting of the five radio controllers along with David Hatch [then Director of BBC Radio], in which we sat facing John Birt and people from [management consultants] McKinsey, and they were proposing these sort of drastic changes to Radio 1, and I said, 'Well, if you do that there will be a disastrous loss of audience.' The man from McKinsey then said, 'On what do you base that assumption?' and I said I based it on twenty-five years' experience.' 'Oh that,' he said, in that tone of voice. Afterwards David Hatch said, 'I don't know how you didn't hit him.'

I remember the controller of Radio 4 at the time, Michael Green, having a letter from somebody when he took over, reminding him it was not his radio station it belonged to the listeners, and it was not his toy or plaything to dabble around with.

Paul Robinson (Former Head of Music Policy at Radio 1, now Managing Director, Talk Radio): Johnny's big mistake was not to have made more change sooner, but Matthew's big mistake was to do too much too quickly. I'd been at Radio 1 four years when Matthew got the controller's job. I applied for it and was unsuccessful and was told I was second. Well, second's fine, but there's no prizes for second. Suffice to say that we didn't agree about a lot of things, although publicly I supported him completely. I do believe it was right to reposition Radio 1.

Radio audiences are conservative. If you gradually import new things into the schedule, then audiences are very accepting and they come to live with it. And then if you take a snapshot over a year or two you see a lot of change. What is not acceptable and doesn't work is radical surgery. People feel a sense of bereavement.

Andy Parfitt: Famously, Paul Robinson's application form to become the controller of Radio 1 found its way into the hands of Simon Bates. Bates said to him one day, 'We know what you've put in there . . .'

Simon Bates: They took the *Golden Hour* off, and if you do that, you're fucked. The *Golden Hour* was a hideous name, and for maybe twelve years I tried to think of a better one. The reason for having a solid hour of records is very simple. You have a high-profile personality breakfast show, you have a volatile audience between nine and ten, on the move – be it going down the dole queue, going to work, listening at home – so you play lots of music uninterrupted. Very simple. The issue is not whether you're playing records from 1996 or 1966 – it's a wodge of themed records. Do that for four months and

79

you will get an audience. Listeners will know that it's the one place they can go without commercials, without a DJ going, 'Oh I went to the movies last night.' Terribly, primitively simple. But if you fuck it around . . .

Equally it doesn't matter who does it. When I went on holiday the figures never went down. Didn't matter if it was a dumb-arse motherfucker doing it – as long as he didn't mess with it. Take it off – death. Listeners go somewhere else.

Johnny Beerling: I feel sorry for the staff that got dumped. No, I don't laugh, I don't take any pleasure out of it, I don't listen to it very much any more. I suppose, frankly, Simon, when you've had to listen to something for twenty-five years, it's quite a relief that . . . you see, when you're a channel controller everybody who works for you expects you to have heard his or her programme, and wants an opinion on it, and I'm a fairly light sleeper and used to listen often in the night, and would drop a note to someone about something I'd heard, either good or bad, so people never knew quite when I was listening. Everyone expects you to have had an opinion on their programme, so there's a tremendous obligation, unless you're out of the country, to listen, all the time, and you hardly ever listen to anything else. So once you stop, and I was channel controller for eight years, once you stop listening it's a huge relief in a sense, you almost go to Radio 4 just by way of a complete contrast, Classic FM or Radio 3. These days I tend to listen quite a lot to Radio 2, Country 10.35, just because that's the kind of music I happen to like, Classic FM, Melody Radio even.

Andy Parfitt: With the Rajar figures you get a book every month that tells you these hard figures, and it's easy to tell if things are going badly – it's obvious. But the figures really are only part of the story. It's some comfort that at Radio 1 we are not judged purely on our Rajar figures, or we shouldn't be. There are other factors: does the BBC understand your strategy? What do opinion-formers think? What does the heritage secretary and his team think about it? If you were in commercial radio, and your Rajars did what ours did, then Matthew would have been out. But as the figures were tumbling, Radio 1 was considered to be doing well in other respects. Some MPs said to us that if we were doing our job properly, the audiences have to go down. They understood that we were taking the network away from the mainstream, and I think Matthew was pleased the way things were going politically – Radio 1 saved, as it were. The problem was, the figures were in freefall for a long time, and showed no immediate sign of stopping.

Matthew Bannister: We quickly discovered that Steve Wright's show simply wasn't working at breakfast. The figures were falling, and our research on it showed that although there was a huge level of popularity for Steve Wright, the format of the show was wrong for that time in the morning. Unfortunately he imported a lot of the stuff he'd been doing in the afternoon, and one of the universal truths about radio is that you listen in a different mode after lunch than you do before it. You want shorter, more topical, faster material in the morning. We were putting a lot of pressure on him to change the format and the music.

Andy Parfitt: *Steve Wright in the Afternoon* was an institution, and he pulled in an enormous share of the audience – about 18 per cent, the sort of share that sends people on commercial radio home sulking. But in the afternoon the preparation had a natural build-up and climax. Steve would come in at about ten, his posse would be around, they'd sit around talking and going through all the papers, they'd write some things over lunch and do some funny voices, and by the time he came to broadcast at three they were all fired up, and the show had a topical and fresh feel.

But at breakfast, they'd prepare a lot of the show the day before, and only came in at 5.45 in the morning, and when it went on air it didn't sound like it was today. Just not fresh enough or exciting. Also, by that time Steve had got to the point where he was saying, 'I know how it all works, don't try and tell me how it works,' and he wouldn't listen. Also he wouldn't play a lot of the stuff on the running order that was given to him from the computer.

Steve had locked himself into a cell, thinking, I'll make this work, I know the radio station is taking a real pounding, and all my mates have gone, but I know how this bloody thing works, and these new people don't. It became a bit of a siege mentality.

It wasn't very long before he quit. I can remember that it was a devastating surprise, and that he used the papers to save himself at what he thought was the expense of Radio 1 and the expense of Matthew. Matthew called me in and said, 'Oh fucking hell, Steve Wright's quit.' It was all sewn up.

Steve Wright (Disc Jockey): Basically I took the job as a favour to Matthew. He said, 'Would you do *Breakfast* for a year?' 'Yeah, sure, I haven't done that one yet.' And as far as I was concerned it was successful. If you look at the figures I achieved, and then look at what was happening to the rest of the network, we held on to it very well. But I felt at the time I'd gone as far as I could go within that format. I could have introduced more characters, but they probably would have been similar to other ones . . . Rather pretentiously, I'd always seen myself as a broadcaster and not just a disc jockey. I wanted to do talk radio, and a television show. It wasn't a question of age or repositioning – I just felt, 'Done that, been there.' I didn't leave for any other reason.

There was no difference whatsoever doing the show in the morning. You just prep up through the night. It was just a question of time: we needed an extra seven or eight months for it to kick in. I only did it for fourteen months, but radio shows need a good nineteen to twenty months to kick in. And it's a question of perception. When Terry Wogan went back on to Radio 2 it took people three years to say, 'He's really great again, isn't he?' Before that it was, 'He's not quite as good as he used to be.' You think that if you have a new show, after three months everyone must know about it, but it's not the case. It's a phenomenon no one can understand.

Unfortunately the pressure was on management to turn it around quickly – but that's simply not the way radio works. It takes time to become liked. My view is always, 'Don't worry, lads, leave it to me, give it some time and it'll be okay.' My leaving was the one departure that was coincidence; had Radio 1 maintained its audience share I still would have left.

Matthew Bannister: There was no warning he was going to go like that. I'd been away somewhere and returned to a note on my desk one Friday afternoon saying, 'Steve Wright wants to see you urgently.' He handed me a letter of resignation, the very last thing I wanted. I failed to persuade him to stay, so I said, 'Well, okay – let's keep this to ourselves for the weekend, and work out how to release the news to our mutual advantage.' He said, 'Yes, fine, no problem,' and within twenty minutes every newspaper was on the line to our press office saying, 'We understand Steve Wright's leaving.'

Later in the evening his agent promised me that he wasn't speaking to the press, but the press were telling us a different story, saying that they were receiving a lot of off-the-record briefings.

After a lot of discussion our line was, 'He's a major talent, and it's not about Radio 1 – it's about his wish to pursue another career,' and we published his resignation letter to prove it. Of course, that didn't really wash with the newspapers, who simply wanted to write that Radio 1 was in a terrible state. We had the editor of the *Daily Mail* on the phone saying, 'I'm holding the front page – if you don't get me a statement now I'm going to run something really damaging about your radio station.' And we had terrible press the next day – 'It's a Wright Off!' – front page of every newspaper – the end is nigh, the final nail in the Radio 1 coffin. It was horrible at the time. At the time I was thinking, 'Oh fuck. What on earth do we do now?'

Polly Ravenscroft (Head of Radio 1 Publicity): We had just begun to get some positive press about Radio 1 at the beginning of January, how it was going to change, and Steve Wright just blew that out the window.

The trick then was to make sure that something bad didn't turn into something horrendous. We had to get together a statement that didn't backfire on us. I started to build up a relationship with Matthew, and unless I believed in what he was doing I don't think I could have done the job, because it was permanently journalists calling you up saying, 'Radio 1 is pretty crap and what the hell's he doing?'

Andy Parfitt: He didn't leave straight away, but just his announcement meant we lost more listeners. Listeners lose confidence in the radio station. They think, 'Well, if my friend on the radio is going . . . If he thinks it's no good, then I think it's no good.'

He didn't want it to be 'Steve Wright loses half a million listeners, he must be rubbish,' he wanted it to be 'Radio 1 loses another half a million listeners, I'm going.' I think he cared mostly about what might happen to his reputation if he stayed at Radio 1 and saw his listenership drop. He was reading a lot of negative press about Radio 1 every day. He thinks, 'I'm part of this, and not only am I part of it, but I'm actually their flagship show – me, Steve Wright, the most popular broadcaster in Britain.' One option is to say, 'Hell, I'm quitting this rubbish,' and that's what he did. It's like when a star striker leaves the football team when you're fighting against relegation.

Steve Wright: To be honest with you I was completely unaware of any panic surrounding my departure. I quit on a Friday, and the next day I had to go to Atlanta, and then I came back to work on the little TV show I was doing. I know it sounds heartless, but I didn't think about it. I do the radio programme for the punters. I was just thinking, 'What am I going to be doing next for the punters?' Radio stations are just studios – they only exist on the radio. What was Radio 1? Was it the studio I worked out of? Was it Matthew Bannister's office in Broadcasting House? Was it the roadshow? My view is, 'Put me in a studio, tell me what the radio station is called, and I'll talk to the punters.'

Part of the success of the afternoon programme wasn't the fact that we were postmodern and smart, it was that we were reliable and friendly. You could switch on wherever you were and be amused and have a friend. That sounds terribly pretentious, but it's true: it's comforting, it's something nice, it's upbeat, we tried only to reflect the good, the funny and the interesting. I think probably in British radio we now lack that. It's become mechanical. We need to update personality radio, so that it doesn't sound naff and it isn't, 'Hello love, where are you calling from?'

What happened at Radio 1 is like a sitcom. If you view it as a sitcom it would be funny. I was happy to be in the sitcom. From my point of view what happened was not personal. It was just professional. It's just a jobbing broadcaster doing a gig. When you do a show you can't think of the exact numbers of people tuning in and how it compares with the last figures – such thoughts are impostors. What people remember is the time you got them through their depression, or the time you helped them with their exams. This sounds like

Steve Wright:
'It's just entertainment. Nobody has a disease.'

Dave Lee Travis speaking. The time you helped them when their husband went to the Falklands, or the time when it was really pissing down with rain and you were the only thing on the air that cheered them up – that's why you broadcast. Everything else is unimportant. At the end of the day it's just entertainment. Nobody has a disease.

Sophie McLaughlin (formerly Head of Radio 1 Marketing, now Head of Strategy and Broadcast Analysis, Network Radio): It was interesting to see Matthew in that situation. We'd been sitting in rooms complaining about Steve and saying, 'Couldn't we get rid of him and isn't he a nightmare, saying the wrong things, doesn't do what he's told, doesn't play the right music . . .' And then when he resigned it was, 'Oh my God he's resigned, isn't this a disaster for us?' That's just panic.

When I arrived in 1994, and Radio 1 was really plummeting, figures were utterly dominant. Not because we were studiously following ratings, but because of the emotional thing of seeing a line on a graph go down like that. It didn't matter what the story behind the numbers was, it was just the demoralizing, frightening thing of seeing a graph like that, going down when once it went up. Liz Forgan was panicking, everyone was panicking.

We had these Rajar meetings in the evening that would assume the air of a war council. Because Radio 1 has such dominance within all BBC network radio figures, because it's the largest one, it meant that share and reach for all BBC radio was suffering. Everyone was, 'Right, Matthew, so what are you going to do about it?' Even Liz at times would falter in her support of the whole thing. She definitely wavered.

I don't think John Birt wavered. John's always been a supporter of Matthew's. It's not as if Birt is a stranger to courting disapproval and making unpleasant decisions. To be honest, he gets more frustrated with Radio 2, because he wants a pop music station for him, where he can listen to the Eagles.

Within the rest of the BBC there was a lack of real understanding about what Radio 1 was or could be, and why it was important. If it had been Radio 4, you would have seen everyone piling in there to get involved and meddle, and say, 'Look, you can't do this, Matthew.' But part of it was people thinking, 'Oh my God, I don't know what to do with pop music – I don't even know if it's important or not. A lot of people listen to it, and we're losing a lot of people, and I can't do anything about it because I don't know what it is or why. So Matthew's got to do it.'

It wasn't just, 'Right, leave it to him to fuck up and then we'll pick up the pieces.'

Liz Forgan: We used to meet and talk about the general strategy, the things that make Radio 1 different from every other pop music station: more live music, a broader spread of music, new bands that you haven't heard before, contextual speech, a variety, comedy and news and other things. The trick then was a tuning exercise to balance and get it all right, and that was for Matthew to do, that was what I couldn't possibly do, I had no sense of what that audience wanted or what it would listen to. The things I thought were funny didn't work on Radio 1 at all, music I loved they hated. So it was a very tough assignment for him. All I could do was protect his back publicly and with the governors and the politicians.

If you're at the BBC I think there is a tremendous pressure on you to let things that don't work go for longer than you would if you worked in a commercial station. Anywhere else you would look at the ratings, and if they were no good after three weeks you'd axe it. At the BBC you're very conscious that one of your opportunities, not to say duties, is to use the freedom of the licence fee to give ideas longer to find their voice or their feet, and I think we did leave some things to go running on too long. I think probably my own instinct is to be too indulgent in that way, because I do so hate to see the waste of talent that is consumed by the demand of the overnight ratings, and I think that's terrible because it produces only a certain kind of very fluent, very easy, very superficial talent and it gives you no chance whatever to find new notes in it, new tones. I don't regret that at all, I think that it's a perfectly reasonable part of growing up for a station.

I don't agree that we changed the station too fast. It had to be done shockingly. It was absolutely impossible to change Radio 1 gradually because actually what we were doing was trying to say to a young audience, who had switched off Radio 1 on the grounds that it was so naff that they couldn't bear to be thought of as Radio 1 listeners, we were saying, 'Please come back.' But it's no good slipping in something credible in the middle of the night and hoping. You had to send out a quite brutal message.

Simon Garfield: At the beginning of 1995, shortly after Steve Wright's departure, senior Radio 1 management gave a presentation to the director of BBC radio and the heads of other networks. This was an annual event, part of the corporation's regular strategy review. The station's listening figures had fallen yet again, from an adult (fifteen plus) weekly reach of 14.3 million in the last quarter of 1993 to 11 million in the last quarter of 1994. The presentation attempted to explain this loss: the station had recently lost its medium wave frequency; there were now 147 commercial stations compared to 120 in 1992, the majority of which played pop music; there were fewer young people in the population, with a greater choice of leisure activities.

The presentation then claimed some achievements ('organizational and editorial problems have been gripped up ... defensible as public service, but still highly popular'), and outlined some aims ('to regain credibility with younger listeners ... to bring forward a new generation of presenters ... to begin the process of marking out a clear territory in the increasingly competitive market'). One section of the presentation was entitled 'When will it all end?', to which there was no answer, but solace was sought in the success of a similar, if less dramatic, repositioning of Radio 2 five years earlier. Those in attendance also got a selection of favourable press cuttings, a counterpoint to the tabloid slaughter. This included a leader in *The Times*, which noted, 'At least Radio 1 is no longer safe and dull. Mr Bannister should keep his nerve under fire.' One page merely carried a headline, credited to *Select* magazine: 'Radio 1 No Longer Crap Shock!' In fact, when originally printed in the magazine, the headline had read: 'Radio 1 "No Longer Crap"?'

Liz Forgan: I didn't panic over figures, although I did get very worried at losing about 5 million, and we did a turn for the governors at about that point which was a bit on the rocky side. If you believe the strategy's right and you really do think that there is an audience who are starved for a certain kind of music product that the BBC alone has the resources to provide, then you have a duty to provide it. I never ever thought, 'This is an unstoppable decline, we're in the soup and must turn round and hire Dave Lee Travis again.'

It is to the governors' great credit, actually, that they let us get on with it, because the figures were quite alarming at some points, and they would have been fully justified in saying, 'Stop this, here's your objective, put the figures up,' but they didn't.

They knew they didn't understand. There was one governor who actually made a great deal of effort to understand, and began by challenging us quite toughly on what we were up to. He kept looking at the figures and saying, 'Listen, this is ridiculous, what's going on? How are you going to get out of this?' He gave us a hard time for a bit and then he was persuaded that things were going to go all right, and then he became very supportive indeed.

Every quarter at the Rajar press conference we had to go and tell the story about yet further decline in Radio 1, which was very demoralizing for everybody and I was desperate to do something about this, and my strategy was to try and get them to put them out monthly, because I thought then the press wouldn't pay so much attention to them, but never managed that and it was just terrible. I stopped going because it was all too thrilling if I went and everybody could ask me questions. It gradually started to calm down as the problems started hitting the commercial stations. But it was a nightmare.

Polly Ravenscroft: The next potential disaster was Bruno Brookes. We put a press release out, obviously not saying that he had been sacked, but then the phones start ringing and the *Daily Mail* is saying that Bruno said that he's 'walked out' and that the BBC's lying. What's he talking about? I remember thinking, There is no way he's going to get away with this, because we were going to keep going down if we allowed our detractors to get away with it.

Matthew Bannister: We were doing a series of events around universities, where we took the evening session on tour, and some bands played in the evening, and then the following day there would be seminars in which a Radio 1 executive and either Steve Lamacq or Jo Whiley would talk about broadcasting or getting into the music business. I was due to talk at Liverpool one Friday, but I had some other business to do earlier that morning in London.

I had to tell Bruno Brookes that life at Radio 1 was over for him. The only way to do that really is the moment they come off air. You can't do it before they go on air, and also it's best to do it with a weekday DJ just before a weekend, because they're not on air over the weekend to be bitter about it.

So I came in one Friday at five in the morning. Bruno's show finished at 6.30. I wrote my speech for the Liverpool conference, and then went down to the studio and said, 'Can you come into my office, please?' Then I said to him, 'I'm terribly sorry, but we're not going to renew your contract, blah, blah.' I named a figure which would buy him out from the rest of his contract – quite a substantial sum. His contract had some months to run, but we wanted to get some new people in – Dave Pearce, who was doing the breakfast show on Kiss, and Wendy Lloyd from Virgin.

I then got on a train to Liverpool, hoping that I could

announce during the Liverpool speech, at which there was some press, that we had signed these new people, and then say, 'By the way, Bruno's going.' I rang up Polly just before I started, and she said, 'We haven't got confirmation from Dave Pearce and Wendy Lloyd that they've spoken to their radio stations yet, so you can't say anything.' I said, 'Well, bleep me when you've got the confirmation.'

So I began speaking, and half-way through my bleeper went. I said, 'Oh that's interesting – I can tell you that we've signed Dave Pearce, Wendy Lloyd and Bruno Brookes is leaving.' One agency journalist realized that they'd got a bit of a scoop, and rushed off to put it on the wires.

But what happened next reminds me of that bit in the Smashie and Nicey film, which starts with the DJs in the controller's office, and then the DJs and the controller rush out, the DJs running down one corridor, and the controller down another, and they both burst into a press conference at the same time, and, at exactly the same moment, the controller says, 'They're fired!', and the DJs say, 'We've resigned!'

And that's what happened with Bruno. The press wanted to know did he jump or was he pushed.

Bruno had gone to Ireland, where he has a castle. I'm in the students' union in Liverpool on a mobile phone with a very bad reception, and I'm getting phonecalls from London which say, 'We've had Bruno on the phone from his castle, and the *News of the World* are pushing cheques through his letterbox in exchange for his story. He wants you to up your offer, or else he's going to tell them everything he knows about Radio 1.' I say, 'Give him a couple more bob, but make it quite clear to him that he'll have none of that money if he speaks to the newspapers.' By this stage Bruno was apparently going, 'They're crawling about in the undergrowth! I'm feeling very tempted!'

In the end we managed to calm him down, and he kept quiet.

Polly Ravenscroft: Gary Davies was another one. His contract wasn't renewed and he again went to the papers. But it's one of those situations where you can't lower yourself to their level. You have to try and get over the idea that you're above this and moving on to better things. I think there was a piece in the *Independent*, and Gary Davies came across as looking quite stupid. This was where things were changing slightly – instead of the newspapers saying, 'How embarrassing for Radio 1,' it was more, 'How embarrassing for another DJ, he's been got rid of and he's just trying to make things look better for himself . . .'

Simon Garfield: In May 1995, Polly Ravenscroft compiled a report summarizing the previous months' PR activities. For December 1994 she was able to write, 'The tide appeared to be turning for Radio 1 after a difficult year,' and she listed an impressive array of favourable coverage on television and in print. Mark Radcliffe had received good coverage; a new DJ, Lisa I'Anson, had joined the station and was interviewed widely, and Chris Morris, another Bannister/Dann success on GLR, was now gaining much attention with his late-night stunts and ruthless parodies. Spoof items featured on the autumn series included a news report on celebrities arriving at Richard Branson's house to watch him have a heart attack, a story about how REM had recorded an advertisement for whale meat, and a competition offering Radio 1 prizes for anyone who sent in a dead local radio 'eye in the sky' traffic reporter. Max Clifford, Donald Sinden, Petula Clark and Martyn Lewis suffered pitiless interviewing. Also, it was reported that Simon Mayo's features were moving towards the centre of his face, and that Jimmy Savile had died. One programme began, 'This is BBC Radio 1 FM and if there is any news of the death of Michael Heseltine in the next hour we'll let you know straight away.' This was followed by a sombre interview with Bruce Foxton, once of the Jam, about which bassline would be most appropriate given the Heseltine news. There had been a few listener complaints, and some outrage in the newspapers, but the target audience found the shows very exciting.

But things changed in the following months.

Polly Ravenscroft's PR Summary: January 1995: General discontent was the mood of the station. Steve Wright's resignation resulted in crisis PR . . . We made the right decision to admit to being shocked yet not in crisis. It was also the right decision for Matthew Bannister to: 1. Not allow Steve to leave on his terms. The press would have thought that was very weak. This would have affected his status in their eyes. 2. Not to do numerous interviews defending Radio 1 (at this particular time). Many journalists were calling for his resignation. Conclusion: A difficult month for Radio 1. Potentially a public relations disaster – when is Radio 1 going to have a stable schedule? How can they get out of this one?

February 1995: Jimmy Savile sued the BBC over the Chris Morris programme – Petula Clark was featured on the same programme. It happened again. Petula sued us too . . .

March/April 1995: It was unfortunate but not surprising that Bruno Brookes said that he had left, rather than having been pushed. This did cause great confusion with the national press. I managed to turn the story around and it did look like Bruno was not telling the truth. Although this was embarrassing, it meant Matthew again looked credible . . . Now was the time for Matthew to do a profile . . .

Matthew Bannister: Often these things are more about the newspapers than what's actually going on. It's the manner in which you announce it in the newspapers, and how it's then perceived, which is almost as important as what happens on the radio. Especially if you're in the gale of bad publicity that we were in the midst of. I think that has a genuine effect on the audience – people don't like to be associated with failure, especially in the field of entertainment. Nobody likes to be associated with something which, every time you open a newspaper, you get 'Fresh crisis at Radio 1, it's all down the toilet and everybody you've ever heard of has left.'

Chapter 5

As It Is

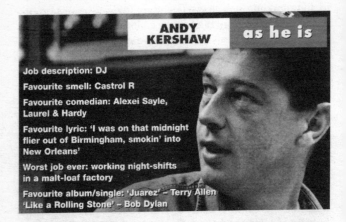

ANDY KERSHAW

as he is

Job description: DJ

Favourite smell: Castrol R

Favourite comedian: Alexei Sayle, Laurel & Hardy

Favourite lyric: 'I was on that midnight flier out of Birmingham, smokin' into New Orleans'

Worst job ever: working night-shifts in a malt-loaf factory

Favourite album/single: 'Juarez' – Terry Allen 'Like a Rolling Stone' – Bob Dylan

SOPHIE McLAUGHLIN

as she is

Job description: marketing manager

Favourite lyric: 'Glen Hoddle he wears a magic hat'

Favourite breakfast: Ready Brek

My life in one line: slightly adrift

Favourite item of clothing: Levi's hipsters – old style

Favourite album: Bob Dylan live at Budokan

Favourite chocolate bar: Dairy Crunch

The marketing campaign:
'You can ask me for a quote, but you're not doing *that*'

Sophie McLaughlin: When I first met him by himself, Matthew displayed extreme determination and no sense of fear. Actually there was a slight sense of fear because the press were getting at him all the time and the governors were raising eyebrows, but he was very confident that his plans would work. He said, 'I've been given the remit to go all the way and it's a bit hairy at the moment but I need someone with good marketing sense.'

I think that it was important that I came from outside the BBC, and that I could look at things in a way that might create a complete split from the past. He talked about building a team that was going to see it through to the end, and he was very inspirational in that way. The idea was that we were part of this campaign to readdress the perception of the station and the injustices of the press.

I was twenty-eight. I had very little of what you might call a pop background. I wasn't one of those people like Chris Evans who was at the roadshow at the age of eight. I was one of those older teenagers who were anti-pop music and resisted watching *Top of the Pops* and didn't see *Grease* until ten years later and things like that. Probably because everyone else was doing it in my school, my own peculiar form of rebellion, I suppose. I certainly didn't listen to much music radio, even when I got the job.

The last campaign before I came majored on changes to the schedules – Steve Wright's breakfast show, Danny Baker. Very traditional: the whole line was that all sorts of things could wake you up, but nothing would wake you up like the Steve Wright breakfast show. There was a man about to fall on a rhinoceros's horn and be hit over the head with a large hammer. It was on bus shelters and posters. It was kind of cartoony.

When you're looking for new agencies to do a particular job there's this research place you can go to to look at past tapes of their work. And I did a shortlist, which included Saatchi's because they had done work for the BBC before, but I must say I never thought that they would come up with it this time. I was thinking that I needed a smaller non-traditional agency, a firm that involves the client in the development of the creative work on an ongoing basis. Three agencies pitched in the end. Saatchi's pitched in this huge boardroom, ridiculously large tables, and they rolled out everyone – head of media, head of this, head of that, flashy this, flashy that. They presented very conventional 'more music' type ads which are quite compelling if you haven't seen the real solution yet. We were going, 'Oh that was all right, and oh look, you see that little guitar they've put in there . . .'

But then we had the pitch from Chiat Day.

John Robson (Advertising Executive, then Chiat Day, now Lowe Howard-Spink Marschalk): Our initial thought was that Radio 1 is a great British institution that we'd grown up with, very dear to our hearts. I'm twenty-seven, grew up in Blackpool, and I saw DLT at the roadshow on the beach. So there was an emotional attachment, and also a feeling that no one had done Radio 1 justice in terms of advertising.

We had several thoughts. Radio 1 represented the sound of England – if you went abroad for a while, and then came back and wanted to know what was happening in music, films, news, you could get back into things pretty quickly just by listening to Radio 1. There was also a thought about the British heritage of popular music, from the late sixties and the Stones, through all the movements like punk and new romantics and the Manchester scene, and Radio 1 had always existed alongside that. We also talked of Radio 1's role within the BBC – we talked about it as a cultural on-ramp: when people become teenagers, there should be a way into BBC radio, and popular music on Radio 1 should be that on-ramp.

Then we went round the building, the old building Egton House, and I remember being surprised at how run-down and unglamorous it was. It was dirty, ramshackle, a rabbit warren, but also studenty and homely. A real contrast to Kiss, where I'd worked, and which was more upfront and shiny, or Capital. It was clear that the reality was very different to the perception that I had had from the press, which suggested it didn't care about music, and Matthew Bannister didn't know what he was doing. The old image totally misrepresented the intentions of the people who worked there.

We presented it to Radio 1 by saying, 'Your station is actually getting better and better, but the press and audience is getting worse and worse. Our idea is for people to see through this, and reverse it.'

In a bar we discussed the idea of doing a documentary, and we talked about it all night, and decided the thing we had to do was to go in and convince a guy who had been slagged off terribly in the tabloids for the last year that what he really needed was to get some journalists into the building to make a film. We thought that was very high risk, especially for the BBC, but Matthew was very laid back about it.

So I went in with a copywriter for two weeks, and we were there while people were still being sacked, and we spent our time just talking to people about how they felt. Steve Wright had just announced that he was leaving, and people were very suspicious of us being in there, especially as we were sanctioned by Matthew. It was clear talking to people how much care and commitment went into the place, how they understood public service radio, and brought to it a rather academic approach. It felt a bit like a music radio university. People genuinely said, 'Yes, I could earn more money elsewhere, but this is where you do real radio . . .' The more I was there, the more of a BBC fan I became.

After two weeks we told Matthew and Sophie that if we could take every person in the UK through what we had just seen, they would think this was a marvellous institution and easily worth the licence fee.

The TV documentary was intended to be a bit like that Graham Taylor England programme – seen by a large audience, and then everyone talking about it the next day at work or in the pub. That would kick it off, and then we planned to carry on with the same characters in print, almost like a soap opera.

But it soon became clear that we couldn't do this due to the regulations over the BBC publicizing itself, so we concentrated on print ads and a documentary shown in cinemas. It was also shown at the front of all the video tapes of *Dumb and Dumber*.

There's no doubt that at least part of the campaign was aimed directly at the press. The problem was how to stop a very negative and gloomy barrage of press comment. The plan was to stop it stone dead. That was the thinking: we had seen the truth, and so much of what the press wrote was misplaced, so we had to come up with something that was just factual, something undeniable. So we just presented what we saw – people talking, real photographs, their real quotes, not posed or fabricated, not really what normal advertising was about. We did a special free supplement for the *Guardian*, and cards for all the DJs which had their picture and a mini questionnaire on one side, and on the other side was a picture of someone from management or production, to emphasize the team aspect. Strategically it was terribly simple – there was no hook or gag or clever message. And it worked. Journalists had no comeback on it. The press improved.

Andy Kershaw: The BBC spent something like over a million pounds on that advertising campaign. The place suddenly became full of marketing and promotions people. I remember one day the record library disappeared, a place where I used to spend many a happy hour. And it was suddenly filled with promotions people.

When they did those postcards for the campaign, I happened to be walking past somebody's desk one day and I saw a picture of myself with this slogan on the bottom which they'd made up. They'd made it up. I can't remember now what it said. But irrespective of what it said, even if it had been something I'd agreed with, it was the principle that they'd put words in my mouth . . . Some advertising johnnies had made up this quote! But then they'd not even had the courtesy to say, 'Look, we've got some advertising johnnies to make up these quotes, is this one all right with you?'

I said, 'What is this?' And they told me. I said, 'Well, you can ask me for a quote, but you're not doing *that*.'

In the end we got something that was okay.

Simon Garfield: For the DJ cards they asked Andy Kershaw to name his favourite smell: Castrol R. His worst job ever was working night shifts in a malt-loaf factory. His favourite lyric: 'I was on that midnight flier out of Birmingham, smokin' into New Orleans.' At the foot of the cards there was white space, designed for the DJ's autograph, which could then be sent back to listeners, or given out at live events.

Some people took it more seriously than others. They asked John Peel about his most overused word: trigonometry. And his favourite smell: the East Anglian night. Sophie McLaughlin, the marketing manager, listed her favourite lyric as 'Glenn Hoddle, he wears a magic hat' and her favourite album as *Bob Dylan Live at the Budokan*. Mark Kermode, the station's film critic, said his life in one line was 'Keep telling yourself it's only a movie.' Jo Pilkington, a documentary producer, said her villain was Liz Hurley and her worst song anything by Bryan Adams. Jo Whiley grew up at 'Miss Selfridge and down the bottom of the playing field at school'. Danny Baker said he'd like to be remembered for his impressive six-octave range, but he knew he would be remembered for his Daz adverts.

John Robson: The most important effect of the campaign was in providing a common visual and cultural identity for the station, and within the station. During this period the atmosphere inside moved from 'Shit, we're going to get fired,' to 'This transformation is pretty good.' It helped other people visualize Matthew's vision. But we were stuck for a name, a pay-off line. Throughout the pitch the name was Behind the Music, until Liz Forgan pointed out that it might mean Radio 1 was behind the times. I had an idea to call it by the address, 1 Portland Place, but then Naresh [Ramchandani, a creative member of the Chiat Day team, which, after a staff buy-out, was now called St Luke's] came up with As It Is, which doesn't mean much now, but it worked for the time.

Polly Ravenscroft: At this time Matthew's PR came into it. I had never met Matthew before he took over, and was gradually getting to know him better. From what I was seeing of him he was a really good guy – quite fun to be with as well as being very good at his job. But the only impression journalists were getting was Bannister the Axe Man.

To look at Matthew he's quite an authoritative figure and could come across as being quite stuffy if he was just doing his Birtspeak. It was quite important for Radio 1 to change that. The way I did that was just to talk to journalists about him when I was out with them. I used to get a real earful about him, about the audience drop and that maybe with Danny Baker and Emma Freud he was making it into another GLR, but I said to them, 'Look, you have to meet him, you can't just talk about him like this.' But then I found that in interview situations Matthew was very formal – to a certain extent he still is. We did an interview with the *Daily Telegraph*, and I said to him before it, 'You can afford to be a bit relaxed about how you come across. I don't expect you to sit there drinking and smoking, but you can allow the real you to come out, because it's not a bad thing and people would warm to you.' And that did start happening, and eventually we went out with tabloid journalists and it was, 'God, Matthew's actually all right, isn't he?' When Matthew was sliding down the banister, Andy Coulson from the *Sun* had never met him.

There was traditionally a problem of being a BBC press officer. You know – how many BBC press officers does it take to change a lightbulb? Answer: We'll get back to you on that one. From my own experience it was like that. We were not encouraged to go out to lunch or drinks with journalists, which I find incredible. Unless you can build up a relationship, how can you expect them to trust or respect you, and vice-versa. You find that they're not just journalists, but quite reasonable people as well.

Rajar and Radio 1 will always be a news story, which I think is fair enough. If I was a journalist I would write about the fact that we'd gone down. But as a press officer you've got to push for the opinion-formers to write that even though we are going down it doesn't matter, trying to put a bit of spin about it. It's difficult. I did find myself thinking, God, it really is bad that we've gone down that much, and we shouldn't – we should be getting all our programmes right. That's when the job gets difficult, when you're trying to spin something you don't really believe in.

Sophie McLaughlin: After the initial campaign we began to use the specialist shows as entry points into the station – we would run special features on Pete Tong, Tim Westwood. We knew that we couldn't just say, 'We're cool, so listen' at the beginning, but gradually people were realizing that the station really had changed. The key element of that was that Radio 1 had finally established what the new music policy was – 'new music first', cutting edge, the only place you could hear the exciting stuff. Sounds corny, all those phrases, but it was crucial to the perception of the station. That, and Britpop coming along. During Britpop, the creative teams at Radio 1 realized, 'Great, what we do has some cultural significance beyond the fact that young people like pop music.' So then the question was, how do they construct an interesting, competitive, compelling show that they're proud of, a show that enables that pride to get on to the air? It was interesting that it just seemed to take so long to get it right, and how difficult it seemed to be.

Andy Parfitt: There was a moment when things changed. A year down the line, having brought in Danny Baker, Emma Freud and older broadcasters who included some journalism in their shows, and with Radio 1 chucking audience away by a million every quarter, we had a couple of days away at a very comfortable place called Warren House in Kingston.

Matthew asked each of his team to prepare an alternative view of what Radio 1 should be. Up until that time I had followed Matthew, implementing the changes that he wanted. He asked me to propose how Radio 1 might be run purely as a youth station, and I came up with something called Wire Free. That was the template of what Radio 1 was to become. It was youth-based, music-based, cinema, clubbing, everything we now do. Someone else did Radio 1 as a twenty-five- to forty-five-year-old album station, and someone did a hell-for-leather very commercial model, a model for what the commercial sector would do with Radio 1 if they had it, which meant getting every big name DJ in town, like Chris Tarrant, to maximize the audience.

My presentation was more persuasive than the others. It was very human, about a very particular sense of the audience, about nineteen-year-olds and what their values were, what they drank, what sort of news interested them, and what they did with their weekends. It seemed to have all the public service virtues – going for a younger audience that wasn't served by the BBC, and it was about supporting new and live music. At the time it was just one option, but retrospectively it seems like the only thing we could have done. It was the only one that excited us all. On the cover of my presentation I put a picture of Hugh Grant with a cat, because at the time he was the man of the moment, and he was friendly, and had big female appeal, and he seemed to embody all the values I wanted for the station. And on my original ideal schedule, Chris Evans was down to do the breakfast show.

We had to do something that would make Radio 1 a robust and proper and thought-out part of the BBC, and if that meant that we would lose more listeners then so be it. Having said which, I could see Matthew taking all kinds of crap in the papers, and it was very painful for him to be losing audience in the way that we did. It is a very awful thing to be publicly vilified.

The one thing we set out to do very clearly after this was to assemble the cutting edge specialist DJs, DJs that gave us credibility and restored the damage done by having a soul programme presented by a white guy, Andy Peebles, and a show presented by a guy called The Man Ezeke, who was a terrible caricature of a black man. The idea was to pick off the very best specialists, and we were helped a lot by Pete Tong. The isolation of success had meant that in the late eighties the single most important aspect of youth culture – the dance and rave scene – had completely passed Radio 1 by. The specialist shows have a proportionately small audience, but the effect that they have on the perception of the station is enormous. So in a sense it was true that we did buy the most credible people off the shelf.

Pete Tong (Disc Jockey): When the management changed I got nervous for a bit; I thought I was doing all right under Johnny Beerling. I knew Matthew vaguely from when we both worked at Capital, but he obviously knew a bit about me. When we met again he was unbelievably encouraging. I became conscious after talking to him and Andy over a number of months that they were meeting me a lot more than most of their DJs. I was somehow very important to them. We would go off to hotels and talk for hours, and in brief they were basically asking, 'What should we do?'

I said, 'You should have a mix show, you should have Westwood on, you should have a jungle show.' They came back and said, 'We want all those things.' I said I'd give them all the phone numbers, but they said, 'No, we want you to do it. You get the shows in for us, as much money as you need.'

I was on Capital when acid house happened in the late eighties, and I instantly became such a major player, because I was the only one on radio really reflecting those times, the only one really championing what was going on at those raves around the M25 and those fields in Essex. So when I came to Radio 1 the obvious thing to do was to spread what I had been doing in the south-east nationwide. I saw it as a massive opportunity, a completely blank canvas. Nobody could now rival my reach.

I was a really big name in the south-east, but the rest of the country didn't really know who I was. I used to phone people up – the Hacienda in Manchester, Venus in Nottingham, Back to Basics in Leeds. These places sort of knew who I was, but the fact that I was on Radio 1 was a big minus to them. They were running the coolest clubs in their cities, and Radio 1 was very uncool. I would then beg them for a chance, not charge them any money, give them a great set, and they'd say, 'Okay, fine.'

Unfortunately, back at Radio 1 loads of people would be coming up to me saying, 'We want you out there doing road-shows.' I said, 'Fuck off! That's not what I do, you don't understand.' Then they said, 'Well, we want to come out to where you go, bring the radio station along with you.' I said, 'Fuck off, you'll frighten the life out of everybody.' It was very much like sneaking into these clubs with a Radio 1 teeshirt underneath, and slowly but surely over a number of years revealing more and more of the logo. That's the way it felt. By 1993, when Matthew arrived, I think I'd already put down the foundations for the revival. And on air, through the *Essential Mix*, every big club DJ in the world got to play on Radio 1, when they never thought they could. But it was a long-term strategy – you can't do it by putting up posters saying 'Radio 1 is now cool.' If you're big and corporate like Radio 1, you don't buy your credibility, you've got to earn it back.

Matthew Bannister: All the research said, 'If you want to dominate London, then Westwood's the man who really matters on the street' [Tim Westwood, rap DJ]. I had a meeting with him at the St George's Hotel, to try to talk him into coming, and I asked him what it was like working at Capital, and he said, 'Well, they just ignore me, frankly. My real frustration is that I have to work round Pink Lady ads, and whenever I want to do an outside broadcast from a club I have to find a sponsor.' I said that working for the BBC he wouldn't have to do that. I explained that the BBC wasn't about getting sponsors, but doing what we believed was right for our listeners. He thought that was fantastic.

The important thing was that we could reassure him that we valued what he stood for, and that we weren't doing it cynically. We said we understood the integrity of his relationship with his listeners, something he's very proud of. He really understands what you have to do on the street to get respect – continuing to go back to clubs and community centres even after you get famous. He didn't want to be seen to sell out by going to a national radio station. But really this was like his real home – he is the epitome of the public service broadcaster. He has a real understanding of people's lives, and he's not above them or patronizing to them.

Once, I took Westwood for drinks in John Birt's office. John said that after all this hoo-ha with Steve Wright he thought he'd have drinks with some of the presenters to show he was on-side. Westwood and John got on like a house on fire. Westwood came out saying, 'I really love working for him! He's my man!'

Paul Robinson: I think the whole music policy was improved. I wanted to tighten it up, make it more competitive, and particularly bring more stationality to it.

What you had at Radio 1 was a series of production teams who worked in isolation. Each presenter had his own producer, own broadcast assistant, and they worked like silos. So frequently you had people chasing the same guests, playing the same records. It was clear something needed to change after the *Gary Davies Show*, which at that point preceded Steve Wright, played a record at five to three, finished his show, Steve Wright came on, jingles, fanfare, played exactly the same record.

I did a number of things. I introduced Selector into the BBC, a computerized music scheduling system. I wanted the playlist records to have a coherence and exist as a continuous strand through the programming, into which you bolted on all the goodies and all the light and shade which was chosen by the producer and the presenter. So in fact you had a sense of there being a character to the station, but then there was colour and different flavours in each individual programme.

I didn't want to take the element of choice away from the producer or presenter, but it was ridiculous that they had complete choice and could play anything at whim, at any time. It was clear that we needed someone central saying, 'I am going to decide what records are played and I will decide the playlist and I will tell you.'

Prior to this, the playlist was a democratic process. Well, I didn't believe in the democratic process, I believed in a benign dictatorship. I thought that one person should have a view about how a playlist should operate, and should shape it so it had some structure and some reason for existing. That was quite different to how it had operated in the past. There was a playlist but they cheated. Producers and presenters chose their favourites, dropped the ones they didn't like, moved things around, so in fact the station had these hideous clashes. The change happened just before Matthew arrived, but I sharpened it up after he came. Remember, Matthew really didn't understand much about new music at all.

Matthew Bannister: Paul Robinson focused the music policy to a certain degree. We certainly got more control of it than anyone had ever had in the past. But I have to say that I wasn't entirely happy with the policy that he put in place. I'd listened to his advice and let him have his head to do it, but we had very heavy rotation of big hits.

That Prince record, 'Beautiful Girl' I think it was called, was on once every ninety minutes and it was driving me mad. There was a very mechanistic approach to it, a sense that if you put everything in boxes then you could add it all up to 100 and it would all come right, and the audience figures would go up again, which, of course, isn't the case. You can use all the tools at your disposal but if you're not sensitive to music and to its effect on the audience then you can't get it right.

So I was getting to the stage where I found that very frustrating, I knew it was wrong. When Liz Forgan came to me and said, 'We think Paul would be very good at this new job we've got, head of strategy across radio. Would you mind if I approached him?' I said, 'Not at all, carry on.' That was when Trevor Dann came in.

Trevor Dann: The way I got recruited was bizarre, because Matthew wanted to move Chris Lycett who was head of Radio 1 production at that point, so he put a headhunter on to it. Now I know how much that headhunter cost, because eventually I had to pay the bill. It cost £26,000, and he could have got me for the price of a local phone call. He could have rung me up and said, 'Trevor, this isn't working, I can't do this without you, let's put the old team back together,' and he just . . . couldn't. My friend Nick Wapshott of the *Saturday Times* has a line on this. He says that it was as if Bannister was in the desert, and he's starving, and there are two things that he can do. He can either take the suicide pill, or he can ring me up – pill or my phone number – and in the end he has to ring me up.

It must have been very difficult for him, because he probably thought, Fucking hell, I don't want Trevor in here, because this is mine now, I'm proving that I can run a radio station, I don't need him this time. So from the very beginning of me coming back it became pretty clear that a distance was being created. I felt that I was treating him like I always had and sort of popping in and saying, 'Go down the pub?' and he was, 'I'm afraid I'm busy today, but I may be able to see you one day next week, please see Sarah and put a date in the diary . . .' Wait a minute, it's me, you don't have to talk to me like this, but I found that that's the tension that has just carried on throughout all of this really, that's why people will say to you, 'Well, of course they hate each other,' but it's not true, and it certainly isn't as simple as that.

Matthew Bannister: It was clear at this time that we really needed a new Head of Production for Radio 1 because the production teams really weren't working according to the new plans and supporting the new talent. And also we needed someone to get a grip on the new music policy, so we began looking and, in the bizarre way of the BBC, it wasn't my job to make that appointment, it was the job of somebody who was Controller of BBC Radio Production. But we sat together and we decided the best thing to do was to employ a head-hunter to look at all the available talent in the market to make sure we got the best person. I was aware that Trevor was around, he'd been doing some work for us as an independent producer, but I didn't know whether he'd be interested. And I certainly couldn't be seen just to shove my old mate into a job at the BBC without asking: 'Who else is out there? Who might be better?' So the head-hunters came back with a field of six candidates who we interviewed and Trevor was one of those. And on the day he did the best interview and that's how we hired him. It was quite surprising to me really, and it must have been odd for him to find that his young Radio Nottingham protégé turned out to be his boss – not once but twice.

Trevor Dann: When they came to me and asked me to do the job [January 1995], I hadn't actually listened hard to radio or mainstream programming for a long time. I had my views like we all do, but I hadn't really sat and studied it. So I sat down and made a conscious effort to listen to it for two or three consecutive days, and it just became clear to me that it was a ragbag, that in an effort to please everyone, it was pleasing no one, because it was falling down a hole in the middle. They were trying to be trendy and still keep the old ELO fans. I just felt that there were never three records in a row that any one person could like, because the playlist was so disparate.

So I came up with a sort of rule of thumb that we should stop playing records made before 1990. And I also said we're going to have to be a bit more picky about what we play: it was no good saying, 'Is it a good record?', we have to say, 'Is it an appropriate record?' And so I had very big fights in the early days about whether we should play a Luther Vandross single. Well, yes, he's popular, but it was an old-fashioned record, so no. Should we play the new Beatles single 'Free as a Bird'? No, because a) it was shite, and b) it just had no relevance. If we're going to be for fifteen to twenty-four year olds, let's be for them. I remember when 'Common People' came out, and I remember Jeff Smith, who was working closely with me, said, 'Oh, I think we should play this, put it on the C list.' I said, 'No, put it straight on the A list.' It's brilliant, and it's exactly what we're about, absolutely about today's pop music. I used to talk about how in the sixties, records that were four years old were considered to be absolutely unplayable, but up to now we were quite happy to play records that were twenty-four years old. So basically I just squeezed it down and focused it.

Trying to bring the margins into the daytime is . . . the audience is not robust enough to put up with it. I remember in the very early days of Matthew's tenure here, when he put Nicky Campbell on the drivetime show with interviews. I had Andy Kershaw in the car and we were both talking about the fact that Campbell interviewed Tim Pat Coogan, the IRA expert, for about forty minutes. At drivetime on Radio 1. I thought, This is GLR! I think Matthew felt, Oh I can give these Radio 1 listeners some stimulating stuff and they'll thank me for it. But instead they just went, 'Err, don't want this, I can get this elsewhere, and probably on LBC or GLR or Radio 4.' Which is why a year or so later he turned it all on its head and went for 'new music first'.

I wrote Matthew a paper, and said, 'This is what I'm going to do,' and he said, 'Brilliant.' I think we maybe talked about records three times in two years: once he asked me why a certain record was being played more than he thought it should, once we had a discussion about whether there were too many boy bands on the playlist, which he felt there were, and once we talked about whether we should play that record by The Luniz called '5 On It', because it was so heavily drug referred.

Matthew Bannister (*Speaking at Bristol Sound City Festival, April 1995*): A combination of demographics and economics is driving commercial radio towards the middle-aged middle class. And, in a sweeping generalization, what those middle-aged middle-class listeners want is comfort – music they already know or that sounds like something they already know. The first manifestation was the emergence of the Gold stations, trading exclusively on the nostalgia of the baby boomers and trying in many cases to re-create the Radio 1 of the sixties and seventies. Next came Virgin Radio, aimed at the album buying baby boomers – the Audi-driving, designer suit-wearing crowd who are always there in force when Eric Clapton plays seventeen nights on the trot in the plush luxury of London's Royal Albert Hall.

Then the market analysts spotted that middle-aged women were ill-served in commercial radio, so they imported Adult Contemporary radio from the USA – playing old hits by Whitney Houston, Phil Collins, Paul Simon – in fact anything as long as it was soft, melodic and familiar. Heart FM in Birmingham is about to become Heart FM in London, and I predict we'll see more of this format if the Radio Authority thinks it's successful.

And as these formats begin to arrive to do battle with the existing commercial FM stations, they begin to move too. They had been differentiating themselves from their Gold sister stations by concentrating on the top forty, but now they too are beginning to move. They are trying to head off the new competition by moving towards the middle ground, playing more established classic hits and taking fewer and fewer risks with new music and artists.

But amidst all this . . . something is happening in music. New music in the UK has never been more exciting and is beginning to find a renewed foothold in that notoriously difficult market – the USA. It is here that we see the vital importance of a station whose only aim is to take risks with new talent and new music, a station which will ignore the bottom line in favour of a major cultural public service. In short, Radio 1.

As the commercial stations cluster in the traffic jam in the middle lane, Radio 1 will speed through the fast lane to take the lead. And as commercial stations fight the competitive battle by throwing money at their potential listeners in big prize giveaways and promotions, we'll simply make the most exciting programmes anywhere on the airwaves. We will be the only place to hear the UK's hot new music – first.

Paul Robinson: Matthew doesn't know a great deal about music. He's not particularly a music fan. He's learnt to say the right things, but when he came in he didn't know anything about music and he admitted as much to me.

He certainly wasn't into new bands, and he certainly wasn't advocating at that point we have to be Blur, Oasis, Sleeper, Prodigy, whoever it is, not at all, that wasn't his agenda at all. His favourite artist was Richard Thompson, and still is. And I remember him lobbying very hard for Richard Thompson to go on the playlist. Frank Zappa was another one.

Pete Tong: Two things helped drag Radio 1 round. One was its commitment to dance music, and then along came Oasis and Blur – manna from heaven.

After a while, I was able to take the radio station with me, so in the day we were playing Oasis, and at night we were broadcasting live from the best clubs in the country. Those two things together just spoke instinctively to young people. If you're on national radio preaching the gospel on a specialist type of music, you better be respected by the core of that scene, and we were. But that's what the Beerling era got wrong – they put DJs on if they liked their demo tape, but the best technical DJs aren't always those that know what's going on.

I'm really proud of the fact that I probably played the first Prodigy record on the radio, the first Leftfield record, the first Underworld record. The other great thing that happened to dance music in the mid-nineties is that whereas in the seventies and eighties dance music was always about the moment, and great records were made by artists that would never make another one, and the scene was a producer medium, now it's a band medium – bands win the Mercury Prize and go on tour and headline festivals. They're all children of the acid house rave scene, and all this helps Radio 1, because it means it can support these bands, and play them early and record them live, so all the traditional Radio 1 resources can actually champion a very credible scene.

Jo Whiley: Yes Britpop was a gift to us, but no one else was playing it at the beginning. When the Oasis Columbia 12 inch came in we put it on and gave them a session straight away, months before they had a hit. We booked them for *Sound City*, the first live radio event they'd done. We were the only people to pick on that stuff and dared to put these bands live on the radio. No other station was interested in them for at least a year.

Rhys Hughes: When I first got there in 1995, the odd Eric Clapton or Phil Collins record would turn up on the script. But Trevor was weeding them out. It was an exciting time. At one playlist meeting the Prodigy's 'Firestarter' came up, and everyone was going, 'Great record, but is it daytime?' I think the vast majority of producers thought it might squeeze on to the C list and get eight plays a week, but Trevor said, 'No, bollocks, let's stick it straight on the A list.' I think Radio 1 helped make 'Firestarter' a number one record. Other stations wouldn't touch it, although they were all very happy to criticize Radio 1 for not playing Status Quo or the Beatles.

Trevor Dann: When I arrived, the playlist meeting was a mammoth squalling affair, at which anyone at Radio 1 was invited, and the people who shouted the loudest got their way. People from some specialist programme would be banging on about stuff, but often the mainstream producers didn't turn up at all. That meant that when it came to persuading the talent to play these records, the daytime producers wouldn't be very supportive. So I said that the playlist meeting should be attended only by those who are going to have to play these records in the mainstream programmes, which brought it right down to being seven or eight people and me, and it became a much more effective meeting, and it meant that when it was published, everybody in the room was signed up to it, and so they delivered the music properly on air. And that meant that for the first time on Radio 1, the playlist was actually what you heard, whereas in the past, for all those years, the big DJs had gone, 'Oh I don't like that one – I'm not playing Shakin' Stevens' or whatever, and they'd all been able to ride roughshod over it.

David Walker (Manager, Status Quo): Mr Dann . . . on behalf of Radio 1, instigated a policy banning any producer from playing our new recordings other than the one play it would be necessary to give on their Sunday afternoon Top Forty chart show . . . abusing his power by unilaterally declaring that Status Quo do not suit the demographic of Radio 1's audience.

Francis Rossi (Singer/guitarist, Status Quo): Issuing the writ was a decision we made as a band. The history is that four or five singles were blanked – hadn't been played for whatever reason. We sent them up to Radio 1, and one hadn't been played because it wasn't enough like Status Quo, and one was too much like Status Quo. Whilst we never expected saturation play, we thought that if we worked to get it into the charts, and did all these poxy promo things that you don't want to do – then at least they'd play it. But no – they're not playing by the rules here.

Matthew Bannister – at least he's been true to his word. He made Radio 1 more élitist. In other words there are less people listening to it. He's given a lot of us older acts a place to go – Radio 2. But there's this stigma attached to Radio 2. Not hip.

We were asked by Radio 1 to come back from the middle of a tour – we were in Switzerland – to do a show with Emma Freud, a midday one-hour live special. I didn't want to do it, but my management said, 'Oh it's Radio 1, they've been good to us over the years.' So we decide to do it. We receive a call two days later, saying, 'It's gone upstairs, and the whole thing's been cancelled.' So what is it Radio 1 has against us? And then Emma Freud leaves the following week.

So all these things are conspiring against us. We're all on the bus in Europe, and we decide to do something about it. We knew that if we did this, most people would say it's sour grapes. We didn't want to do it, but it would have meant letting another single go. It's very hard to explain. The action seemed to be the only way to get through to our own fans what was going on. We thought we had nothing to lose. If the record would have been given even a little bit of play, then we wouldn't have said a word. They could have still kept us out.

So we went for it, and I suppose in retrospect it was a bad move. The lawyers came up with the angle that we'd done a show for them for free to celebrate their twenty-fifth anniversary, and that they owed us. Again we didn't want to do it, but we were persuaded. 125,000 people. They said that before the gig we were voted the band that most listeners wanted to hear live. And then a while later we get the word from above that we didn't suit the demographics.

Trevor Dann: We knew absolutely nothing at all until a press release landed on our desks saying, in very portentous language, something like, 'Tomorrow at the Langham Hotel a major group will announce a major action.' It didn't say 'against the BBC'. Then it turned out it was Quo, but we still couldn't work out what they were doing. Then they had their big announcement and we were utterly bemused by it. I remember thinking, This is funny, and it's really working for us, because a great spotlight is being shone on our attempts to turn Radio 1 around. A band who are in some quarters a bit of a joke, and who represent so much of what we were trying to get rid of, were drawing everyone's attention to what we were trying to achieve.

They issued two writs, one seeking a judicial review of BBC policy, in light of what they claimed was Radio 1's announcement that it was a Top Forty station. Of course that's something we had never announced. The other writ sought damages for the fact that we hadn't played their record even though it had got in the Top Forty, and which they felt had therefore damaged their sales. Let's not forget that the record in question was not one of those great old Status Quo records: it was a hopelessly incompetent remaking of 'Fun Fun Fun' by the Beach Boys, and it was actually recorded with the Beach Boys – a pub version. That afternoon the phones went bonkers, and I did lots of interviews. One particular one they picked up, in which I said that what they had done was a publicity stunt. They then issued a third writ, citing me for defamation.

Over the course of the next year or so the case for judicial review was thrown out by a judge in chambers, and the other two were settled. One of the agreements of the settlements was that we couldn't talk about how they were settled.

Francis Rossi: Maybe we played into Bannister's hands. It brought a very high profile to the idea that this was going to be a station for young people.

We used to be unique in this country in that we had a coast-to-coast radio station. If your song did get played this morning, you know that every fucker from Lands End to John o'Groats had a chance of hearing it. Now the way radio is going, you don't.

I like current music. I liked 'Love Is the Law' by the Seahorses on *Top of the Pops*, but I can't deal with the fact that it's 'new', because there's no way – it sounds like a cross between the Beatles and Badfinger. I liked a recent Wallflowers record, and 'Gangsta's Paradise'. But mostly with rap [*blows a raspberry*] – I'm not interested. I don't see that the street culture of LA has anything to do with West Drayton. I play CDs in my car. I play Tori Amos, although I always did like a girl who sings with her legs apart.

Chapter 6

I've Decided to Destroy it Myself

Evans and Bannister:
'That was the defining moment
... the moment it stopped
being "Radio 1 is shit" '

Trevor Dann: I think I'd only been at Radio 1 for two weeks when Steve Wright resigned, perhaps ten days. Matthew busily negotiated with Steve to stay on, and all of us – me, Andy Parfitt, everybody, just kind of went into a huddle and went, 'Who the fuck are we going to talk to?'

Absolutely out of the blue, and quite separately from all this I thought, John Revell rang me up. He had been working at Virgin Radio as their launch programme director and I think was now looking for new things. We had not parted on fantastic terms from GLR, but he said, 'Look, I'd really like to see you again, and I'd really like to be seen coming to Radio 1, I think that'd be a really groovy thing to do, let's go and have a pizza.' So he came in, I showed him around, we went off to Sergio's and sat and had a bowl of pasta and talked, as we would, about Chris Evans, because he was our mutual contact.

It was soon clear that Revell was working with Evans on various things, and we began to talk about what was going to happen after Steve left, and I think it gradually dawned on me that Revell was an emissary from Evans to find out how the land was lying and whether it was worth them having a bash at going for the breakfast show. So we kind of loosely discussed it, and I think I probably said something to John like, 'Well, frankly, I think Matthew would be interested – get Chris to give us a ring.'

I came back to the office and I went straight to see Matthew and said, 'I've just had lunch with Revell, he says Evans might be interested,' and Matthew went, 'Oh brilliant, I'm going to ring him now.' And he went behind his desk, and I remember this so vividly, and he rang Chris's home number and left him a message, and that was it.

Matthew Bannister: I thought, Well, why not just ring him up? I hadn't seen him for nine months or so. So I called him, and he said, 'I know what you want to talk to me about – come round to my flat this afternoon.' He had a flat in Docklands, overlooking Tower Bridge, on the penthouse floor, with views both ways. He'd just been to rehearsals for *Toothbrush*, and we had a cup of tea, and I said, 'I'd really like you to . . .' and I was about to give him this spiel about 'to your advantage and my advantage', and he said, 'You don't have to sell this to me – I'd really like to do it. The way I think about this is that I should always do things that make me so excited that I want to go to the toilet. I'm so excited about doing the Radio 1 breakfast show that I have to go to the toilet now.' He said, 'I want this, but I want to produce it myself with my own company, just give me overnight to think about it.'

So I left, incredibly excited. We spoke on the phone the next morning, and he said, 'I'm definitely going to do it, sort it with my agent, and get Matthew Freud involved.' Matthew was his PR, and he came to see me to talk about how we were going to promote the show.

I was then rung up by Matthew the next Saturday, when I was down at my cottage in Sussex. He said, 'This is beginning to leak, and we better make a big splash. What I want you to do is come up to London, and we'll stage a photograph for the *News of the World*, where they can appear to get a secret shot of you and Chris doing the deal.'

So I drove up to London in the car, to where Chris was rehearsing *Toothbrush* in the LWT studios. An extraordinary business. The photographer came up to me as I got out of my car, and said, 'Hello, are you Matthew Bannister?' I said, 'Yeah.' He said, 'I'll come with you then so that we can stage this secret shot.'

So I went in to find Chris, and watched the rehearsal for a bit, and then we went into the canteen, and they found a balcony outside where the photographer could hide behind a bush, behind some railings, and me and Chris came out through some French windows with our plastic cups of tea on to this rather crap balcony with wooden picnic tables. And then we sat down and pretended to do the deal, which of course we had done already.

Sadly, it didn't make the *News of the World*, which I was disappointed about, having dragged myself up from Sussex. But then it was a full page in the *Sun* on Monday, the same blurred pics with me and Chris looking rather dishevelled, with the headline, 'The million pound cup of tea'.

That was the defining moment, the turning point in our PR. There's no doubt that that was the moment it stopped being 'Radio 1 is shit', and started being 'something exciting's happening at Radio 1'. And from all the stuff that's been written about us, that's the one page of newsprint that I'll keep.

Matthew Freud (Public Relations Director): Unofficially I suppose I've represented Chris all his life.

The first show he produced in London was my sister's. I met him through that. He was a funny, geeky, strange boy, very wide-eyed. We vaguely kept in touch for eighteen months, and then I helped him get an agent when he got the Power Station job; I signed him to the Noel Gay company. When he got the TVam job he came to see me, and I moved him over to [agent] Michael Foster at ICM, and I got him a lawyer. Just being helpful.

I'd given him a little bit of help about his PR, about how he might work his profile, and when it was worth doing it and when it wasn't. When he got the *Big Breakfast* job we took on Planet 24 [*Big Breakfast*'s production company] and helped launch it, and so officially I started representing him then.

We took a very strategic view, and said, 'Entertainment is about very long careers.' At the time we were very conscious of Jonathan Ross, and how it's easy to allow your publicity to adversely affect your career very early on, just by doing too much and by satiating the media appetite for who you are. We took a view that once we established him as a star, we would be very, very regimented in the control that we'd take. It's such a preciously guarded profile.

The reason Matthew paid the money he did for Chris was not entirely because of Chris's talent, but because of Chris's media equity. Radio does not have many personalities. Radio is seen either as a stepping stone to TV, in which case presenters lose their personalities to a certain extent to television, or careers stall at radio. And the media does not regard DJs, even a Radio 1 DJ, as being fantastically newsworthy.

There was a very important conversation I had with Chris around *Don't Forget Your Toothbrush*. This was his big shot, and he'd just done the first and rather disastrous pilot – a total horlicks. We spent about three or four hours very late one night talking about how a programme can basically market itself. The concept emerged of a word-of-mouth check on each show, the idea of looking at a programme after you'd done it and saying not, 'Was it a great show?' but, 'Are there one, two, three, four things that people would be talking about?' In the States they call them watercooler moments, people standing round at work or in the pub the next day saying, 'Did you see . . .?' or 'Did you hear . . .?' Since *Toothbrush*, every show that Chris has ever done has always had these moments. Quite often they're put in gratuitously, and effectively they're what allows you to do your own marketing. If two million people have watched your show, and they then go and talk about it rather than just passively viewing, then the audience will grow. That's how Chris has built his audience in everything he's done. It's all geared around giving people something to say, and the press something to write. And I've never had to say to him, 'Could you please give us something more to work with?'

Trevor Dann: It was all terribly exciting, and then came this awful moment where Matthew said, 'Basically the good news is he'll do it, but the bad news for you is that he doesn't want to work in-house, he wants to do it as an independent.' Because in his GLR days he had done a weekend afternoon show for Radio 1 for thirteen weeks which he had not enjoyed, and I think he felt that the restrictions of the BBC were such that he wouldn't be allowed to flourish. My thing was, 'You can't let him, don't let him do that, Matthew, because you've just brought me in to make this department better, and get the atmosphere humming, and if you take the breakfast show away from me and give it to an independent you're not giving me a chance, and if I have Chris I can prove to everybody how this is now an exciting place to work.' So anyway, he said he was unable to persuade Chris.

Matthew Bannister: Chris absolutely insisted that the only way he would do the *Radio 1 Breakfast Show* was through his own company, Ginger Productions, and that wasn't a strange thing for Radio 1, we already had independent productions – the Tim Westwood show was independently produced and several others – and they'd been very successful. Chris was adamant that he wouldn't work in-house for the Music Entertainment Production Department, and I agreed to that because that was the terms and conditions on which he said he would come. I remember having to go and tell Trevor about it, and I took him for a drink, and I said, 'Trevor, great news, we've got Chris Evans, it's fantastic. But the bad news for you is that he insists on it being an independent production and he won't do it through your department.' I think he resented that decision. He felt that it had in some way undermined his authority and so he set about knocking the Chris Evans show internally and stirring up feeling against it and there was bad feeling between him and Chris and John Revell. So much so, that I remember once Chris storming into my office and saying he wanted to kill Trevor, he was going to put him up against a wall, get him by the throat and hit him. And I had to calm Chris down and really smooth over that situation because Chris was very emotional about the way in which he felt he was being dealt with by Trevor. And it came to situations later where he felt that when the show was a success Trevor was claiming the credit for it, when in fact Chris felt it had been Ginger Productions, Chris Evans, and John Revell who had made the show a success. So there was a very difficult and tough atmosphere .

Chris Evans (Disc Jockey): I said to [Bannister], 'If I'm going to have to take a risk, so are you. You are going to have to be totally committed to the show.' If my friends had found out I was joining Radio 1, they would have locked me up in an asylum.

Matthew Bannister: Several years before, he had come to Radio 1 for a Sunday afternoon show which he absolutely hated. He rang me up one day for advice on whether he should leave. They'd taken all the spontaneity out of the show, made him put everything on tape to stop him offending anybody, and he'd been ticked off for not being a team player. He said, 'I really can't stand this any longer, I think I'm going to get some TV work, shall I leave?' And I said, 'Yes, absolutely, it's the best thing you'll ever do for yourself.'

Johnny Beerling: The show was not a great success for several reasons. I think the producer was wrong for Chris Evans, a personality clash. And he wanted it to be like his GLR show, which wouldn't really have worked so well outside London. And he wanted to do whatever he wanted to, without adhering to the usual formats or accepted ways that we had of doing things. I suppose you could say it was a foretaste of what was to happen when he came back, although he was a very big star by then.

Matthew Bannister: The initial fee of £1 million came from them. It was a question of us working out if we could afford it, but he wanted to have a deal that was the biggest deal ever done for a radio show, and all of this for PR reasons, and for his own ego reasons. The figure did rise to £1.4 million, but that was the sum paid to his production company Ginger, not his own fee. We did a list of all the independent production contracts that BBC radio had that year, and whilst Chris Evans was at number one in terms of the size of it, in terms of broadcasting per hour he was about number thirty-five out of fifty. We got a huge volume of output from him, two and a half hours a day, five days a week, compared to a drama on Radio

4 which might be ninety minutes for £15,000 to £20,000. His entire production company got – what? – about £7,000 a show.

For the breakfast show I was extremely keen to avoid the pitfalls that we'd fallen into with Steve Wright. I had negotiated into the contract a clause that said he must play all the records that we chose in the order that we chose them, and that he must play the trailers at the given times.

We negotiated the clocks with John Revell, who was to be his executive producer. It was very tightly formatted to begin with – it had absolutely fixed, regular features – *The Kids are All Right (But Only If They Are Completely Wrong)*, *On the Bog*, *Personality or Person*, which was famous people being asked ordinary questions like, 'How much is a pint of milk?' We also agreed that Dan McGrath would be the sidekick, and I don't think it had Holly on at the beginning. That just evolved from her role as a researcher.

We did three pilots. The discussion we had most about was pace. And from the start I didn't like this character he had called Charlie Manning, who was an unfunny northern comedian that Dan used to play. It didn't work because it was just bad jokes. So we had a lot of debate about that. I allowed him to keep it in because Chris was sure it would develop, but in the end we dropped it after three or four months. I didn't like *On the Bog* very much: It was Chris and Dan allegedly on two toilets side by side, and there was dripping water behind them, and they were talking about some aspect of modern life. Again it was a bit childish and contrived. But we didn't change much.

On the first day [24 April 1995], we had the world and his wife outside the studios. We filmed a bit of it for the As It Is campaign, and there's a great bit where Chris goes to some photographers, 'Don't bring those bad vibes into my happy studio – I wouldn't come into your workplace and be miserable and horrible like that.' It was a wonderful morning.

Liz Forgan: I knew about Chris Evans because I was at Channel 4 when he did the *Big Breakfast*. I saw that show on paper and I said, 'This show cannot work because it has nothing in it, there's no river to sail the boats on, you've got six good ideas for items, but every morning for two hours . . . what is the background, what is the thing that's carrying it?' And it was Chris. I said, 'Don't be silly, no one person can possibly do that,' and he did. I've just never seen a performer with that absolutely unending spring of charming, sweet, crazy, zany, creative, endless babble and vision that Chris had. He really has an extraordinary form of creativity out of nothing, which is exactly what you want on a radio programme. I just thought he was a complete and utter genius. Of course, things happen to geniuses.

The money – well, it was big but it wasn't that tremendously big. People forget that Radio 1 was a very big deal for the BBC in the sense that it brought a critically important audience of young people who didn't use the BBC very much, and they're the future licence payers of the Corporation. Matthew was triumphant when he got him, and so was I delighted for him, because he'd been through a long time of absolute slings and arrows, standing up at platform after platform while people sneered at him and rubbished him and accused him of being everything from a lackey of John Birt to a talentless . . . it was terrible and he took it wonderfully. I knew that Chris would just turn everything round, and it was worth the money, no doubt.

Matthew Freud: Chris understood very early that his media equity was the single most valuable commodity that he had. He reasoned that because he was going to be around for a long time we would use the media for our own agenda rather than theirs. Fortunately, those agendas meet quite often.

We're quite good at making sure that what is effectively one story elongates over a long period of time. We do that by leveraging access to him, so for a number of days it's kind of, 'Do what we want and you'll get him,' so then you've got the media working very hard to show you how supportive they're being, then they get him. And then, because they've built up reader interest, you're then able to disseminate information through them for the next two or three weeks. On the breakfast show we had coverage for virtually the whole run, and for four and a half months we had uninterrupted daily coverage.

The skill is to milk and bleed the story. You work out how many different layers there are. The rule of thumb is that you only ever give a story as much as it needs: any extra information that is not going to impact on the size of the story, you hold that back. So the news that Chris Evans is going to Radio 1 is going to run, and then next day speculation about how much Chris is going to be getting is also going to run, so there's no point throwing it away too early. It all depends on the level to which you can deconstruct a story.

Simon Garfield: In May 1995, Radio 1 management drew up several 'position papers' analysing its future approach towards listeners, non-listeners, national and specialist press, students and opinion formers. The overall aim was consistency, and the clear delivery of a simple message: Radio 1 has changed dramatically, and was now hip again, and was worthy of your attention.

The arrival of Chris Evans represented a significant part of this transformation, but was far from the only factor; it was hoped that his arrival would shine a light on all the other exciting but less newsworthy aspects of the station: the specialist DJs, the coverage of live concerts and festivals, and the social action campaigns focusing on drugs, AIDS, exam pressures. 'Cracking this [credibility] issue will guarantee our future success,' one of the position papers argued. 'Listeners must feel they are listening to the most credible station in the UK. We need to raise the profile of the station as a whole by deploying the personnel of the station – the experts – producers as well as presenters . . . We need to organize events such as workshops in schools, another *On Campus* tour, the *Essential Mix* tour and Westwood's *Live Rap Show* which demonstrate Radio 1's unbeatable expertise in these areas.'

Under a section marked 'Resignations', the documents said, 'Stress that the station is more than just individual presenters. It is a fact of life that people sometimes change jobs. Prepare contingency plans.' In a section on the roadshow it stated, 'Let's hope nobody resigns on stage.'

In future press coverage, 'We must maximize accessibility of key presenters to do the right sort of interviews. We do not want 'Me and My Body', but we do want 'A Day in the Life'.

In terms of listening figures, it was considered important that, 'We must not lose our nerve in being confident about our radio station to the national press. We are still the biggest pop music station in the UK – double the size of our nearest rivals.' There were also plans 'to prepare for a drop in the listening figures next quarter. Plan statement if Chris Evans fails to deliver increased audience. Move away from figures measuring success.'

Elsewhere in the corporation, Broadcasting Research was preparing a detailed survey into the effects of Chris Evans. At the end of June 1995, ten weeks into the new show, 551 people aged fifteen to forty-four were asked what they thought of him. Most listeners found the show good to wake up to: almost 90 per cent agreed that it was lively, funny or enjoyable, and about 30 per cent believed it was getting repetitive, irritating and too noisy and chaotic. Seventeen per cent agreed that it was too smutty.

Research of this nature usually closes with listeners' own observations in their own words, often the most entertaining element of the survey. Here, listeners found that Evans 'comes up with really unusual things, not like other presenters', and 'he's dynamic and takes risks – and he treats you like a normal person. He is not pretentious.' One listener enjoyed 'the childish pranks which make you forget the world's troubles'; another found him 'more lively, with better music' than Steve Wright. But some people thought he was 'a ginger-haired irritating git'; 'some of the things Chris Evans says are disgusting'; the show was 'crude, bawdy, unintelligent, unprofessional'; 'the man needs psychiatric help. He's totally manic, with no sense.'

Matthew Wright: Chris Evans was so important to Radio 1 because every other appointment that had come through in the new Matthew Bannister regime was pretty much deemed to be a failure or never populist. I mean Emma Freud and Lisa I'Anson – a great DJ and everything else but she's never going to be the queen of breakfast shows.

Despite the fact that one could argue that he's an obnoxious, arrogant whatever, at the time he joined Radio 1 he was enjoying the warmest popular appreciation of what he does. It was just so unusual that a guy that had a high profile TV personality, albeit on a Channel 4 show, should decide to go to Radio 1 at a time when everyone's writing it off as a doomed, failing exercise. His decision to join gave the station a kind of rubber stamping, his own personal rubber stamping of the changes Matthew Bannister was introducing. Incredibly important. Then of course it was actually a bloody good show, at least at the beginning.

At the *Mirror* and the *Sun* he was the first person we would want to write about. You're not gonna get endless copy out of – I shouldn't pick on her because she's lovely – Lisa I'Anson. The new Radio 1 people had no public profile, or they were seen late at night on TV on cultural reviews. So at long last the tabloids had somebody that they could actually write about who the public have heard of and are interested in. So from the day he arrived, it happened – we were all away with endless stories.

The fact that he also chose to go down the sort of Howard Stern route meant that there was a story every day. The Evans thing linked up into a publicity team that's behind him because journalists cannot cover everything. You cannot listen to the whole show when you're coming into work, especially if you also want to listen to Virgin and Capital. So you are automatically in the hands of the PRs. And it was not just the Radio 1 press office, but Freuds – far more aggressive, far more proactive, basically spoon-feeding.

I think the whole radio industry is still benefiting from that moment because it's become increasingly obvious that people are getting interested in radio again.

Jo Watson (Broadcast Analyst): When Chris started we did some more research of our own, and the results were split fifty-fifty. People loved him or hated him, but it was clear that there was going to be a big churn [audience switching from one station to another] and that he was going to have a massive effect on the figures. And when the Rajar figures came in – a massive effect. All the additional research we did was extremely positive – you just don't get presenters who are scoring that highly in research.

Simon Garfield: On the first day of his new breakfast show, Evans had serenaded listeners with 'Welcome Home', the sappy ballad by Peters and Lee. The message was, 'It's okay to listen to Radio 1 again – no shame any more.'

Although the audience figures were on the increase shortly before Evans arrived, in part due to the new music policy, his first full set of figures were remarkable, and were the cause of much relief among management. In the space of three months, breakfast show listeners increased from 6.1 to 6.81 million. The figures fell in the next quarter (July–September 1995), but then increased to 7.19 million in the last three months of the year. In the first three months of 1996 the average monthly reach stood at 7.36 million. Several months later he told Bryan Appleyard of the *Sunday Times*, 'We didn't get half a million more listeners, we got 7.5 million new, younger, hipper listeners. We changed the demographic profile of that station.'

Inevitably, Evans's performance increased the listening figures for the station overall, but not as fast as he increased his own ratings; it was clear that other shows on the station were still not performing as well as comparative shows a couple of years earlier. Management realized that if Evans was to leave, they would have serious problems again. From an average weekly reach of 10.5 million listeners in the three months before he joined, the next quarter increased to 11.07, and then to 11.21

million three months later. A year after he joined, the figures for listeners aged fifteen plus stood at 11.25 million. The figures for listeners aged four plus increased from 12.28 million in the first quarter of 1995 to 12.87 million a year later.

Internal BBC research, conducted a year after Evans's arrival, suggested that not all his listeners were happy with what they heard. Out of 375 people questioned, 23 per cent believed he made too many crude jokes, while 52 per cent agreed that he was too smug and self-interested. Forty-eight per cent agreed that he criticized people in the media too much, but 91 per cent reckoned that he still made them laugh. Thirty-three per cent thought they were listening more than they were six months ago, and 12 per cent thought they were listening less. People were asked what they would do if they were Matthew Bannister. Three per cent thought Evans should be sacked; 11 per cent felt he should be stopped going quite so far; two-thirds thought he should be allowed to carry on exactly as he is; a fifth thought he should be given more freedom.

Matthew Bannister: It did get to the stage where I was lying in bed with the covers over my head, thinking, 'What's he going to say now?' The classic one was the Brussels sprouts joke. 'What do Brussels sprouts and pubic hair have in common?' 'You push them both aside and carry on eating.' He told this at five to eight on BBC national radio. We said to the papers, 'I don't think Chris understood the implications of what he was saying.'

Polly Ravenscroft: That was awful, that morning. The press were going, 'Come off it!'

Matthew Bannister: To be honest with you, we never had a cross word – not in ten years. We would have a proper discussion. On the pubic hair joke he said, 'Hands up – Matthew, I was wrong.' We would always talk intelligently about what the parameters were for the show. I wasn't running the show thinking this must be a Methodist chapel. I wanted it to be controversial and near the edge, and my job was to be the edge. And to point out to Chris every time he banged his head on it. There were many things that were controversial but absolutely defensible, a lot more of those than the six or seven tiny incidents that we had to apologize for, or I had to apologize to our listeners for. Much of it was just good fun – Chris threatening to expose the name of his plumber who had done a terrible job on his house, a very funny piece of broadcasting.

But the show evolved very fast. All the features and fixed spots that we'd talked about swiftly dropped away. Chris was exhilarated and frightened – the thing about fixed spots is that they give you something to cling on to – you don't need to invent, invent, invent. But after a few months virtually all the fixed spots had gone and it was live soap opera.

Simon Mayo: I thought it was great. How much he got paid didn't bother me. If you want Ronaldo to play for your team you pay £15 million, if that's the price that has to be paid. I've never been one for that kind of snipey attitude to it.

For most people he was the person from the *Big Breakfast* and *Don't Forget Your Toothbrush*, and they hadn't heard what he did on radio. I always thought he was fine on television, but he's much better on radio. The ultimate reason why Chris was great for Radio 1, or any radio, is that I can't think of many people around who kids listening to the radio would think, 'I want to be like that.' That's what I felt listening to people like Noel Edmonds, and I think he will have inspired a lot of people to go into radio and be a DJ. He was never ashamed. He said, 'I'm a DJ, and I'm on Radio 1.' It was his life's ambition to do the breakfast show. He wanted the biggest audience possible and he was cool, and to that extent he represented what Radio 1 wanted to do.

I enjoyed doing the handover, it was a big challenge. I remember one time I was just getting in the shower at home, before I came in to the studio, and he said, 'Right, coming up next we're going to do a survey on how many people working on this show have been faithful to their partners in the last year,' and there was complete silence, and when he came back after the record it was never referred to. So for the handover I thought I'd say, 'You know that survey you were going to do . . . well you never went back to that . . .' And then we decided that we wouldn't do that, or I was voted down by my producer.

We ran a thing for ages which eventually we called Chris-demeanours, about people who'd seen him behave badly. It was me reading out a letter about Chris being seen drunk, or 'Chris had done this', it was like a *Confessions* thing. You could hear the trepidation in his voice at nine o'clock. It'd be nine o'clock, and I'd just sort of go, 'Dear Simon . . .' and he'd go, 'Oh no . . .' What he didn't know was that we were getting the stories from his ex-wife, and from his producer, and from his family. It made for compulsive radio. That's what we aspire to – finding those moments that people will remember, links that people will remember, events that people will remember. Part of that is playing all the best music, so you remember the time you heard the new Radiohead album, but what I spend most of the time doing is thinking of things to say, features to do, that will make unmissable radio. Chris just had thousands of ideas a day, would write them down on bits of paper, and for him it came naturally, but some of us work harder at it.

Chris used to have this jingle to the tune of the 'Banana Boat Song' – you know, Day-O! 'Mayo! May-ay-ay-o! He works until lunchtime so we're off to rob his house.'

Matthew Bannister: We had the *Ginger Grand Prix*, another fantastic thing. There had been a grand prix on the television on a Sunday, so on the Monday morning Chris is talking about it, and says, 'We should have a London Grand Prix.' He got out a bit of paper on air and started working out the route. Piccadilly, then Trafalgar Square. They kept on doing this through the show, and by the end of the programme it was,

'Well, let's do it on Thursday. We'll get the police to close the roads, and you the listeners can all come. I'm going to drive my Bentley, Dan's going to be on his motorbike, and someone will be on rollerblades, and we're going to set off from the Mall, and we'll paint the grid on the Mall.'

And they did it. They got the police to close off the streets, and about 250 people turned up in their cars and motorbikes, and they drove the route of the London Grand Prix at 5 a.m. on a summer's morning. Quite wonderful.

And there was the morning when he forced Dan to propose to his girlfriend on air – incredibly uncomfortable to listen to. On the last day before he went on holiday he just pushed and pushed him, and got the girlfriend on the phone, and he happened to have Andy Coulson from the *Sun* in the studio. I went into the studio myself at 8.30 during the programme and said to Dan, 'Are you all right?' because he was under such pressure. The fax and phones are going absolutely crazy – people saying, 'Go for it Dan,' or 'Don't give into this pressure.' In the last three minutes of the show he said, 'Yes, I'm going to get married to her,' and she came through on the phone, because she was in the car on the way to the studio. Chris had also offered to give him a free honeymoon, and all sorts of financial inducements, and I think he kept his word.

Chris said to me after the show, 'What they'll all be talking about in the papers and the pubs is, 'Was I right to do it, to put him under that kind of pressure?' Chris asked me, 'Are you happy with this?' I said, 'Yes – it's the most compelling radio I've ever heard.'

But the problem with it was that towards the end he became increasingly convinced of his own immortality. There were times when he talked for twenty-five minutes without playing a record, which just gets on your nerves, frankly. And he got increasingly obsessed with talking about how rich he was, and how many houses he had bought, and how he had been out with his showbiz chums. He had changed so much from a guy who started out with this feature *Personality or Person*, asking celebrities what the price of Jaffa Cakes was, because he thought it was funny that they were out of touch with real life, to being a personality himself. He couldn't possibly have had *Personality or Person* at the end, because you could have asked Chris and he wouldn't have known the answers. He started on the people's side, but then he lost touch, and towards the end of the year it tipped over into self-indulgence.

Chris Evans: I used to think that if you say something on air that provokes a reaction – whether people hate it or love it – then that's all that matters. But it's not all that matters . . . I would say things that were just too rude or aggressive, or horrible even. I could probably have understood why people were angry at the time, if I'd stopped to think, but I don't think I would have done anything about it because I wouldn't have cared.

Simon Garfield: Chris Evans was due to celebrate his thirtieth birthday on 1 April 1996. Freuds, which Radio 1 referred to as the Agency, and which was charging the BBC £7,500 a month for its services, had prepared a list of possible April Fools to mark the occasion, and presented these at a meeting with Radio 1 press and marketing. To add an extra twist, one of the Freuds people suggested that the prank could be played on 2 April, thus avoiding journalistic paranoia on the day itself. The ideas included Chris making a fake marriage proposal on air. 'The subject could be any number of celebrities,' one document noted '– Cher, Jon Bon Jovi, Claudia Schiffer. The comment would be something like: "I would just like to forward this message to someone very special to me . . ." thus fuelling the press into finding exactly who the mystery person is.'

Another plan was for Evans to tell his listeners that he had written a screenplay that had been bought by Hollywood, featuring all his regular breakfast show team. 'The Agency would hold a photocall outside Broadcasting House with Chris in a director's chair and loudhailer for all national newspapers and picture agencies.' The third proposal was for Evans to announce, 'He has conquered everything else, so it is time for him to run for parliament.' A Freuds man suggested Evans say, 'You've heard of the Reds, the Orange and the Blues, now it's time for Ginger too.'

It was also hoped that surprise guests would appear throughout the show to sing 'Happy Birthday', including Shaun Ryder, Noel and Liam Gallagher and Cher. Des Lynam was to have turned up with a large birthday cake. 'Chris will also receive 30 birthday gifts throughout the show, the final gift being an "abusive" card from Matthew Bannister, who will then give Chris the following morning off.'

Three weeks later, on the first anniversary of the start of his breakfast show, there were to be more scams. It was planned that more people would show up to sing 'Happy Birthday', and twenty journalists would receive a gift from the show, possibly a mini birthday cake, a dummy or a printed nappy.

But a few days after these proposals were discussed, an account manager from Freuds wrote to Radio 1 with some disappointing news. 'Chris is loath to put too much emphasis on the first birthday, as he sees it as too self-indulgent. However, if Matthew were to arrive in the studio with a cake/champagne and/or a present, we would have sufficient ammunition to gain publicity in the *Standard* and the following day's papers.'

Matthew Freud: As soon as we go on air, that's when access stops. What we then do is unit publicity. We have a team of publicists who are in the studio throughout the show, every single day, and within twenty minutes of Chris coming off air they have a story list of all the things that he said that are possibly of any interest. Then it feeds back into a team of five or six people who spend that day going round all of the nationals and regionals to make sure that we get as much content-based coverage for each day's programme. It's extremely successful.

Media ultimately is total navel-gazing. It becomes this self-perpetuating thing whereby the media, especially the tabloids, does something which the media report, and then other media reports that. You get this universe that exists totally outside real life, which was not what it was set up to do, but it has discovered that it can exist in completely its own environment. It makes its own news, and Chris is a one-man media industry. On Radio 1 it became a complete cycle, because he said something that was reported, and then he would use the papers next day on air to describe them writing about him.

My company is the oil in that wheel. On an ongoing basis our role is to make sure that whatever someone is writing about Chris we are either feeding it to them, enhancing it, spoiling it or blocking it – whatever we have to do.

John Birt: I think Chris Evans is a genius. I've always thought that. I think he's definitely one of the great broadcasters of his generation. For the overwhelming majority of the time he was absolutely marvellous to have around and is delightful, witty, a life-force and really stimulating to listen to.

One per cent of the time he stepped over a line which people working for the BBC shouldn't. Maybe even less than 1 per cent of the time. In an organization like this you have to worry when somebody finds it hard to work within your set of guidelines which are published to the world. We say to the public, 'These are the values, these are the standards of the BBC,' and it's very important we stand behind them. So nobody takes lightly transgressions of our editorial principles. So it was about how we tried to work with Chris to make sure that he stayed within them rather than stepped outside them.

But there was no . . . I mean there were some strong expressions about this, but I wouldn't say that there were differences of view.

Simon Garfield: Matthew Bannister and Radio 1 press and marketing people often reviewed the media's reaction to Evans in their regular Communications Group meetings. Generally, they were thrilled with the new attention, but sometimes there was a cautionary note. 'Chris Evans must not be built up as the panacea to the station,' one set of minutes noted. 'Matthew also keen that the "Chris is out of control" line be squashed.'

Trevor Dann: We had a lot of playlist problems with Evans. Matthew would say to me, 'Well, I really like the playlist all day long, but when Chris is on he doesn't seem to keep to it. Will you go and speak to him?' In the initial negotiations over the playlist, John Revell, who thought he knew a thing or two about playlists, having run Virgin, said to me, 'I'm not playing all these bloody new records, this is hopeless, Chris doesn't know anything about new music, he wants to play records he likes and feels comfortable with, banging out great oldies by the Police and Bryan Adams.'

Within a matter of weeks that had been completely turned on its head, because Chris had come back into the music business, and he wanted to appear very hip, and suddenly it was, 'I don't want to play all these old records, I only want to play Black Grape.' Chris and Revell and his team were all basically twenty-five- to thirty-five-year-old white people, and they all liked indie and guitar pop, which is why you never heard any black music on the Chris Evans show, never any dance unless it was sort of Prodigy or Chemical Brothers white student dance, but they just didn't like Shola Ama or R&B, and I found that a real problem. Radio 1's proposition is that it is about generality, it's not about niche, because everyone else does niche.

Matthew Bannister: The Scottish trip was just brilliant. In London he was going on about how the smog was getting to him and how he had catarrh, and London was horrible in the summer and we have to get out of here. On the Tuesday I said to him, 'Well, why don't you really do it? We can get the most remote BBC radio station in Scotland, and you can do the show from there next week.' He thought that was marvellous.

So we got Radio Inverness, and the team went into overdrive to put the logistics in place, and they were fantastically helpful in Scotland, and within days the whole team had decamped to Inverness, which didn't quite know what had hit it, because the world's press also came. This was at the extraordinary height of Evans's controversy. By this stage

Chris had developed a policy of never talking to the press. If they were nasty to him he slagged them off on air.

The week was a brilliant piece of broadcasting. They went to the local village hall to judge a talent contest. I spoke to Chris every day, and he was going fishing with the chef from his hotel, and they hired a speedboat, and the press hired a speedboat to chase them up Loch Ness, and then the second week they decided to live on a boat.

At one point this guy Tich McCooey, who had his own local show on, had tried to get his own publicity out of this. He had turned up while Chris was in a meeting with his accountant and John Revell in a hotel. Tich McCooey turns up with a photographer to try and say hello to Chris, who told him where to get off. Chris then went on the air the next day and slagged him off in a very aggressive way and said something like, 'You're a tinpot nobody, I could buy you tomorrow, my researcher earns more than you . . .' – a really vicious attack. I thought this was wrong – really patronizing, offensive and nasty. Chris told me afterwards, 'Tich McCooey was completely in the wrong, he tried to harass me, he's a public figure so he deserves what he gets, playing in the public arena with me.' We had an argument about that. Chris had every right to slag this guy off, but not in the way he did, suggesting he was worse than the dustbin at Chris's heel. So I did ring him up and tell him off about that.

Chris Evans: He took me to breakfast one day and we were talking generally. I asked him what the breakfast was for, and he admitted it was about the newspaper reports. He said we had to do something about the bad press because he was getting so much flak from the governors.

I said, 'Matt, I've got to tell you, I never react to anything because then we're being led, and I've always led myself . . .'

He said, 'You've got to help me, Chris. It's becoming increasingly difficult to defend you every day to very powerful people, and I'm running out of excuses.' I told him he'd either have to keep defending me or get rid of me. He said, 'I can't get rid of you.'

Simon Garfield: Frequently, mostly in jest, Evans would have a go at Bannister on air. He called him the Fat Controller; he accused him of being out of touch. One comment, in October 1996, displayed a little more aggression. By this stage, Bannister had become Director of BBC Radio, Liz Forgan's old job, a promotion that entailed having overall authority over all the national radio networks apart from 5 Live. He remained day-to-day controller of Radio 1.

Evans told his listeners that he'd been talking to Bannister. 'Look,' he said, 'how ungrateful is this guy? We save his job, because before he joined he was frankly slipping down the bannister, he was out on his ear. We turned the station around, we make safe his job and now . . . we also get him the job of Radio 2, 3 and 4 . . . and now yesterday, after eighteen months of doing the show, he decided to give us a pep talk all of a sudden. All right, well thank-you very much. After we've . . . got you your promotion, now it's time to keep the breakfast show in line. Well thanks a lot, Matthew.'

Trevor Dann: I'd put in for this new job as Head of Music Entertainment that I'd kind of helped to design myself, after the split between Broadcast and Production in 1996. And then, before any announcement had been made by the press office or me or anybody, so I don't know where it came from, Lisa O'Carroll in the *Standard* wrote a couple of fairly careless paragraphs saying something like Dann to be head of pop for BBC, and described it as another triumph for the triumvirate that used to run GLR: Bannister's now this, Dann is now that, Evans's now that. The implication was that I was the unseen guiding hand that had had a lot to do with Evans's success.

Evans is clearly not best pleased with this idea, and next morning he has a rant on air. The first I knew about it was when I got to work that morning, and people said, 'Did you hear Evans this morning?' and I said, 'No,' because I'd stopped listening by then, I just couldn't stand his arrogance. People said, 'Oh, you should get a tape,' so I went down the corridor and got a tape, and I heard it.

Chris Evans (on the *Breakfast Show*, 7 November 1996): God, I got up quite angry with the music business this morning, and I'm getting even angrier now. But listeners please, please, please hear me out on this one. It's very important that you hear this. I've just read a report from last night's *Evening Standard*. Have you read this, John?

John Revell (Producer): No.

Chris Evans: Let me read this to you. The *Evening Standard* in London last night – often breaks a lot of media stories, and then the national daily papers pick up on them the next day. It says, 'Top job for invisible man of Radio 1. The man who brought Chris Evans to Radio 1 was today rewarded with responsibility for the BBC's entire pop music output, from Radio 1's chart show to BBC1's *Top of the Pops*. Trevor Dann . . . [*sharp intake of breath from John Revell*] . . . who turns forty-five today . . . has been the invisible hand of success behind Radio 1 since he joined three years ago. He has quietly stopped the ratings freefall and helped the controversial Evans with record ratings.' John?

John Revell: Sorry, Jamie just put something in front of me. Can you read that line again?

Chris Evans: 'He has quietly stopped the station's ratings freefall and helped the controversial Evans win record ratings.' This is Trevor Dann.

John Revell: Aaah, that's who's been doing it.

Dan McGrath (Producer): But he's invisible – you can't see him doing it.

John Revell: I wondered who'd been doing all that behind our back.

Chris Evans: Oh God!

John Revell: Who wrote that? Lisa O'Carroll? Lisa, for goodness' sake . . .

Chris Evans: Sort your life . . .

John Revell: What is it with her? Why don't you become the cooking correspondent?

Chris Evans: Here we are . . . 'His appointment as head of BBC1 music production highlights the extraordinary relationship between the Radio 1 controller Bannister, Evans and Dann.' Extraordinary because we unreservedly loathe the man.

John Revell: Pretty much so.

Chris Evans: Well you especially, John. You hate his guts.

John Revell: Yeah, and he hates mine, and he makes that quite common knowledge that he hates my guts.

Chris Evans: And since we've been here, this man has made our job very hard, very difficult sometimes.

John Revell: Indeed. When was the last time you had a conversation with him?

Chris Evans: Seriously? About seventeen months ago.

John Revell: About this show?

Chris Evans: Probably not, no. He's always scared to talk to me about this show. Unbelievable! He's got in our way more times . . .

John Revell: Can I just have a look at that?

Chris Evans: . . . he's tried to put this show down more times than anybody else I've come across. And now apparently he's the invisible hand of success behind this show. I'm sick of this, John. I am. I'm boiling over. Sorry about this – we've got to read this, go on John. [*John Revell mutters as he reads.*] Go on, soak it up, John.

John Revell: He hasn't been here for three years . . .

Chris Evans: I don't know what's going on. It's gone mad – everybody's gone mad. It's 7.23 . . .

Trevor Dann: I thought, 'Right, this will not do,' so I rang Revell, who wouldn't take my call. I spoke to Dan McGrath, his producer, who said, 'I can't talk to you about this, I've been told not to discuss it with you.' So I found the piece in the *Standard* which I also hadn't seen up to then, and I went to see Matthew.

I went there fully intending to say to him – this is the week when somebody like Eric Cantona or Ian Wright had been suspended for two weeks or something for being out of order – I went in there fully intending to say, 'Matthew, there is a limit to what you can let Evans do, this is not satisfactory at all because he's libelled me on the air. It's all very well, you know, he can have a go at me and he can call you the Fat Controller, that's all part of the hurly burly and joshing tradition of DJs, but this is a bloke having a go at my professional standing, and I want you to do something about it.'

That was what I was going to say. So I went to see him, and he sat at his desk, which is not his style, and he said, 'Sit down, Chris is furious with you, what the hell have you been doing?' And I went, 'Er, hang on, I've come to say you should do something about *Evans*.'

He said, 'I've had Evans on the phone and he's absolutely livid about that story you've given to Lisa O'Carroll.' So I explained what had really happened, and he just wouldn't see it. He had a complete rant at me and he'd never got cross with me in his life before, and there he was, just getting redder and redder and going, 'You've done all you can to undermine that show, they hate you and I hate you,' and he just got livid, and that's just about the last professional conversation we've had.

At that point, unknown to me at that stage, Evans was beginning his whole 'I'll only sign for four days' routine, and

Matthew was beginning to get the stuff from upstairs about 'You've really got to sort this out, Matthew.' Even though he had now got this big new job, he was under a lot of pressure from what Evans was saying. The show was off-beam on a number of occasions. It went from being truly brilliant to truly awful quite quickly.

Matthew Wright: I think Evans soon recognized that not only was he doing the breakfast show on Radio 1, but he also had a national voice. And I think he started abusing it, I don't think there's any doubt about it. I have no problem with the notion of trying to shake up a breakfast show and making it different and original and harder-hitting and everything else, that's fine. But you just started to get the feeling that after a while there were less innovations coming through on the show and more reliance on slagging people off, just being offensive.

You're generating new interest, fitting the Matthew Bannister plan of bringing in younger people all the time, which is absolutely right. But at the same time you're also starting to repel people. And, more significantly, you start getting the feeling that Evans is actually doing it because it's helping his own profile more significantly than perhaps Radio 1.

The thing was that in Scotland it just reached . . . it was such a bloody . . . it was so obviously offensive and unpleasant and unnecessary that I think that's when it really registered in the public consciousness. Basically they were just louts up there, that's how it came across.

I can't say it's awful and I condemn it, I don't. But that 'Wake up, it's a beautiful day with Radio 1' started to change into 'Do we really need to listen to this sort of loutish unpleasantness?'

Trevor Dann: The audience had begun to turn off . . . people were going, 'I can't listen to it any more.'

Matthew Freud: Scotland was a mistake. It was nasty. He did descend. How much did Matthew tell you? There was one day when he quit. He came off the show one day and said,

'That was a great show, but I've had it, I'm leaving.' He'd become very negative, very cynical, he was attacking people, and it had become quite a nasty programme. I think listeners were aware that something weird was going on, that there was this really dark side coming out of this programme.

So the media reflected that, and some turned against him. We issued a couple of writs against the *Mirror*, which we'd never done before. They said he'd been sacked, which he clearly hadn't been. I said to him, 'You're sort of self-destructing. You are allowing the media to destroy the idea, the icon, of Chris Evans.'

So the next day he came in to see me and said, 'I've decided to destroy it myself. I'm not going to let them do this slow death, I'm just killing it. As of today, Chris Evans no longer exists. I'm never going to broadcast again, I'm never going to do another show.'

He went from me to tell his agent, and from there to Matthew, and then he went from Matthew to Michael Grade. On the way to Michael Grade he called me on his carphone and said, 'I've changed my mind. I've decided I'm just going to be positive.'

That was the end of the dark period, the beginning of the reconstruction. Now everyone's forgotten that he was the most reviled man in the country for six or seven months.

Andy Parfitt: At the time of Chris's departure Matthew and I were very close, the closest we'd ever been. He was the best man at my wedding. We went through the situation again and again. 'What should we do? What should we do?' Chris had become increasingly difficult to manage on air, he had become very ill, we had given him a new start time, we had given him a new contract with a bucketload of time off. We were organizing our whole programme year around when Chris wanted time off. The whole of the radio station was going to work for him. We thought we'd gone all the way we could, and then one Thursday afternoon this letter arrives.

Paraphrasing, it says, 'If my boy has to turn up tomorrow morning then that's it, he's giving notice.'

Matthew seems to think that because it started happening through his agent they lost contact and stopped talking to each other, and the seriousness of the situation wasn't really comprehended. We felt, How could we run this radio station and keep our heads up if we were going to be held to ultimatums like this, with twenty-four hours' notice? It wasn't a macho thing, just a question of authority: is the Radio 1 brand bigger than the fact that Chris now wants to have Fridays off? Matthew was deeply saddened by the fact that it was a personal thing.

Matthew Bannister: We had a fantastic year and a half of wonderful, creative broadcasting, but then I began to get very concerned about it. It coincided with his period of ill-health.

He was on holiday and his agent rang up and said, 'I don't think he's well enough to come back, he is just about well enough to do *TFI Friday*.' He had exhaustion, he was over-stressed and over-tired. I went to see him in his dressing room at *TFI Friday*, and he was white and sweating. I said, 'Take the next week off, and go and see my doctor.' I also said, 'We'll cut the show by half an hour, so it starts at seven and not six-thirty.'

He said, 'Oh that's great, thanks very much,' and I think I actually went round at the weekend and saw him at home as well, just to see how he was on the Sunday. And he wasn't looking much better, and he hadn't been eating properly and all that sort of stuff.

At that point he was also beginning to talk about, 'It's Fridays that are the problem.' He'd have this adrenalin peak at 9 a.m. on the Friday morning after his breakfast show, and then have to climb another mountain by seven that night. So we also renegotiated a new contract for the next year, which gave him thirteen or fourteen weeks' holiday, double what he'd had before, and also agreed a schedule that he had to take them at regular intervals. And we agreed a pay increase of not insubstantial proportions.

He went to see my doctor on the Monday, and the doctor obviously did a good job with him and sorted him out mentally, I think. It was more getting the advice . . . the sense that there was somebody there to help. And then he went on *TFI Friday* and showed all his pills that the doctor had prescribed.

I thought, 'Well, I've solved that.' He did get better, and he did take the right medication, and gave up drinking and smoking for a time. Back on the rails, he came back with renewed vigour.

As far as I was concerned, what happened was another incident that he would then make television out of, make radio out of, and it appeared that he just completely lived in broadcasting. So whilst I was aware that he was under some pressure, I didn't think it was that serious, because I thought he'd just got a bug or whatever. So I think things went on until Christmas and then he was due to have some time off. I don't think there were any major problems between then and Christmas, aside from the usual kind of headlines that he'd said something on the air, and a certain sense in my mind that he was talking far too much. I remember one incident where he just talked for twenty-five minutes, and you were shouting at the radio, 'Put a record on!'

He then had some time off, and he did *TFI Friday* on the Friday before he was due to come back to Radio 1, and he found it a wonderful experience.

It was partly my view that if something had to give maybe it should have been *TFI Friday*, maybe they should have cut into the run of that and given him more breaks from it, but that never seemed to be an option that Chris was prepared to entertain. So I think it was on the Monday that he came back from the Christmas/New Year break, I got a call from his agent, Michael Foster, saying, 'What about him having Fridays off?'

Once again I said, 'Michael, that's something I can't do – I can't have a breakfast show that only runs Monday to Thursday, and in particular I don't think I can be seen to give another concession to Chris, because it's already quite a difficult thing to manage both publicly and in the station.' He said, 'Well, have a think about it, as this is quite important to Chris.' There was no sense of, 'You've got to sort this out this week,' or whatever.

I said to Michael that I'd really like to go out for breakfast or lunch with Chris to talk about the show, and he said, 'Chris won't meet you until this is sorted out, because this is a business issue and he doesn't want to have to discuss it with you because that's what we do together.'

At this time Chris was also saying things on the air like, 'I'm not going to do the roadshow this year,' just suddenly out of the blue, which again got in the newspapers, and that was the first I'd heard of it. And then I was over at Yalding House, talking to Andy about something, and Sarah [his personal assistant] came in with a letter which I opened and it was from Michael Foster. And it said that under their contract with us they now give us ninety days' notice to quit, unless Chris is given tomorrow off and every Friday off for the rest of the contract. I should say also that in previous discussions there had been absolutely no question whatsoever of getting them to reduce the money as a result of giving them less hours and more holiday.

Chris Evans: I asked for Fridays off for six fucking months. One whiff of what they thought was dissent and that was it. It was a sincere request: 'Give me Fridays off and I'll do everything better.' I get paid five times as much for doing one day of TV than for a whole week of radio. And to do the radio I get up at six in the morning. Well, the only reason I'm doing that, Matthew, or anyone else with half a brain, is because I want to. All they saw was that I was getting paid £1.7 million a year for the radio which, okay, is a lot of money, but it's not if you're earning five times as much on the TV. I said, 'Please let me stay. Please, Matthew.' And he went, 'I'd be seen by the governors as not being in control.' Bollocks.

Matthew Bannister: All of a sudden there was this gun at my head. I rang Michael and said, 'Are you serious about this?' and he said, 'Yes, it's an ultimatum, Chris either gets tomorrow off, and every other Friday off, or it's ninety days' notice to quit.'

I said, 'I can't give him Friday off tomorrow,' and he said, 'Well, we'll have to stand by our decision to quit.' I asked whether I could talk to Chris, and he said he would try to find him. There was a series of phone calls, where I kept ringing him back saying, 'Have you found Chris yet?' and he said he couldn't find him. Then the press office just got deluged with calls from the national press saying, 'We understand Chris Evans is leaving.' I could only assume that it came from Ginger Productions, because the only person who knew apart from me was Andy who was with me in the office all through this period.

So I rang Michael again and said, 'We can't have this, I've got the press waiting for me to say something, we're going to look complete Charlies if we don't say either no or yes pretty quickly.' I said, 'We'll start drafting a press statement, but you must find Chris.' But he'd gone out with John Revell and they'd switched their mobiles off. I was told he'd gone to a pub somewhere.

We drafted a short press statement which we sent over to Michael for him to check and he changed a couple of words. It said simply that Chris had given us ninety days' notice to quit because we wouldn't give him Fridays off. And I think it was about two o'clock in the afternoon when we finally released that, not having been able to find Chris, and with the phones going absolutely bananas in the press office, because Michael was absolutely adamant that there was no way round this situation, and it was non-negotiable.

I later found out that Chris had gone to Needles Wine Bar

round the corner from us, and that he was very quickly closeted with Andy Coulson of the *Sun*, giving him an interview for next day's paper. The interview had a certain amount of dignity, actually, I mean he didn't use the opportunity to slag us off, but basically it said that he'd been forced out because he needed to have Fridays off, and I'd been completely unreasonable about it. And then I think he went off and went to Groucho's and had a lot to drink with the team, but they did come in next morning to do the show.

I came in early myself and sat in my office just in case anything completely horrible happened. On air Chris said he'd been forced out and wasn't it outrageous? At that stage it was difficult to judge his mood from listening to him on the air. He was playing sad songs, including 'Please Release Me (Let me Go)'. I went down to the studio after the show, because I thought I've got to speak to Chris, this is ridiculous – we were all over the front page of the tabloids and we hadn't spoken about it. So I went down and walked into the studio where there was a pretty highly charged and emotional atmosphere, and I said, 'Chris, I'd really like to talk to you,' and he said, 'I don't want to talk to you, I'm fucking angry with you,' and stormed out past me, and went out into the street and that was when he was photographed, which was the front cover of *Private Eye* actually, him walking out carrying a book, and 'I'm quitting while I'm big headed' was the caption.

That felt horrible to me, because I really hadn't ever had a genuinely cross word with Chris in knowing him for all those years. I'd never had a situation where I'd thought he didn't respect me and I didn't respect him, and where there was any sense of personal animosity. It had been a friendly relationship when we were working together, and a sort of friendly relationship when we bumped into each other in between at parties or whatever. So that was quite a shocking thing to have experienced, because he was genuinely vehemently angry, and there was no knowing what was going to happen after that because as far as I was concerned he was a completely loose cannon and he could be talking to journalists . . . whatever, and saying whatever he might want to say, and of course he's a much more powerful figure in the tabloid newspapers than I.

Chris Evans: The perception was that I was taking the pee because I'm a hard-nosed bastard out for everything he can get. It's not true. I didn't want to leave . . . Matthew Bannister just thought I was trying to put one over on him. I wasn't being lazy – I wanted to do a great four days on the radio and a great TV show. In the States, loads of jocks do Mondays to Thursdays. It's a way of getting your weekend DJ known, by starting him on Fridays, and the audience will befriend him and listen at the weekend.

Matthew Bannister: In the end we decided the only approach we could take publicly was to be light-hearted about it, and so I said in a meeting, 'Why don't we take the lightboard in Piccadilly Circus and take out an ad for a new DJ?', which we managed to do and I think people saw that as the right response and a rather un-BBC response to make. Rather than sitting in our ivory tower and issuing short statements through the press office, we thought we'd go out there and talk to our listeners and certainly to the press, and say, 'You know, we're sad about this but life goes on, Radio 1's still here, and we've still got a sense of humour,' which I think probably did us some favours.

Then I had a call from Michael Foster who said, 'I've just walked through Piccadilly Circus and seen this ad and Chris'll go mad,' and I said, 'No, no, no, just tell him that it's not about him, it's just about us having to carry on and it's a joke and it's meant to express warmth.' We put up something like 'New Radio 1 breakfast show DJ wanted', and we put, 'Ginger hair an asset', which I told Michael meant that Chris was still welcome to change his mind.

Then we had to decide what to do about Monday, because clearly there was a possibility that he might not show. I mean it's one of those things where you don't know. He might have come in and gone on absolutely as normal. On the Thursday Michael was adamant they were going to do the ninety days, absolutely adamant.

We had to get Kevin Greening to stand by as a replacement, and I rang Chris's home on the Sunday, and he picked up the phone, and I said, 'Hi Chris, it's Matthew.' He said, 'You know I can't talk to you,' and then there was a silence and I said, 'Well I can talk to you, and I really want you to understand that I'm very sad about this happening and if there's anything we can do to sort it out let's talk, please give me a ring at my house in Sussex on this number, 01428 . . .' and then he just put the phone down.

I realized this wasn't exactly a good omen. In the evening I rang John Revell's house, to find out whether they were going to come in on Sunday, and a strange person answered the phone, not his wife, but a bloke I'd never talked to before, and I said, 'Is John there?' and he said, 'I'll just go and see,' and he went off and said, 'He's just putting the children to bed, can he ring you later?' Which of course he never did. And then the next morning Revell phoned Clive Warren, the on-air DJ, and said, 'We're not coming in.' I think it was sort of 5.15 or something, about an hour before the show was due to be on, or maybe an hour and a half.

There's no hard feelings, it's all totally all right, but it had to end some time. It's a shame it ended this way, with all that publicity, which of course wasn't bad at all for Chris. It happened so fast, and the real problem was not being able to talk to Chris through it all. One day it was all, 'Okay, we'll sort this out, a business deal, no hard feelings, we understand, talk to the contract people about serving the ninety days . . .' And then the next day it was all emotionally charged and – what is it that nuclear reactors do? It had all gone critical.

Clive Warren (Disc Jockey): Chris called me at about ten past five – the famous phone call. Or rather John Revell called. He said simply, 'We're not coming in today.' I said, 'What do you mean? Do you mean just this morning or never again?'

Andy Parfitt called me up after the show and said, 'Can I have a word with you?' I went to his office and he said, 'Tell me exactly what John said.' So I told him, and he said, 'Was there any laughter in the background?' No. He said, 'Tell me again – did it sound like a wind-up? Were they in a pub? Did it sound like a one-off or a final thing?' I told Andy the exact conversation about four times.

Andy Parfitt: I got Kevin Greening out of bed, and came in with him to help produce his show. I chose the first record, the only record I had ever chosen directly on Radio 1. It was Oasis: 'Don't Look Back in Anger'.

Matthew Wright: Evans's ego was . . . I think he just went absolutely crazy. Everybody you speak to that knew him at that time, apart from the most insipid and loyal puppy dogs, would just say that he became a complete megalomaniac bastard.

I would think the primary factor was that he was over-working, coupled with the fact that there were too many fawning people surrounding him telling him how wonderful he was. I think he sort of blew his top. Matthew Bannister gave Chris Evans an awful lot of support in the preceding years, and I think that Evans behaved like a shit to him and I can't think of any other way of describing it – a shitty, disloyal, unpleasant, selfish thing to do. Now he's still a success-ful radio DJ, he's still a successful TV presenter, so maybe those are the qualities that you need, but quite frankly I'd rather be a decent person than end up like that.

At that precise time there was a huge, huge public sympathy for Matthew Bannister, overnight. With the appointment of Evans people were saying, 'Oh he's getting it into gear,' but I don't think Matthew necessarily got as much credit for that manoeuvre as he deserved. And losing Evans just made people think that Matthew Bannister's a decent bloke who's doing his level fucking best to get Radio 1 working again, and he's just been shat on by a friend he offered a great break to. I think Radio 1 has benefited from that warmth.

Chris Evans: I'll never forgive Matthew for what he did. Actually, I probably will forgive him but I'll never agree. I think he made a mistake, and I know Matthew really well, he's an intelligent man, and that wasn't him that day. That person who said what he said wasn't him. I think he actually changed for a while. I wouldn't be so grand as to say I took that job as a favour to him, but I wouldn't have done it for anyone else. I said I'd do it if he backed me all the way, and he didn't.

Jo Whiley: Chris Evans brought it all together for us at Radio 1. When he left it was almost like someone dying.

Chapter 7

Something Wrong with the Sample

Mark & Lard aka the Ra-Gnomes aka the Shirehorses:
'. . . after two weeks all the listeners had gone'

Simon Mayo: No other show matters like the breakfast show. For listeners, breakfast shows have to be there for a long period of time if they're going to work – two, three years minimum – that's the only way to enter into the public consciousness. Chris only lasted about twenty months, but Chris was always the exception.

When he didn't show up on that Monday, and Kevin Greening did the show, at the handover I asked him, 'Are you in same time tomorrow, then?' and he said he didn't know. And then after the show I got a call from management saying, 'We want you to do it.'

The problem for me was that I was in the middle of filming *Confessions* and I'd always said I didn't want to be doing the breakfast show . . . that was another thing. One of the reasons I wanted to come off the breakfast show in 1993 was that we were about to start filming *Confessions* and if you got up at four o'clock in the morning and then had a TV show to film on Saturday night, and a kid, I found that very difficult. So this time I said, 'Well, what do I get out of this? I don't want the gig because I've done it, I don't need the aggro of getting up at that time because I've got this TV show.' You know – I'm the loser. They were saying, 'It would help us out enormously.' They were beseeching me to do it, so I agreed to do it just to the end of the week. Also, they offered the most money to do it.

I had a great time. To do the breakfast show and not care was a very liberating experience. Chris hadn't cared because he didn't need the gig, I didn't care because I didn't actually want the job full time again. We started the show with the theme music to *Never Say Never Again*, the James Bond film. I could do the show four or five times better now than I did in '88. We were in hysterics a lot of the time. It was just going to be for a week, but then they offered me more money to do it for a month.

Kevin could have done it for a month himself, but I imagine they asked me because I'd done it before and people knew who I was. The truth was that Chris was neither the saviour of Radio 1, nor was it the death when he left, but you had to make sure the figures didn't slump right back and lose what he'd built up, so I guess I was the safest option.

When it was announced that Mark Radcliffe would be taking over I only wanted to give him all the support and encouragement I could. There is a problem about DJs talking about other DJs and not have it come across all snipey. The one thing that I've always said is that when I do leave Radio 1, I don't want to become a sad old tosser, and I don't want to become embittered so that all I ever do is slag off other people. So I'm not going to do that. But what I'm saying is, the worst time to take over the breakfast show is when it's been popular and successful, and Chris had an unbelievable profile, not a huge audience in terms of Radio 1's history but an unbelievable profile in the press. Mark and I would never hope to achieve that . . . the very worst time to take over. Like Ken Bruce taking over from Terry Wogan – what can you do?

Mark Radcliffe (Disc Jockey): We'd been on a night-time show for three and a half years and were looking to move. The people who loved it really loved it, and we didn't want it to just become routine, and we wanted to get off while it was still intact and fresh. And also, it's a job: we wanted to change our shift pattern for the sake of our life. We didn't want to work at night.

Simon Garfield: Radcliffe's time on the station began in 1983, producing sessions for John Peel. He then moved back to his native Manchester to work as head of music at Piccadilly Radio, but began DJ-ing again to relieve the boredom. He played an alluring mix of music on his Radio 5 programme *Hit the North* and his first Radio 1 show *Out on Blue Six* in the early nineties – a brew of garage, psychedelia, punk, comedy guests and poetry.

Radcliffe had first met Marc 'Lard' Riley when he produced his band The Creepers for John Peel (previously, Riley had been in The Fall), and their friendship developed after Riley became a promotions man for various indie bands. On air they made a strange pairing – Radcliffe dominant yet downcast, Lard the rather fey stooge. Lard liked to finish Radcliffe's sentences. They were both very funny.

John Peel: I thought Mark Radcliffe was just magnificent when I first heard him on *Hit the North* and *Out on Blue Six*. I always used to suggest to people that we ought to be using Mark Radcliffe a lot more. Clearly a clever man, but one has to say that putting him on at breakfast seemed like a fairly suicidal decision.

Mark Radcliffe: Eventually we convinced Matthew that the afternoon would be the right place for us. We didn't want to move to the weekends, and so we agreed to do four to six on weekdays. We were quite happy with that, and the contracts were being drawn up. One Monday we were in here recording a song, and the phone went and it was Matthew.

He said, 'Chris Evans has just left.'

I said, 'Oh right. Not entirely unexpected.'

He said, 'That leaves me with a bit of a problem, really. I kind of think I'd like you to do the show.'

I said, 'I kind of think I wouldn't want to, really. I'd be quite happy doing the afternoons.'

He said, 'Oh, right. To be honest I hadn't expected that, that you'd turn it down.' Because if you're a disc jockey, I don't think it's the sort of thing you're supposed to do. But at that point it didn't seem right for us. There was so much pressure riding on it. I put it to Matthew that whoever followed Chris Evans was being given a poisoned chalice, because Chris was so popular that whoever followed it would get a kickback from it. Not because you were no good, although some might argue that point when it came to us, but just because you weren't Chris Evans. Matthew assured us that if we did take the show, they would support us to the hilt and they would underwrite it in terms of a period of time. But I said I really didn't want to do it.

Mark Radcliffe:
'We could skydive naked
off the Eiffel Tower. . .'

Then he and Andy came up one afternoon and took me and Marc out to Frank's in Altrincham. He said, 'I would consider this a personal favour if you would do it, and also I'd like you to think about the sort of radio station that you want Radio 1 to be, because if we don't have you two on we're going to go with a much straighter show.'

So we said we'd think about it over the weekend. We went home and talked to our wives about it. I phoned Matthew back and said, 'We don't think the money's right. We don't want to get up early, and have no wish to do it.' Then we put a price on us doing it, the sort of price that I thought they'd respond with, 'Who the hell do you think you are?' But they didn't. They said, 'All right.' We were a bit trapped then.

Matthew Bannister: Looking back now, of course, it wasn't perhaps the ideal choice, but it was the best option at the time.

But I didn't think it would be a three-year job. The first thing that struck me about the show was that while self-deprecation was a very endearing quality late at night, and 'We're a bit crap and we can't really do this . . .' had sounded very funny and entertaining in a cult late-night show, there's something about the history of the Radio 1 breakfast show and people's expectations of it, that means that self-deprecation can quickly turn out to be rather unnerving to a listenership that's expecting to be woken up with a confident laugh and so on.

There was a lack of ambition about the show, which once they were at breakfast became quite exposed in a harsh white light, whereas at night irony and tangential references had made them into a cult success. I had thought in all good faith that Mark and Lard had such a strong double act that had been going for so long, and were keen to make the transition into the mainstream, that they would pull it off, that they would take on some of the characteristics of operating in the daylight as opposed to in the dark. And indeed they tried very hard to do that, but in the end it began to sound very inconsequential to me, and the Radio 1 breakfast show is expected by its listeners and observers to be in some way agenda-setting for the day, and of-the-moment in some way – the exclusive play of this and that sort of stuff, and even when they had those things they threw them away.

We started to have sort of brainstorming sessions with them, saying, 'We want big ideas . . .', although what I consider to be a big idea they didn't necessarily see as a big idea. In their sort of slightly-ironic-about-being-a-DJ way, they didn't want to shout about anything in case they looked like they were getting like DJs.

I think you'll find that history will rewrite itself, but I think that they were actually quite excited by the challenge at the outset, then daunted at the interest of the press, which was obviously not at Chris Evans levels, but was pretty consistent for a time. When they got on to this, 'It's not as bad as we thought it was,' phase, and found they had some things they actually liked doing, that was when they were at their most relaxed.

Simon Garfield: They began the breakfast show by giving away a van. Regular items included features called *Bawling out with Alan*

Bawl, in which a caller would nominate someone to be slagged off in a very high voice, *Dobbins or Bobbins*, in which a caller had to tell real horse names from fake ones, and *We Love Us*, in which a pop star or soap star had to answer questions about their band/soap. Regular characters included showbiz reporter Max Beaverdong, Rabbi Lionel Blair, who answered phone-in problems and had a thought for the day, and Fat Harry White, who advised on matters of love.

Commenting on the positive reaction to their earlier breakfast show try-outs as Chris Evans's holiday replacements, Marc Riley told an interviewer of the emergency music that Radio 1 has on hand to play after the death of a member of the royal family. 'And I thought that would come on after ten minutes of our stint. But they let us go on broadcasting.'

Riley's musical experience and Radcliffe's love of drumming came together when they wrote and then broadcast parodies of hit songs. Under various spoof names that collectively became the Shirehorses, and with the help of their producer Rhys Hughes and engineer Chris Lee, they gave birth to 'Plums Drop' (a version of Hanson's 'Mmmbop'), 'Lardy Boy' (Placebo's 'Nancy Boy') and 'You're Gormless' (Babybird's 'You're Gorgeous'). The running gag was that it was the established groups who had in fact ripped off the Shirehorses' original songs. The Shirehorses opened the 1997 Glastonbury Festival, shortly before their stage sank into the mud, and they signed a deal with EastWest Records to make *The Worst Album in the World . . . Ever . . . Ever!* It seemed to be a part of their life they enjoyed most.

Mark Radcliffe: Before we started there were no real discussions with Matthew or Andy. I didn't talk to anyone apart from Rhys and Marc. We were left alone to do the show we wanted, and now I think they feel that they left us alone too much. At the time they felt that they'd heard the deps [deputy broadcasts] we'd done when Chris was away, and they were fine, and they'd done some research, and people had reacted favourably.

But I always thought it was a high-risk policy putting us on full time. Before we began I did mention to Matthew and Andy that we really were very low profile. That was partly because our lives were run-of-the-mill and dull, and also because that's the way we like it. I told them, 'You're going to struggle to get the tabloid interest, especially as we're in Manchester.' If there are any openings or receptions for anything in Manchester I don't go to them anyway. But I always thought that people would like us because we were the antithesis of Chris – instead of being the Flash Harry who was going round the London clubs with Gazza, it was two regular blokes who went for a pint and went to football, and I thought people would get off on that. But not enough did.

The only thing the media seemed to be interested in was our private lives. I wasn't ready for that, and I found all that very difficult to deal with. We met with Matthew Wright and Andy Coulson from the *Mirror* and the *Sun* so that they knew us and so stories would go in. Us going to Rome for the England game was really an idea dreamt up just to generate publicity. But there is only a select group of people that the tabloids are interested in. At the top you'd have Princess Diana, the Spice Girls, Chris Evans, Tony Blair. But whatever we do . . . we could skydive naked off the top of the Eiffel Tower and nobody would take any notice. The classic example is doing all these photos in Rome, of me and Marc on scooters, and me and Marc making pizzas, and not one photo made it into the papers. We're just not a tabloid species, and when Radio 1 realized that we never would be, that was our fate sealed.

Polly Ravenscroft: Before they even started it had got to the stage where his ex-wife had the *News of the World* knocking on the door, and somebody had gone round to Mark's dad's house. Mark was saying to me, 'I can't bear this – it almost makes me want to say I won't do it.' I said to him, 'It won't be like this forever, I promise.' Then I managed to persuade Mark to do an interview with Matthew in the *Mirror*, but it's quite difficult to explain to him that this is the right thing to do. He must have thought, 'Why am I being made to do this?' But it is better to give one interview, and then a lot of it goes away. Marc Riley used to be a PR, so he knows the game exactly. We really did try to get stuff in the tabloids, but it never felt right.

Matthew Wright: I travelled up to Manchester to meet them. The premise was, do an interview with Mark and Lard, and have a chat with Matthew Bannister as well, who was also up there at the time. Giving all respect to Mark and Lard, I was much more interested in what Matthew was telling me than they were. He spelt out his vision, and it was the first time I'd ever fully appreciated what he was trying to do. I wouldn't say it was a road to Damascus thing, but it was the first opportunity either of us had had to exchange our views. And by the end of it I felt myself totally in line with Matthew Bannister's thinking. Not totally, but certainly over 80 per cent in line. We went to Mash and Air, then back to a hotel room. Everybody was plastered by the end of the evening and he was as plastered as anybody else. It was clear that Matthew Bannister was not your typical BBC corporate figure. He was making an effort.

In terms of coverage in the *Mirror*, I think Mark and Lard benefited enormously from the friction that had developed between the *Mirror* and Freuds re Evans. Absolutely enormously. The history of it was, whenever Freuds had an Evans story they went to the *Sun* first. If they did any interviews for Chris, it was always with the *Sun*. If we hadn't got a problem with the way we were dealt with by Freuds over Evans, we would never have done a quarter of the stuff we did on Mark and Lard. It was definitely a vengeful thing, that – keep weighing in because we knew it would wind Evans up, and it did.

But Chris Evans would prostitute anything for media attention and Mark and Lard were totally the opposite. Chris Evans talked about how he was looking forward to getting his divorce when he was on a live TV awards show. It's such a personal thing, why would you possibly want to say it to the awards audience, let alone on TV?

Mark and Lard were the absolute opposite, particularly Mark Radcliffe, very shy, very unhappy at being pushed into the front line. And also I think, they're not idiots, they knew damn well that the way they were, the way they worked was not going be a commercially, audience-winning, successful breakfast show.

But I think everybody involved in Radio 1 would just say thank God for Mark and Lard, they stepped in at an incredibly difficult and unfortunate moment and they didn't do at all bad. There were vast sections of that show that were totally unintelligible, it was like Dada radio, it was fantastic, highly enjoyable, but if you want to bring in a big audience to Radio 1, it was the last thing you needed. And although Matthew Bannister assured me, and had me almost believing, that audience figures were not important, at some point they become important. You can only go so far down before they become very important indeed.

Rhys Hughes: They left us alone for the first three months. They let us just get on with it. But then there were bits of tinkering that came from London about how we needed to play more bums-on-seats tunes. Fair enough, because I think that Mark, coming from that culty late-night thing, could have a bit of a problem playing some of the records.

Mark Radcliffe: They had tinkered as you'd expect them to – it was the flagship show of the station. But then there was this kind of meeting. We all expected the audience to drop, and it did of course, and one of the things I had said to Matthew before we started was, 'You've got to promise me that when the figures drop you won't panic.'

Matthew Bannister: What finally happened was that we did the research on them which showed that basically the best reaction they were getting was from a minority of people who saw them as a cult. The average reaction was indifference, and there were quite a lot of people who . . . it did their heads in having people shout at them in the mornings.

Jo Watson: After four weeks of them starting at breakfast we did some more telephone research – about 300 people. Even then there was the feeling of 'Bring back Chris Evans', but there still wasn't this feeling that it would have such an effect on the figures. We knew they would drop, but not that much. People were saying, 'Oh, they're loud and they're stupid and we don't get their humour,' but the positive comments by far outweighed the negative.

But when we did the qualitative research – the focus groups – some months later, it was completely the opposite. There were very few positive comments. The focus groups were eight groups of eight people. A research company would find these for us: they might take the electoral roll or some other database, and call a household up and say, 'Do you have someone aged between fifteen and thirty-four, do you listen to the radio?' We had a mixture of people who listened to Radio 1 two to three times a week, and lapsed listeners who used to listen to Chris Evans. We sent those people tapes, and asked them to listen to a week of the breakfast show. And they just didn't get Mark and Lard at all.

We did groups in London and Manchester. People were saying, 'We don't like their irony, they have a stupid sense of humour.' We couldn't understand that, because they're bloody funny people. But it was because people just can't listen to them at that time of the morning. They just felt it was a lot of noise, and they genuinely weren't hearing them – a real problem.

The music – it was seen as an indie-based programme, but that wasn't necessarily seen as a negative. They had this real core of loyal listeners, but it was very small. That tended to be the student bloke – mainly blokes. One group in London, we had to stop the group in the end, because we couldn't get them off the subject of Chris Evans.

I went to the London ones. Sometimes they're done in people's houses, but I always ask for a viewing facility so that people at Radio 1 can come down and see it for themselves, so they know that the guy's not lying when he comes in and presents it. The respondents are told that they're being filmed, and that there are people behind the mirror, but they're not told we're from Radio 1. It doesn't seem to restrict them at all. They're sat in a lounge environment, on sofas, and there's booze. There's a place in Bromley, and there are two in Hammersmith that are really plush – leather sofas. With me were Matthew, Andy, a guy from the agency and Ian Parkinson [Radio 1 managing editor], quite crowded. I think it's important that they hear it from the horse's mouth. These were in the end of June/beginning of July. We made a few changes on the strength of the research – they slowed down, they weren't as manic. People really want to be guided through the morning, something easy to listen to, and Mark and Lard weren't.

After the focus groups Andy and I and the guy who did the research went up to Manchester and sat down with Rhys, the producer, and Nick Ware, the Manchester editor. We went through it all in some detail, a difficult situation because we didn't have any good news to tell. We didn't keep anything from them. Rhys was disappointed, but I think he knew what the faults were.

The next morning on air, Mark and Lard were saying, 'We've heard that all our listeners think we're crap. So we've got our own focus group in.' They had one person there, and asked him, 'What do you think of us?', and this person went 'Great' or 'Crap!' So they did have their little dig, despite the fact that they had specifically been told not to.

People are cynical of research. A lot of people don't understand it, and only believe it if it's something they want to hear. If the views are negative they say, 'Well there's something wrong with the sample.' But if they go up, 'Great! This research is wonderful.'

We've done a lot of work on presenters, always monitoring

their plus and minus points, and I've never actually presented the research directly to a presenter. I've always done it through a producer, and then the producer goes on and massages the ego. Very difficult people, these artistes.

Sophie McLaughlin: From a marketing point of view the problem was that they're night-time people. Not only were they in a night-time slot but they're dark, they're dark characters, they've got a kind of black sense of humour, they're in Manchester which is dark, metaphorically, compared to London which is bright lights.

With marketing and press there has to be a certain complicity from the DJ, an appreciation of the game. If you're going to succeed in making people into bigger names than they are, they've got to be prepared to turn up at the parties and the premières and be a bit of an arse. Quite rightly, of course, they believe that's naff, being like that, but that view doesn't really help them, or us.

They didn't need or want it enough. Mark's got married, lives in Manchester, loves Manchester, got a new house. The fact was the breakfast job didn't come naturally to them, they didn't have an instinct for it. People at that time of morning want clear signals as to when to leave the bathroom, when to leave the house – they want the time, the travel, the weather, and more music and less of this barrage of talk. But the problem is, how you do that without reducing their zest and taking their character away?

I went up there and we talked about how we could do a TV trail campaign that would really blitz the weekend, make people look forward to the show on Monday. If it had all gone better I would have made something out of their peculiar looks – a Beavis and Butthead type thing – and I would have played up their buffoonery, rather than try to make them cool.

They are more self-effacing than some other DJs, but however self-effacing you are you don't get to be a DJ without having a huge ego. They do like the idea of having a trailer made for them, or a press add, and then they're terribly precious about how they look in it.

Andy Parfitt: We were expecting a drop and we modelled it, and we thought we'd lose about 800,000 in reach, total, and we didn't know the timescale of that loss but we thought it would be quite quickly. But we lost consistently month on month on month, losing something like 400,000 listeners in reach every quarter. It stabilized for a while and I thought, Right that's it. But then we got some more bad figures, and I was the one who went to Matthew and said, 'Look, I think we're going to have to do something, we've lost another 400,000, and there are no signs of it stopping.' And the qualitative research was quite devastating.

Simon Garfield: Those interviewed were asked to draw pictures of the images that came into their heads when they listened to Mark and Lard. Mark was depicted as a matchstick figure, while Lard was invariably a small round man, the opposite of his true build. Some were asked to write a letter to their producer. One read, 'I feel your programme Mark and Lard does have potential, but they need to remedy some aspects of their show. I feel they need to slow down and make the show less chaotic ... play more music, cut out the poetry section, entice more people to take part in competitions with bigger prizes.'

Many people seemed to want less noise. 'It's just shouting and talking across each other . . . It's like they are in the back of the room shouting ... It is a sensory onslaught ... They seem to shout from beginning to end ... They get lost in their own conversation ... They should talk to us and not to each other ... Dour and nasty types – I want to wake up in a brighter mood ... Attitude without the charisma.'

The research concluded that although Mark and Lard were adored by many loyal listeners, there were many barriers to be overcome before they achieved mass appeal. 'Although Mark and Lard have been seen by a few on *Top of the Pops* they are not yet felt to be real personalities. This means it is easy for them to be seen as 'want to be' types or people who have not quite made it, i.e. second rate.'

Andy Parfitt: I went up to Manchester with Matthew and talked through the research in very frank detail with Mark and Lard, and they listened to it very carefully. I remember Mark saying to me, 'Yeah, look I know it's got to move more mainstream,' and I think that they did have a real intention to change. We had a discussion about the mood of the show, about how they sounded, how Mark could vary the tone of his presentation – just the sort of conversation that a producer has with their broadcasters, really.

Mark Radcliffe: When Matthew and Andy came up here, Marc picked them up and drove them to the pub in my village. We sat at the back next to the pool table, and Matthew had plaice and chips. Le Gavroche it's not. They said, 'We believe in the show, but we want to make some changes.' The new Rajar figures were about to come out, and they'd got wind that they were low. So we made some changes, and took some characters out, and moved the *We Love Us* quiz, which they thought was strong, we moved that into a more key position, and we made a lot of other changes. And *Brat Pop* was dreamt up, with these kids singing songs from Blur and the Prodigy. So this was all agreed and written up and faxes went backwards and forwards.

Then they had the official Rajar figures in the papers, and I remember them saying they were down, and a Radio 1 spokesman said, 'We are right behind Mark and Lard.' At the time I said to someone, 'That's like the football chairman giving a vote of confidence to their manager, and you think, 'Well, that's him doomed then.'

It sounds arrogant, but I never thought that we were so great that nothing must be tampered with, and we were learning as we went along. I know sometimes we had a tendency to talk too much, but I thought people liked us talking.

But the focus groups . . . I couldn't believe it. We were changing policy on the basis of six people observed behind a two-way mirror in a terraced house in bloody Chelmsford.

Chapter 8

She Really Likes Music

Andy Parfitt: 'You know in your heart when a show is not working'

Mark Radcliffe: Anyway, we then went on holiday for two weeks. I went to Cornwall, and Kevin Greening did the deps. And of course in the second week Princess Diana died, which in retrospect sealed our fate too.

Kevin Greening: I heard the news in a club at half past four that Sunday morning. Word got round that there had been a crash, but Diana was okay. I forgot to tell the people whose chill-out I went back to that there had even been an accident. It hadn't registered as important. We had a chill-out until lunchtime, and then I went back home to sleep. I was woken by a call at about seven in the evening, from Andy Parfitt I think, saying, 'You know she's dead?' I watched the news all evening to get my head around the enormity of the story.

The question on Monday morning was, 'Without any features, and mostly sombre instrumental music, how do you make it sound like a breakfast show?' I'm not blessed with the discursive talents of Chris Evans or Danny Baker. I can't talk for ten minutes on any subject; I need the three and a half minutes that a record's playing to think about what I want to say for the following thirty seconds, and get it just right, and get off.

I remember coming in very early on the Monday, and going through every station on the dial, really to find out what not to do. Some commercial stations were saying things that didn't feel right. The lesson was not to talk about anything else in the news, and to make a joke about anything was obviously just falling flat. So at seven o'clock we went on air and just tried to tap in to what people were feeling, this mass hysteria. And day by day we thought it would get easier, and the grief would be less, and we could gradually reintroduce features and some humour, but it didn't happen like that.

Jeff Smith (Head of Radio 1 Music Policy): I was on call that weekend as duty executive. The phone rang at about half past four, I was zonked, and the particular words were, 'Dodi's dead, and Diana's critically injured.' I was half awake – 'You must be joking.' We had Annie Nightingale on – the chill-out zone. They'd started playing some of the obituary CDs. I got a cab, and I was in just before five. The news in the cab was that she was dead.

There's a set of three emergency CDs in a little cupboard in each studio. CD(a) has sombre-ish mainly instrumental music, CD(b) is a mellower vocal-driven selection, and CD(c) is a let's-come-out-of-it scenario and move on. But they're designed for your average royal person dying. If the Queen Mum died we'd have our normal CDs, and probably be out of it much faster than with Diana.

For Diana, the obituary CDs that we had didn't really seem good enough, and I was already working on newer ones, based on more contemporary ambient music, and with some string-driven and operatic elements. So I started rotating these five or six tracks, and added to them through the day. And from the e-mails we got the audience said they quite liked the selection. So we played tracks from the Apollo *Four Forty* album, and 'Sabres of Paradise', and the film soundtrack *Merry Christmas Mr Lawrence*, tracks without vocals to enable people to have their own thoughts about things. I think people found it relaxing, a haven from all the talking heads and ghastly photographs. We played one particular track out of all the news bulletins, 'The Aloof'.

Gradually we introduced George Michael – 'You Have Been Loved' and Massive Attack's 'Unfinished Sympathy' and 'Missing You' by Puff Daddy, 'Everybody Hurts' by REM and 'Don't Go Away' by Oasis. Originally when I heard the George Michael song I thought, Radio 2 record, but it worked for us in the circumstances. I think we did do something different from other commercial stations. Capital played classical. I think we played music from our people. A lot of our DJs were genuinely choked. Lisa I'Anson was crying, and Jo Whiley clearly really felt it. And with Mayo, it brought out the real broadcaster and the desire to interact with people.

Mostly we had praise for what we did. The main criticism came from people who felt we should have gone to rolling news like the other stations. But we had made the decision months ago that if anything like this ever happened – although we were really thinking about the Queen Mother at the time – we would go our own way. Strangely, three or four years ago we practised what we would do if Fergie had died in a car crash. We actually talked about how we'd bring the music down when we heard about the crash and she was just injured, and then how we'd bring it down more if she had died. Unbelievable now.

The music changed throughout the week, reacting to the latest news. When the news came through that the driver had been drinking we had to drop 'Tubthumping' by Chumbawumba and watch what we were saying about drinking. By nine o'clock on Wednesday morning I thought it was okay to get back to our basic scheduling, with the exception of certain records. There were a couple of unfortunate tracks. Jo Whiley had a free choice, and played 'There is a Light that Never Goes out' by the Smiths [which has a line about the possibility of a double-decker bus crashing]. Nicky Campbell played 'Let it Be' and 'Imagine', and a Velvet Underground track which I'm not sure was quite right for our audience, but he was sincere and honest about it.

Nicky Campbell: We just handled it properly, not mawkishly. That's when people appreciate us – the best broadcasters, who also happen to be playing pop music on the radio. When I heard Chris Tarrant [*adopts smarmy voice*] – 'Oh yes, Diana, what a great friend of Capital Radio, the last time I saw her she was, er . . . anyway, up to you Russ in the Flying Eye . . .' 'Yes, Chris, we've lost a great friend here at Capital Radio, oh she used to have us on, 95.8 Capital in every room in Kensington Palace . . .' I just thought, 'Fucking hell, it's a different world.'

Kevin Greening (*on air, 1 September 1997*): Good morning, this is BBC Radio 1, my name is Kevin Greening, and I don't know about you, but I'm not feeling very funny this morning. This is no ordinary Monday morning, and this is no ordinary breakfast show. It's as simple as that. [*Plays 'Lifted' by the Lighthouse Family, 'Don't Go Away' by Oasis.*] As a mark of respect to Diana, Princess of Wales, the normal breakfast show has been suspended. Let me assure you that the mood behind the scenes at Radio 1 is the same as its public face today. [*Radiohead: 'High and Dry'*] We're letting the music do the talking today. We've been struck by the unspeakable news just as much as you. We all just sat around on the floor reading the newspapers in disbelief this morning. [*Blur: 'The Universal'*] The newspapers are printed up in black borders, and some of them are going to be the same papers that in a few weeks' time will be asking us to part with more money for more telephoto lens pictures, this time of someone new. And when they do, let us try to remember how we feel today.

[*The following morning*] I thought I'd be feeling better by now, but it still feels so weird. We DJs are a pretty cynical bunch, as you can tell from our shows, but this is different. Clive Warren is still here. Chris Moyles is talking to him, and normally DJs here avoid each other as much as possible. But today we're talking, and of course there's only one topic of conversation. Zoe [Alpass, broadcast assistant] is here this morning, but she might as well not be, she's a wreck. So we won't be doing the normal features, and the jokes have been suspended for the foreseeable future.

Matthew Bannister: We rang commercial radio to talk to them about dropping the Top Forty, and they said if we'd drop ours they'd drop theirs, so we dropped it. I mean, we would have done so anyway whether they had or not, but we just wanted to check what they were doing, and we took the view that what we should do was just constantly update the news, and keep the sombre mood going.

I haven't heard a single complaint about Radio 1, not one single complaint. I mean we've had complaints about Radio 3 taking too much of Radio 4 on the day of the death, which I think is probably right, and a lot of complaints about Radio 4 doing too much, but my sense of it was that this was a young people's story, and when you went to Kensington Palace you saw young people and young children, and Radio 1 was really important to it. Of the people who listened to BBC radio coverage of the funeral, the biggest number listened on Radio 1, according to the research. About 20 per cent, ahead of Radio 4, which is where you'd expect everyone to go for the state occasion, but instead they listened on Radio 1.

Jeff Smith: The plan was for Mark and Lard to come back the day after the funeral, but it was decided to keep Kevin Greening on for an extra week. The thinking was that Kevin understood the mood completely, and that Mark and Lard couldn't possibly really understand. Not knocking their professionalism, but for somebody who had been away for a couple of weeks to react to something they hadn't been a part of would have been very difficult.

Kevin Greening: It was put to me by management that even after the funeral the issue wasn't completely put to bed, the pain was still fresh. The suggestion was that they didn't want Mark and Lard to stumble off the plane and say, as they had every right to do, 'Hey, what's been going on here? We're not here and there's been a bit of news!' That was the only way that they could have approached it, and it would have sounded disrespectful, although not purposely so. They had a lot of catching up to do, and for the listener it would have been, 'Well, we've been through that process.' That was how it was put to me. But I suspect that they'd been doing some research on the deps that I'd been doing, and the Diana thing had completely driven a coach and horses through that research, so I think keeping me on was as much about finishing the research that they wanted to do . . . and perhaps thinking of me as a possible replacement full-time.

I first did the deps for Mark and Lard the first time they went away in April. If you're an up-and-coming player rather than someone who's on the wane, there's always the suspicion that you're being given the try-out as a possible replacement. But my first try-out on the breakfast show was for Steve Wright, and clearly nothing had come of that. Admittedly, I did do a miserable job of it, a nervy failure.

For a few weeks before Mark and Lard came off, there were whispers that I might be being lined up, but these sorts of things fly about a lot. Only my partner was convinced that I would get the show.

Matthew Bannister: The softness of Kevin struck the mood perfectly and fit with the sort of music that we were playing in that week. His feeling was genuine and sensitive, no doubt about it. We felt that the harshness of Mark and Lard, coming back to get us out of that mourning, was going to be too much.

Mark Radcliffe: I came back from Cornwall ready to start work on the Monday morning. I'd been incommunicado, so when I got back there were messages on the answerphone and faxes, all saying they didn't want us on the next morning. They wanted Kevin on to help take the audience through this.

I did think this was strange. I talked to Marc and my wife and I even called my mum, and I said, 'There's something odd here.' We could have gone back on. I felt insulted, at the best, that they didn't think we were able to cope with it, and that we couldn't change our tone at all, that we were seen as a one-trick pony. But everybody said, 'Oh no, you're being paranoid, there's nothing in it at all.'

Matthew Bannister: Then we got some new monthly figures, and the audience for Mark and Lard had dropped a further 400,000 in the second month, whilst the Radio 1 figures in general had gone up. So we thought, We can't go on like this, it's a flagship show, it's affecting the whole schedule, we have to make a change.

Mark Radcliffe: When we did finally come back we were on a daily conference call with London. After the show on Monday I phoned Andy and said, 'What do you think? Do you like the changes?' He said, 'Yeah, fine, not bad at all,' and we had a chit-chat about a couple of things.

On the Tuesday I phoned Andy and said, 'What do you think about the show?' He said, 'Yeah, it's all right. Anyway, me and Matthew want to fly up and see you tomorrow.' I said, 'Have we got the sack?' and he said, 'Oh it's not as bad as you might think, but I don't want to say any more, and I'll see you tomorrow.'

So I put the phone down, and said to Rhys and Marc, 'They're coming up,' and I think we all knew then that something major was afoot. We had twenty-four hours in which we speculated: Would they sack us completely? Would they move us to another show? But we had pretty much worked out that we were off.

Simon Garfield: The following morning, Mark and Lard welcomed Kylie Minogue to the studio. She read the traffic report: long delays on the M25, some cancellations on the Fishguard–Rosslare crossing. On air, Radcliffe read her an interesting story in the papers: Radio 3 was distributing sweets with 'silent' wrappers to its audience at live recordings, so that listening enjoyment would not be impaired. Then he said, 'But here on Radio 1, because the music's so crap, we've got these extra-loud wrappers. We're going to play this record, which is on our fantastic playlist, and we'll see if we can obliterate it entirely by crinkling these wrappers.' And they did, drowning out the first few seconds of 'Sunchyme' by Dario G, a big hit in the clubs. When it ended, Radcliffe said, 'That's a great record, and we're only saying it wasn't so we could do a joke with Kylie.'

At the end of their show, shortly before their meeting with Bannister and Parfitt, Radcliffe played a Shirehorses song called 'The Hapless Boy Lard', loosely based on the Nick Cave–Kylie Minogue duet 'The Wild Rose'. The second half went:

[**Radcliffe:**] On the second day I was pissed off with him already,
When Roger Bannister called me on the phone,

He said, 'Bruno Brookes had to go, you can have your own
   show,
But you'll have to bring Lard, you can't do it on your own.'

[**Lard:**] I got started in showbiz on Radio 1,
And after two weeks all the listeners had gone,
But at least it's a start, it's a foot in the door,

[**Radcliffe:**] Now I'm stuck with this tosser for evermore.

[**Lard:**] They call me the Hapless Boy Lard,
Why they call me that I do not know.

[**Radcliffe:**] Because you're a fucking lardy-arse cunt,

[**Lard:**] Yes, I suppose so.

The expletives were deleted. At the hand-over, Simon Mayo said,
'That's a fine record. Remember Laurie Lingo and the Dipsticks and
"Convoy GB"?' [a hit pastiche by Dave Lee Travis and Paul Burnett].

Later that morning, the choice of music on the breakfast show
came under discussion in London. Jeff Smith, the man responsible for chairing the weekly playlist meeting and programming
every mainstream show, was feeling a little upset.

Jeff Smith: They've got to the point now where they do what
they want. We give them a list of records to play between seven
and nine o'clock, but they tend to do what they want with it.

Before they went off on their holidays we took quite a
strong overview on the show. I would look at the music and
made sure they followed the running order, and Andy would
look at it editorially and talk to them about what they were
saying. And towards the end of that, before they went off,
they were sticking pretty closely to the list we gave them.
They wouldn't like some of the songs, but we weren't giving
them certain records we knew they didn't like – they'd
already given us a list of certain artists they didn't want. But
since they came back . . .

The playlist that we've got now, even if all the records

aren't absolutely fantastic, every record on the playlist now does some form of job. I have to push myself away from it a bit, away from being head of music policy, and ask – is knocking the playlist fun and anti-establishment and do people like that? I've been referred to on the show as a clerk compiling this list in London, and I guess it is a bit mathematical and precise because we do use a computer and we do rotate the list, and programme in certain criteria.

But it pisses me off when people have a pop on the air about the playlist, because they help choose it. I find it amazing that there are big stations like KROQ in Los Angeles which is a twenty-four hour a day playlist station, and the DJs love to play the records, because they completely believe in the music that they play. And I don't see why we can't have a radio station like that here.

Yeah, 'Sunchyme' by Dario G. That record is on the A list, and has been on six weeks. The problem is that the presenters get tired when it comes to six or seven weeks. But if we're going to actually get the listeners we have to do that – because you have to make a radio station familiar to an audience. But DJs sometimes don't think before they talk.

They don't play as many records – they drop records. They make the excuse of running out of time in a particular half hour. They say they've dropped a record because they were running long, a lot of DJs claim that. But as a DJ you can make time work however you want to. If you don't want to play a record, you drop it from a half hour by playing more of another record or talking more.

I think the breakfast show is such an intensely personal thing. If you get up at that time of the morning to do a show, for the nation, one half of you is an experienced production person, but the other half of you says, 'This is my name and I stand for something, and I don't want people to think I play crap music. I want to be known for only playing good music.' But it's a bit childish – why not just be professional and play a good range of records whether you like them or not? They drop, they change and they add. So we haven't got the same show we designed.

I get very annoyed about it. We do a lot of work. We design the show around them – no Kavanagh or Boyzone records in there when there should be, and then things still get dropped and done in a way we haven't agreed. I wouldn't mind if we had audience ratings rocketing through the roof, but we haven't.

But perhaps we're changing something that can't be changed. That's why I find it difficult to say to them, 'Well you *have* to play this Kavanagh record, or you have to play this record by this other boy band.' If you get in the way of what they do, you might as well not have them on. Perhaps it's our fault that they're there. Unfortunately, Radcliffe and Lard don't seem to be catching the audience at all.

Mark Radcliffe: Towards the end, the relationship between me and Marc – everything that we actually do, that they had liked and what they had wanted for the breakfast show – they decided they didn't want. So it became obvious to all of us that really they should have someone else doing it. They'd lost that belief in what we were. It really wasn't a pleasant feeling to know that we'd lost that confidence from the top. We always had that. In the end I didn't know what we were supposed to be doing.

It really was a relief when it ended. It was like getting parole. The only downside of it was the public disgrace of having failed.

We went for a cup of tea at the hotel next door. Matthew said, 'I'll tell you straight what we want to say. We want to make a change to the breakfast show.' He said, 'We're going to give it to Kevin, but there's someone else going to do it with him.' He said he wouldn't say who. We said, 'Is it Zoe Ball?'

Funnily enough, we'd suggested having Zoe Ball on our show doing a showbiz thing. One of the things levelled against us is that we're a bit laddish, and we thought, Let's have a woman who's a bit London and a bit glamorous. Some names were mentioned, and one of the names suggested by us was Zoe Ball. She'd always said that she liked the night-time show that we did, so we knew she was on our wavelength. We actually said, after our first holiday, 'When we come back, we'll do a pilot with Zoe Ball,' but it all went very quiet after that. I can see why now.

So we said, 'And do you have a job for us?' and he said, 'Yes, I'd like you to do two to four in the afternoon.' Previously I'd been talking to someone up here who said, 'Have you thought about what you'd do if they offer you other options?' I said, 'Yes, I imagine I'd say, "Thank you very much."' Because I need a job. I do bits of TV and bits of writing, but what I am is a pop radio DJ, and who else are you going to work for? And I get paid very well for it – Matthew was a gentleman on that score – he could have wrangled about contracts, but without question we were paid up to the negotiated breakfast show rate until the end of the first year [£250,000 per year].

Andy Parfitt: It was all of our concerns if the audience went down, not just their fault. I really wanted to be listening to every second of it, so that they felt I was really taking an interest in every single thing. I've talked quite a lot about research, but your heart tells you as a listener and as a professional in radio for the last God knows how many years, and you know in your heart when a show is not working. And I think that the programme became completely soulless really, because they were no longer doing the things that we know that they do brilliantly well, which is just going off on one, seeing what happens and a joke coming out of it. So although the formats of the programmes I thought improved no end, I think that the heart went out of it.

We managed it with the press very well, but you can't in the end keep them from writing the story that everyone's turning off this breakfast show. In the end they'll write it. You can go on for a certain length of time saying, 'Well, it's Chris Evans's audience leaving, and they're absolutely right for the schedule,' but it was pretty drastic what was happening, and you have to stop it for the rest of the network, you have to arrange the network in a way that you believe will arrest that. Once we decided to take Mark and Lard off the breakfast show, we were absolutely clear in our minds that we must keep them on the radio station because they're famous DJs and they're very good.

Everything you do in a schedule change has a knock-on effect, and we had to do perhaps half a dozen things simultaneously to make sure everything didn't fall apart. When we made the decision to take them off it was an amazingly fast thing, and I think we've got very good at it. Yeah, we have had so much experience at doing it.

Trevor Dann: They thought that Radcliffe and Lard would be exciting because it was a good show, but Matthew made exactly the same mistakes as with Danny Baker – he bought a brilliant show and put it in the wrong place, on the wrong network. Many of us could see that whole Mark Radcliffe situation coming – that's not hindsight, but everybody I know professionally in the business thought it was reckless and suicidal, and we were all proved right. Matthew would probably get the credit for being brave, but it's a pretty off form of bravery.

I did feel genuinely sorry for Matthew, because it is a terrible feeling to be running a radio station and the figures are dropping. Because Radio 1 is on all day long, you can't get away from it. It's all-pervasive, it's on when you get up in the morning, it's on when you go to sleep at night, and it's terrible to have a station that's going downhill. I do admire them for admitting their mistakes, even though they haven't actually admitted that they were mistakes . . . It's like when a football chairman puts the wrong manager in, and you go, 'What the bloody hell have we got this old tosser for?' And when he finally sees sense and fires him, part of you is really pleased that he's seen sense, and another part of you goes, 'Well, why did we have to waste that stupid period of time with this bloke running the club?' Because Radio 1 got relegated briefly. I am more optimistic about it now, but there was quite a lot of damage to undo.

Matthew Bannister: We took them for a cup of coffee across the road, and obviously they knew what was coming. Or they had guessed. Mark Radcliffe said, 'We told you we'd be crap on the breakfast show and we were.' But they were very nice about it, not unpleasant at all, very professional. Mark summarized it by saying, 'Okay, I got moved from the post room to accounts, but I've still got work.' He said, 'Obviously it's not nice to be associated with failure, and we're going to look a bit bad in the papers and so on, but on the other hand we've got a new show,' and we started to talk about the new show and what we might do in it. Mark then went out while we were having coffee, and got a good luck card and signed it and asked me to give it to Kevin.

Mark Radcliffe: We did feel let down. I would say that having made the decision to put us there, they should have held their nerve longer, but then I don't have people with their foot on the back of my neck, watching the graph fall. We hadn't wanted to do the show, and we had been asked to do it as a favour to Matthew, and we did it, but then we felt we'd earned more loyalty. I think we did feel stitched up at the time.

Rhys Hughes (*to Radcliffe*): You handled it very well – that show when Lard hid all the papers with the news of Zoe – you took it on the chin completely. Ours wasn't the shortest breakfast show, you know. Mark Goodier – three months, mate.

Simon Garfield: The news of Zoe Ball's appointment achieved what Mark Radcliffe never did – front page coverage. The fact that Kevin Greening would be co-presenting caused minimal interest, although some papers did mention the fact that he was gay, and would be doing all the hard, technical work. The Zoe Ball news also overshadowed the announcement that, after ten years with the station, Nicky Campbell would soon be leaving to join Radio 5 Live.

On the same morning, 18 September 1997, Radcliffe revealed his *Headlines of the Day*, a regular item about bad tabloid puns. 'The coveted number one slot goes to the *Mirror* with several huge pictures of Zoe Ball who's apparently got some top new gig with loads of cash and a brand new alarm clock thrown in for good measure. Onederful! It's . . .'

Lard [*quoting*]: 'I'm Zoe Happy!'

Radcliffe: And so are we! [*Plays record.*] It's eighteen minutes to . . .

Lard: . . . Nine.

Radcliffe: Fair enough! [*Does the travel, plays more records, including another Shirehorses track.*] That's more or less it from us today. Just in case you missed it, Zoe Ball and Kevin Greening will be with you for breakfast from Monday 13th October, and we wish them every success. Our last show will be in Rome on Friday 10th October, the day before the England–Italy game, as good a place as any to bow out. Thereafter we'll be on between two and four. Thanks for listening. It was fun while it lasted – for us, anyway. [*Plays Echo and the Bunnymen: 'Nothing Lasts Forever'.*]

Simon Mayo [*sobbing*]: Love you, Lard! Love you, Mark!

Radcliffe: All right, Simon, how are you?

Mayo: Love you, Mark!

Radcliffe: Ay now, don't give us any of that nonsense.

Mayo: Mark!

Radcliffe: How are you?

Mayo: I'm fine – I'm just going through the papers. It's extraordinary coverage . . . quite extraordinary coverage. I don't remember *you* getting all this.

Radcliffe: That's what they're after.

Mayo: Have you not got a cleavage, Lard?

Lard: I'm working on it.

Radcliffe: He has got a cleavage, but not *there*.

Mayo: Have you ever seen this kind of coverage before? Ever, ever, ever?

Radcliffe: Extraordinary.

Mayo: And is this you as well [*reads headline*]: 'BBC staff in revolt . . . Open war at the BBC as stars revolt.' Is this because you've been moved?

Radcliffe: Well, that's what we were hoping, but it turns out to be a newsroom reorganization.

Lard: I tell you what, Simon – Zoe and Kevin, they're talented. You've seen Zoe in all the papers. And if she did telly she'd be brilliant. But she's not as good looking as me, and you'll never take that away from me.

Mayo: That's very true. Describe how much better looking you are, Lard.

Lard: Loads.

Mayo: Yes, I think you've convinced me – it's a winning argument . . .

[*The following day*]

Radcliffe: Morning, everyone! Well, we turned in! First we'd like to say thanks a lot for all your e-mails of condolence. We're not going to read them out, because that would smack of self-aggrandizement, something we haven't done nearly enough of in the last few months. Later in the programme we've got Posh Spice Victoria Adams on *We Love Us*, a chance to win some pyjamas . . . and there's *Ask Lard* in which Our

Kid solves your homework problems – all the top-quality items that have made this show so dispensable.

Mark Radcliffe: I never wanted the show in the first place. I never wanted to get up early, I never wanted to pretend at being famous. Marc did feel a bit differently. Marc is proud of the shows we did, and he's right – we couldn't really have done anything else. We did the only show we could do, and once they started to change it we did a less good show. So he doesn't see it as a failure, but I do.

Rhys Hughes: It depends on how you judge it. If you judge it solely on ratings, then yes, it did fail. But if you ask, 'Was it creative and imaginative and exciting?' then I don't think it did fail.

Mark Radcliffe: I think Marc was right when he said that people who liked it would remember it for a long time.

Rhys Hughes: What used to freak me out with Evans was that he was going on about his huge salary all the time, and hanging out with Oasis. I thought that if you were a milkman in Doncaster on fifteen grand a year, you'd get very pissed off, but now I think that actually maybe that's what people do want to hear. The antithesis of that was Mark and Lard, two ordinary blokes, but perhaps in the morning people do want big showbiz.

Mark Radcliffe: We used to be upfront, but now we're in midfield, the two old warhorses. We're the midfield holding operation. And the Shirehorses thing has been great fun.

The Shirehorses just began with us doing a few songs in the evening, and then a few more on the breakfast show, and then people kept on saying we should put them all on a tape. The Glastonbury date came out of a need for publicity, the fact that we weren't in the gossip columns. Doing Glastonbury was thought of as one way we could get some attention.

Our last show will be supporting Blur, which seems like a

good way to end, and after the last song the plan is to just put our instruments down and slope off without a fuss. I think you can say the same about the band as you can about us: 'Well they turned up on time, and they were no trouble.'

Rhys Hughes: The other thing is that as soon as we knew we were being taken off, the breakfast show started sounding so much better. They relaxed, and they went back to doing what the two of them were best at – bouncing off each other. I think the last month of the breakfast show we flew – I think it was a great show. There is an argument for saying, 'If they had left it for another six months, would things have turned around?'

Mark Radcliffe: I'm glad we came off, because the pressure on Matthew ultimately got too much to bear. They lost that belief in themselves. I would have hated to have stayed until February, which would have been a year, with worried faces every time we had a meeting.

Rhys Hughes: Caroline Sullivan in the *Guardian* called it the greatest breakfast show ever. But the *Sun* didn't – that was the difference. I think it was a BBC2 breakfast show, not BBC1.

Mark Radcliffe: We were never breakfast show DJs, though we pretended to be for a while.

Simon Garfield: Just how badly had the breakfast show performed? Two weeks after Radcliffe and Riley moved to the afternoon, a Radio 1 management team met in Matthew Bannister's office to discuss the latest quarterly listening figures, and how best to present them to the press the following day.

Every three months, Rajar held a press conference for media reporters, at which all the latest BBC and commercial radio figures were announced, and at which a representative of BBC marketing and the independent networks each gave a brief presentation and took questions. Sometimes the questions were rather hostile, particularly if a journalist detected a good story (which inevitably meant a disastrous performance by a famous DJ or network). In the past four years Radio 1 had provided journalists with a great deal of copy, first when the audiences plummeted, and recently when Evans reversed this trend.

This quarter the news was grim again, though not as bad as it had been: the last Rajar headlines had all reflected the fact that Radio 1's weekly reach had fallen below 10 million listeners for the first time. The figures also showed just how poorly Mark and Lard had faired: Chris Evans's last quarterly listening reach stood at 6.94 million; Mark and Lard's fell initially to 6.33 million, and then to 5.53 and 5.01 million, although there were signs of a slight upturn at the time they were canned. Andy Parfitt, Polly Ravenscroft, Jo Watson and Sophie McLaughlin (who was to give the presentation to the press the following day) had a difficult job on their hands.

Sophie McLaughlin: [*going through the figures*] Okay, reach down 170,000, and share up 0.4 of a percentage to 10.1 . . . year on year we're down 1.7 million. I think we should say something like, 'Although the loss appears to have slowed considerably, we're still in a very competitive market.' We should say that after a very turbulent time, this is a relatively stable quarter for Radio 1, with reach falling very slightly and share slightly up. And they're listening for longer.

We could say, 'As you all know, we have introduced a new breakfast show with Zoe Ball and Kevin Greening, and Mark and Lard have moved to the afternoon slot.' And we won't get industry standard figures on the new shows until next January.

Andy Parfitt: What's the overall picture on the breakfast show?

Jo Watson: Quarterly, Mark and Lard have lost 460,000 among four-plus. Among fifteen-plus they've lost 380,000.

Andy Parfitt: I hardly think it's a story for them now, to say, 'You've got rid of Mark and Lard because they've lost a lot of audience.'

Polly Ravenscroft: You should also say, 'We're talking about the future here. We've just got a brand new fresh breakfast show with Zoe Ball and Kevin Greening, and we're moving on.'

Sophie McLaughlin: So we're still the biggest breakfast show . . .

Jo Watson: But *Today* may have overtaken us.

Sophie McLaughlin: We're still the biggest *music* breakfast show, with over 5 million listeners.

Polly Ravenscroft: They probably will ask, 'What are you going to do if Zoe and Kevin don't work?'

Sophie McLaughlin: So . . . the justification for taking Mark and Lard off . . . 'Was the breakfast show losing faster than the station as a whole?' Yes. So I can just say that.

Andy Parfitt: But you should say that it was not just a function of the audience. It was that the audience were telling us, not only through Rajar, but also the qualitative research, that they liked Mark and Lard but they were wrong for that time of day. In the afternoon slot there are less formatting restrictions and it's more suitable for them as broadcasters.

Polly Ravenscroft: So when they say to you, 'You said last time you were committed to their breakfast show,' you've just got to say, 'We were committed to Mark and Lard.'

Andy Parfitt: We *are* committed to them.

Polly Ravenscroft: We could say that they only wanted to do it short-term. It was just a bit shorter than we expected . . . You might get a question like, 'Isn't it a shame that Nicky Campbell's gone – are you expecting Mark and Lard to perform as well as him in the afternoon?'

Sophie McLaughlin: Can we say that Nicky wanted to explore other career opportunities, and it's great that it's within the BBC? And Mark and Lard is a very different show . . .

Andy Parfitt: I don't think we want to box ourselves into, 'Oh they'll do as well as Nicky Campbell.' Just say, 'It's too early to say.'

Polly Ravenscroft: And clearly we think the show's going to work, which is why we put them in that slot. We said that last time, though . . .

Sophie McLaughlin: Shall we say that we planned for them in that slot in the first place?

Polly Ravenscroft: Yeah, that's the one. The original plan was for them to be there.

Andy Parfitt: How's the Top Forty?

Jo Watson: The share is up, but the reach is down.

Sophie McLaughlin: We can say the same thing as last time – there are many more stations taking the Pepsi Chart Show – how many stations was it?

Jo Watson: About sixty.

Polly Ravenscroft: And say we're broadcasting the *official* chart.

Andy Parfitt: It has nothing to do with the performance of the show – it's just that more listeners get registered as being Pepsi Chart Show listeners.

Sophie McLaughlin: What's breakfast show listening like overall?

Jo Watson: I need to check this, but it looks like Chris Tarrant has lost over half a million. It was 2.6 last quarter, and now it's 2 million. That's 24 per cent of Capital's audience!

Andy Parfitt : On share terms, Capital overall have lost 3.2 per cent over the last quarter.

Sophie McLaughlin: That's always good for a question . . .

Jo Watson: Russ and Jono on Virgin have lost almost 200,000.

Sophie McLaughlin: Okay, what do we think the Zoe and Kevin questions will be? 'Can they save the station?'

Polly Ravenscroft: Or, 'Are you not selling out having Zoe on with Kevin?' And, 'Isn't Kevin the DJ, and is it true you've just got Zoe for publicity reasons?' But we can say that she's a talented broadcaster.

Jo Watson: Popular with our target audience.

Sophie McLaughlin: So we say, 'She's a key BBC talent. She really likes music . . .'

Andy Parfitt: Credible indie music.

Sophie McLaughlin: She was on the cover of *Melody Maker*, wasn't she?

Polly Ravenscroft: She was also voted by *More* magazine as the most popular person among their readers. She's been to all the festivals this summer – you can't say she doesn't know what she's talking about when it comes to music. They might ask, 'What are you going to do if their audience freefalls?'

Andy Parfitt: You say, 'It's just too early to say. They've only been on the air for ten days.' Say that both presenters are on long-term contracts. We've got them for twelve months.

Sophie McLaughlin: What does our own research show?

Jo Watson: Massive churn, our listeners trying Virgin, Virgin listeners trying ours, commercial listeners trying both, so the figures are going to be all over the place. High approval of both shows, but particularly high approval of Radio 1's breakfast show amongst fifteen to twenty-four year olds.

Sophie McLaughlin: Just to recap: Have there been any particular success stories in other parts of the schedule?

Andy Parfitt: Oh yes. Stability and improvement. Saturday mornings up, Sunday evenings. *Dance Anthems* has put on 3 per cent, hasn't it? [*looking at figures*] Jo Whiley up by half a per cent, drivetime up by half a per cent, the *Evening Session* hasn't gone up . . . Saturday morning up . . . the weekend dance schedules up across the board – Westwood is up by 1.5 per cent, and Rampling is up by 2 per cent. Good. It's a result, and the schedule is looking really good now.

Sophie McLaughlin: So what are the three key points to get across?

Polly Ravenscroft: New breakfast show, new beginning, new Britain!

Andy Parfitt: Strong weekends.

Jo Watson: Strong performance for fifteen to twenty-fours.

Sophie McLaughlin: And key schedule changes beginning to work.

Simon Garfield: The following day, at the Institute of Practitioners in Advertising in Belgrave Square, about thirty journalists gathered to see what the excuses would be this time.

A man from Rajar explained that this quarter listening had been down overall, possibly due to Diana (perhaps people turning to television coverage, although everything was blamed on Diana in the last quarter of 1997), and probably due to windfall shares enabling more people to go abroad on holiday or buy computer games and televisions for the bedroom.

Sophie McLaughlin did her bit with a computer presentation: BBC radio claimed 47.5 per cent of total listening, despite the introduction of seven new commercial stations between June and September 1997. The total reach of all BBC networks, including local stations, was 26.32 million.

Overall, the skill seemed to be in presenting the figures in such a way that every station had at least something good about it: reach and share were the ideal indicators, but year-on-year figures could also be emphasized, as could a particularly strong performance of a particular part of a schedule. At the very worst, a lousy performance might be offset by a promising showing in a particular age range, and a suggestion that losses appear to have stabilized. So Radio 5 Live did particularly well, with reach and share up year-on-year to 4.9 million and 3.4 per cent of all radio listening. Radio 2 reached 8.6 million listeners each week, and year-on-year gained 250,000 listeners aged forty-five to fifty-four. Radio 4 enjoyed a 100,000 increase in reach to 8.3 million, and a half per cent share increase to 11.2 per cent. Reach and share were stable on Radio 3, remaining unchanged from the previous quarter at 2.3 million and 1.1 per cent.

Radio 1 'continued to dominate the market for fifteen to twenty-four year olds'. Forty-two per cent of this age group listened for at least five minutes each week, and an additional 100,000 fifteen to twenty-four year olds tuned in in the last three months. Reach fell slightly to 9.5 million, but listeners stayed tuned longer, and share rose by almost half a point to 10.1 per cent.

There followed a presentation about the commercial sector (a 50 per cent share of all listening, Talk Radio doing well, Virgin and Atlantic 252 stable, Classic FM slightly down), and then questions from the floor. *Broadcast* magazine wanted to know how Sophie McLaughlin might explain Radio 3's poor performance year-on-year. The problem lay in daytime mornings, she said, which were being reviewed. Live music and the proms did well, though.

The *Daily Telegraph* asked, 'What was happening to Radio 1 breakfast show figures in this period? It seems to me that when we spoke last quarter you expressed full faith in Mark and Lard, but then shortly afterwards you binned them. At the time the graph was really plummeting down, and now seems to have bottomed out in terms of reach and share, and I wondered if perhaps you'd binned them too soon.'

Sophie McLaughlin: I think 'binned' is a little bit strong, given that they're one of our afternoon star pairings. Undoubtedly Mark and Lard are extremely talented broadcasters, which is why we've put them on in the afternoon, which was actually the original slot which we had all planned for them, and the slot they actually wanted. But it would be fair to say that reach to the breakfast show was falling faster than reach to the station overall, so we did have to do something about that.

Daily Telegraph: How fast?

Sophie McLaughlin: I don't actually have the detail on that, but I can let you know afterwards.

Press Association: Is there anybody here from Capital to tell us what happened there? That's quite a loss.

Woman from Capital: This is traditionally a low quarter for us, anyway. But what actually happened is that we really believe that the death of Diana had a really big impact on our figures. We veered from the playlist probably more than any other station. We usually play very upbeat hi-energy music, but for about three weeks we played very slow, sombre music. We knew it would have a very strong impact on our figures, but because we had a very strong feeling towards Diana at Capital, we had to respond to people's phone calls and faxes. Our helpline was just brimming over with bereaved people. Perhaps we carried on a bit longer than we might have wanted to. We'd be very surprised if the figures didn't jump back next quarter. Also, Chris Tarrant was off for an exceptionally long time because he happened to break his wrist.

Sophie McLaughlin: I would just like to make a point about playing sombre music. Radio 1 also changed its playlist appropriately to match the tragic events of Diana's death, and actually it doesn't seem to have affected us too badly. We got a lot of letters and e-mails about how appropriate people felt the music was, and they felt supported during this time. I think it's swings and roundabouts.

Sophie McLaughlin (*A few days later*): In some ways doing the Rajars is the worst thing ever – such a peculiar situation. You have to look smart to project the right image, and I just pretend it's not me up there. Deep inside I've always felt that if you tell the truth it's much better. You don't get caught out and you don't make a fool of yourself. So I find it very difficult to be confident giving a spin on something.

Commercial radio put even more spin on than us, because they're effectively packaging up a number of different results, all of which are patchy, into one presentation package. Their whole thing is a spin by definition, whereas we have to separate the performance of the individual networks, which makes them exposed.

I don't think that many journalists understand the figures, certainly not the tabloids. But there is always that boffin with the beard, a Broadcast man I think, a trainspotter, he spends ten minutes before the conference with a calculator. It's far easier to answer a straightforwardly aggressive question, but what's far harder is when someone asks a normal question, or a non-question, like, 'Radio 4 is 4.2 and last quarter it was 4.4.' You just think, Yes, fine. You've obviously added it up. What do you want me to say?

The BBC is definitely caught up in a sort of ratings schizophrenia. There's this kind of intellectual and also visceral feeling that the BBC doesn't exist to be driven by ratings, it's non-commercial, it's creative, it's distinctive, all the rest of it, and that does run through the core of the organization. But people do react to figures very emotionally. When the figures go up, it's all, 'We're pleased to say the figures have gone up. It's fantastic!' And when they go down . . . It's a very complicated equation.

These days, figures are increasingly being used as PR tools. In the past, figures were less dominant as measurements of success or failure. They were less sophisticated, and life wasn't as competitive.

Trevor Dann: As a public service broadcaster over twenty-odd years, I've heard myself say two contradictory things.

I've heard myself say, 'Yeah, I know that show didn't do very well, but it was really good, it was a quality programme and the people who liked it really liked it.' And then I've heard myself say, 'Oh I know it was shite but it got 8 million,' or whatever. And the thing about the BBC is that you can call it both ways. You can say, 'Our job is to serve the public, and we've just served 20 million of them, aren't we great?' or you can say, 'Our job is to serve the public and we've just served 0.6 of a million who wouldn't otherwise have been served.'

Public service broadcasting can be a terrific thing, and terribly valuable, but a lot of hokum is spoken in its name. The memos that come round about figures – you can write them according to a template. If the figures go up a bit, the memo says, 'Fantastic news, congratulations everybody, there's been a 0.1 per cent increase in share. And let's all be very pleased, and Virgin have gone down but we've gone up, and Heart FM suffered badly . . .' and there's a real sense of triumphalism and crowing. And then the next quarter, template B is used which goes, 'Latest figures show a slight fall, of 2 million or whatever it is, and there may be some negative press about this, but I think it's important to remember that x has done very well in his new slot against a very competitive background, and that anyway figures don't really matter, because what matters is the quality of the programming, which we all know is of the utmost.'

They play it both ways and I don't attack them for that, because we've all done it. But I just do not accept that the BBC is not obliged to do popular broadcasting. The idea that Radio 1 was weak in the argument against privatization because it was popular is piffle. The problem was that when you went out and you asked anyone under twenty-five if it was any good, they said, 'No.' It was popular with people who are much older, but the job surely was to make it popular with younger people, not to make it trendy – that's two rather different things. Aiming for an *NME* reader was . . . it was just too small a target, I think, and they needed to be broader than that, and keep being popular, being a bit silly, being . . . all those awful words that we now despise, like zany and wacky and fun. We quite rightly deride them because they're the shibboleth of another era, but actually people of sixteen, seventeen, eighteen do actually quite like people to be zany and wacky and fun. They don't use those words necessarily, but some of those values are what they tune into the radio for. This is not the World Service after all. People who are fitting exhaust pipes at Kwik Fit, they would like to be entertained.

Chapter 9
The DJ Might Explode

Chris Moyles: 'May as well throw the fat boy on . . .'

Simon Garfield: Once a week, usually on a Thursday afternoon, management would gather in Andy Parfitt's office for a strategy and planning meeting. The deputy controller would normally chair, and Bannister would show up only rarely, kept away by the demands of his other job. Privately, Bannister would tell his colleagues that since he became director of BBC radio, Radio 1 had become a part-time concern, something he would do mostly in his spare time.

Parfitt's office was one of the largest in Yalding House, the former BBC reference library that Radio 1 had occupied since September 1996. The three studios were below ground, the DJs and producers and assistants occupied two open-plan offices on the ground floor, and management, press and marketing camped on the first floor, cramped by computers and faxes and hi-fi. It was not a glamorous place in which to work.

Given the proximity of the on-air talent and management, the two groups mixed infrequently. Indeed there was a bureaucratic barrier between them: a distinction between Broadcast and Production, a Birtian efficiency-seeking reform of 1996, which entailed separate management and separate channels of control. There was a distinction, too, between the network (controller, deputy, press and marketing, music policy) and creative commissioning; for decades Radio 1 had commissioned in-house, but since Producer Choice had been introduced in 1993, it had been obliged to buy its programmes from the BBC's Music Entertainment department (about 70 per cent) or from independent companies or other BBC departments.

In 1997/98, Radio 1 had a budget of about £19 million a year, of which roughly £7 million was spent on copyright payments to record and publishing companies. The remaining £12 million did not include the cost of news, marketing or transmission, but covered all management, running and talent costs. As elsewhere within the BBC, Radio 1 was under pressure to cut costs at the rate of 5 per cent each year to free funds for digital broadcasting.

The weekly network management meetings were the one forum in which all future programmes and general station policy was discussed, and much of the ninety-minute session was spent updating each other on how they'd been spending their week – which band had said yes to a documentary, what the new logo might look like, when the new mental health campaign might start, whether it was possible to broadcast from *The Clothes Show Live*.

They sat in wicker chairs around a small table, beneath a huge poster of Jo Whiley advertising Radio 1's Sound City festival in Oxford, a *Radio Times* cover of Chris Evans, an Oasis poster. Heavy traffic noises from Great Portland Street streamed in even with the windows closed. Occasionally, in the course of a few months' uneventful meetings, topics would emerge that engaged the participants in a more illuminating debate, but mostly it was the daily drudge.

There was the possibility of broadcasting a U2 concert from Sarajevo, but the cost was prohibitive. 'We can only pay £30K, which is £10K an hour,' Kate Marsh, the programme editor, says. 'They know we really want it. I think £35K is our absolute limit. If we don't do it, it's not going to happen for the rest of the world, because we're the ones taking all the trucks.'

The Shirehorses planned to release a single, but the station could play it only if there were good editorial reasons. The breakfast show couldn't do it, because that would just be advertising, but if it gets into the Top Forty that would be okay. 'Have you heard it?' someone asks. 'Their version of "North Country Boy"? It's really terrible.'

The Shirehorses are going out on tour for a week in a double-decker bus, and there will be a tribute band in support, possibly the Pulp tribute, and there might be a comedian. 'We're in negotiation with Frank Skinner and Harry Hill. Obviously we can't offer them much money, but the bonus for them is that they'll be on the show the next morning to plug whatever.'

In week thirty-six the station would have the exclusive first play of the new Spice Girls single . . . In the following week they're doing 'We Love Us' on the breakfast show. In week forty-four there's a Spice Girls weekend, including a documentary. [In the passages that follow, each new paragraph denotes a different speaker.]

There will be a thirty-year anniversary party on 29 September, possibly at Kenwood House, but they may have too many rules, like no smoking. Everyone's been e-mailed, but few have replied. 'John Peel still has no idea what e-mail is.'

The *Sun* are definitely coming to the breakfast show in Rome. '*Loaded* are playing Blur in a five-a-side, so we'll try and get them both to come to the club in the evening.'

The new dance weekend launches soon, and there are plans to give away free promotional CDs. 'Pete Tong's a bit tepid about it. He's afraid of cluttering the market, because he already has his *Essential Mix* CDs out there.'

'Isn't he being a bit precious? It's only a thing given away with a magazine.'

At the funeral itself, Elton John will sing a new version of 'Candle in the Wind', beginning, 'Goodbye England's Rose'.

'Fucking hell, no.'

The Brit awards

'We've been asked which award we want to sponsor this year. It seems the Best British Newcomer is the prime one. After the show I thought we could do a sort of Brits breakfast into the breakfast show. It could be a bit like in America with the Oscar breakfasts, where on TV they just have guests dropping in on the way back from the parties . . .'

'My view is that we should have a very strong presence this year. Last year I'm not sure we were that committed to it. It would be quite nice if we can try to ease Capital out of it.'

'This is my concern as well. They are gradually trying to take it over. They have got the New Single, which we let them have last year, and I was thinking of taking that back off them this year, but as it's probably "Candle in the Wind", I thought we would let them have it again.'

'If we can make a significant commitment to them this early, maybe they will leave Capital out in the corridor.'

Steve Lamacq wants some leave

'He does need some holiday, as he hasn't been off for a very long time, and he might explode.'

The *Radio Times* needs billings for the new shows

'Okay, just *Judge Jules*. We don't want a stupid title like the other ones.'

'No *Lovegroove Dance Party* or something?'

'Don't knock it – it gets us an 11 per cent share.'

'And what about Zoe and Kevin's breakfast show?'

'The Radio 1 Breakfast Show with Kevin Greening and Zoe Ball. In that order.'

'At the moment they just write, "7 o'clock, Mark Radcliffe". So you want it to say "7 o'clock, Kevin Greening"?'

'Well, it should be 6.30 for a start. They're being paid for 6.30.'

'So it should be "Kevin Greening *with* Zoe Ball", or "*and* Zoe Ball"?'

'And.'

'In the afternoons, should it be "Mark Radcliffe and Lard", or just "Mark Radcliffe"?'

'It's Mark Radcliffe. Simplicity, simplicity. We can always add silly names later.'

'For breakfast, I'm thrilled to say that the newsreader will be Tina Ritchie. Which is just absolutely fantastic. The major feature of the new programme will be Zoe's entertainment news and gossip, and for that we're having a Net person working late to provide audio and written material . . . It's going to be great!'

'At the beginning, we should endeavour to keep Zoe and Kevin on as long as possible without a break. They're allowed eight weeks.'

'Kevin's got some leave booked in the second week of December.'

'I think we should ask him to cancel that, and say we'd like him to work all the way to Christmas.'

'I think there'll be six records per half-hour. It's important that it sounds like a breakfast show. I think with Kevin, because he's such a slick operator, he might even be able to get another one in.'

'We've got the front cover of the *Radio Times* with Zoe and Kevin for the week of 13 to 21 February, but it'll be out before that, to coincide with our Rajar week.'

The World Cup

'It's clear that our World Cup coverage does hinge on the cooperation of Simon Mayo, and him feeling confident with our plans. We went through them with him, and his single and very important point is that he feels dreadfully exposed, and that he's been talking to some friends like Gary Lineker, who have said, "You are fucking mad if you think you're going to do a roadshow in front of a lot of blokes who are pissed out of their minds and going to watch a game, so don't do it."'

'Clearly it's important for us to know that we can guarantee everyone's safety.'

'Off air, at one end we could do a sort of Torquay Roadshow, with live interaction, guests, live bands and competitions, and then at the bottom end we'd simply put videos on the big screen, and Mayo would do the music and introduce the occasional band and then run off again, i.e. not him wandering around on stage in a big suit – almost treating the roadshow like a huge ghetto blaster and pressing play, without Mayo necessarily having to put his head above the parapet.'

The Spice Girls

'Virgin are handling everything at the moment because the Girls haven't got any management, and they have asked us what we want to do with them next. I said it would be nice to broadcast one of the days on the European tour, either the first date in Vienna at the end of February or the first or last UK date. Virgin have said that the first one might not be possible because clearly they're going to be a bit nervy about it.'

'Let's see . . . Madrid . . . Lyon . . . Arnhem . . . Dortmund –

we could do the breakfast show from Dortmund.'

'Could we get them to co-present a show?'

'They're going to be knackered.'

'By the way, Jeff has just put the Rolling Stones on the playlist.'

'It's the "Deep Dish" mix. Being played by Pete and a lot of our specialist programmes. It's called "The Saint in Me".'

'The kids will think they're new.'

Marketing

'I thought we should do some marketing activity in March around the breakfast show, just coincidentally of course in the last month of the first Rajar quarter. We'll probably use the national press, built around a big competition. So if anyone has a corking idea that will last through an entire month . . . Where will the Spice Girls be in the last days of March?'

'Antwerp.'

'Oh God – we'll pay *you* . . .'

'. . . to sit through the Spice Girls.'

'Shall we talk about this Concorde thing? We thought we could run a massive competition on the breakfast show, with the prize of going on Concorde to New York for two or three days. And also do a show from Concorde. We'd build the competition up throughout March. Do you remember the competition that Chris had on his show?'

'They were going to go to Cher's house, weren't they?'

'No, they were going to go to Prince's house – to go and call him a purple git.'

'In the end you couldn't leave your house because you had to listen. I think if it's rehearsed enough and done properly, something like that could be very exciting. In terms of cost, there is a way in which we could get Concorde very cheaply with some deal, but clearly we have to be careful that there's no conflict there. And I have already said to British Airways that there is no way that we would be able to say "Thanks to British Airways".'

'Do we know what the competition is?'

'Not the mechanics, no.'

'You give it away seat by seat, don't you? You fill up the plane row by row, and you announce to a winner, "And funnily enough the person sitting next to you will be . . ." who may be someone from a band or someone from the show, so it's double the whammy.'

'You could put the seating-plan on the website.'

'If we left on a Friday, couldn't we take all the daytime shows?'

'You don't actually have to go anywhere on Concorde. If the fun of the competition is filling the seats, you could just fly around for a bit and land back in London.'

'That's not as exciting, though, is it?'

'For the competition you could phone up various people in New York who have different sorts of jobs, like somebody who works at Grand Central, and ask them off air what colour underpants they're wearing. The person who's doing the competition doesn't know the answer and has to guess. If you call up and say "red" and the ticketmaster at Grand Central has said red beforehand, then they win the prize. Then you get the entertainment factor of people at home thinking, "That's interesting, will they get through to the person at Grand Central?" but of course he's already said it on tape.'

'And you could have a tie-break on air. By that point it's actually quite sad when someone loses – that's just as good on the radio.'

Win Noel Gallagher's guitar

'I'm not joking, but we've managed to get hold of a Noel lookalike wig and some eyebrows.'

'And who will be wearing that?'

'Zoe. To launch the competition.'

'Callers have to phone up and play an Oasis song using a strange instrument of their choice.'

'Does Noel know we're doing this?'

'Yes. He's keen on it.'

'We should try to get him to come.'

'That's a brilliant competition. We should take a photograph with all these lookalikes and Noel, and you have to spot the Noel.'

'He won't come, will he?'

'He's got a great sense of humour, but there probably is a limit.'

The Christmas party

'It's going to be at Stables Market at Camden Lock. The Shirehorses will be coming down to play. Fun, fun, fun. We think it will cost about £6,000–£7,000.'

'What do we normally do about the business of using licence payers' money for our own parties? I think everyone has to pay for their ticket.'

'People will always whinge and bitch if they have to pay to go to their own Christmas parties.'

'We have to be careful, because it's Christmas and not much news around, and the papers are on the lookout for which BBC department is going to spend a fortune on Christmas parties.'

The new bags

'They'll have the BBC Radio 1 logo here and a little tag here ... We could have done duffels or satchels, but I had a word with some producers and presenters, and they agree that the good thing about the record bags is that they say "Music". They cost about £6 each.'

'The whole point is that they stop giving out crap on air. The bags should replace the prizes they're giving out now. You know, when Clive Warren goes, "Hey, it's twenty past one, and we've got a few crap videos to give away ..." They should say, "This is a Radio 1 prize," with the emphasis on the station, not on the shite videos they happen to have been sent that week, and then in the bag they can put a few CDs or whatever.'

'Which programmes still have budgets for prizes? I think

we ought to quantify how much money we give them to give away crap on the air.'

Chris Morris will definitely be returning to the station

'The series is from Talkback, but they're now talking of delaying delivery by a few weeks, so that they can do a few either side of Christmas. That's just Chris playing silly buggers. Tell them I want it before Christmas, all of them . . . There's going to be a very bland trail for it, just Chris going, "What are your dreams? Discuss them on the Radio 1 Dreamline." Then he'll give out a number. Clearly, no one should find out it's him.'

'We'll definitely get press calls on that.'

'Say that we're not planning to broadcast them. Say it's an experiment for a new Radio 1 series. The working title is *Plankton Jam*.'

'Will that be "Chris Morris's *Plankton Jam*"? I think it should be. You need Chris Morris there.'

'I'm negotiating with him. In the *Radio Times*, Chris wants it described as "ambient stupid", which I've said no to. It's a floaty, dreamy kind of surreal experience. I'm so excited, and I haven't heard the pilot yet. He won't send it to me.'

[The series became *Blue Jam*, broadcast at 1 a.m. on Friday mornings to wide critical acclaim, but an audience of only about 100,000. The shows featured stretches of trip-hop and ambient music punctuated with warped, fantastic conversations, such as the doctor who cured his patients' ailments by kissing where it hurt, and parents discussing how they organized bloody combat between their eighteen-month babies. One show was a few minutes short of an hour, the edited passage judged unsuitable for broadcast at any time.]

[Four months later] 'I have some money left, and I'll be advertising *Blue Jam*. I've had some conversations with Chris Morris. He *is* mad, but we're forging ahead anyway . . . You are right about the paranoia.'

'You do realize that if it's not fit for broadcast it will be pulled?'

'So I might have advertised a show in Thursday's press that doesn't go out?'

'You might. A show will go out, but it might be a repeat.'

'That's quite serious. I have to supply copy by the Tuesday before, because it'll be colour, but you're not going to know by then? So why don't we spend it all when we repeat the show two days later?'

'Maybe that's better, because I can tell you, if it's not fit for broadcast, it won't be broadcast.'

'Chris has told me that he'll deliver the first one two weeks before.'

'That's what he said last time.'

'But we had a long conversation about it.'

'Last time we got it with ten minutes to go.'

Core values

'I thought we might start talking to all the presenters, in order to communicate what we thought we were about now, and what the core values were, and what they thought about us. I thought one thing we could do in advance is a questionnaire like the one the agency did for As It Is. That was quite engaging.'

'The questionnaire thing might be going backwards. Simon Mayo will think that this is some silly form of communication. To be honest, the breakfast show this week – they're in a bad mood anyway and they feel like the honeymoon period is over. A lot of the time what they actually want is people showing interest in their show – they need you and Jeff to go and see them.'

'It seems to me that we have been woefully inadequate in saying to Mark Goodier, Judge Jules, Pete Tong, Dave Pearce, essential things like, "Our target audience is fifteen to twenty-four year olds, and then twenty-five to thirty-fours, and this is why . . ." The same as I did with the breakfast show yesterday. I'm sure that's only the second time that that's happened to them in their whole time at Radio 1.'

'I think you really have to make an effort to take a team out for lunch and then go through everything, and make it clear that we're not just going out to get pissed.'

'Between the six of us we should be able to pick off the whole station in less than eight weeks. And it's not enough just to tell them what their Rajar figures are.'

'There's no point just talking at them. We have to make sure that they don't just go back afterwards and say [to other producers and presenters], "Yeah, have you been taken out for lunch yet, have you been got by upstairs? They're obviously not happy with the show . . ."'

'Before your meeting yesterday, the whole breakfast show were shitting themselves that they were about to get bollocked. It's really easy for us to think they're fine, but they get really worried.'

'I'd quite like to do that branding thing. It makes things quite clear about how you define a world. Once you've got that idea in your head . . . this is the Radio 1 world. It was this whole idea about how you have a brand, and how it has character. You know, "If it was a newspaper what would it be?" or "If it was an advert what would it be?"'

A new DJ

'We really have to find a new swingjock, someone who can dep on a number of shows. I tuned into Tom Clay [name changed] last week and it's just "click" – straight off with the radio.'

'Well, he's on the way out, don't worry.'

'You put it on and think, "What *is* this?"'

'I switched it straight off.'

'I think if we're going to hire a new DJ to use around the schedules my feeling is that it should be Clare Jones [name changed]. Clare has got lots of potential. I've heard someone here be snotty about her because she was once on in-store radio.'

'She will need some serious presentational assistance

before she goes on air, just in terms of Radio 1-ness.'

'I think the thing to do is to meet with Clare Jones and speak to her about what she might want to do, and I think we do a direct swap between her and Tom Clay. We've persevered with Tom and it's just not . . . it's hopeless.'

'Is there anyone here who is spending a solid week travelling the country listening to who else is out there? It's silly of us not to be doing that.'

'We always have this problem that if we find someone we're not absolutely sure about, there's nowhere we can hide them away in the schedule to try them out.'

'It ought to be done in a systematic way. Rather than just taking a pot-shot at 140 stations we ought to go to Rajar and look at people's performance amongst fifteen to twenty-four year olds, like we did with Moyles. Moyles's figures confirmed his appeal. We need to commission it as a project.'

'We all know that we ourselves would be better than Tom Clay. We can also get some press out of it – there's no reason why we shouldn't be seen to be looking for new talent.'

*

Andy Parfitt: I get loads of tapes from young DJs every month, all wanting to be on Radio 1. I normally set aside a few hours every month to listen to them, go through a few minutes of them all, and we have two standard replies which Jo [Lamb, his assistant] sends out. One is, 'Heard your tape, thanks a lot. We liked it – let us hear more soon.' And the other is, 'Thanks for your tape. It's not quite right for us.'

A few weeks ago somebody hacked into Jo's computer and altered the last letter to read, 'Thanks for your tape. It was really shit.'

Before we realized this, about four letters had gone out. Obviously we sent these people another letter immediately, explaining that someone had done this as a prank, and three out of four of them I think have taken it in good heart. Unfortunately we are currently being pursued by one man who has taken immense offence, and won't let it drop. We've given him a full apology, but he wants more than that, although exactly what isn't clear. He says he might go to the newspapers.

Chris Moyles (Disc Jockey): When I was at Capital I got a call from someone who said they were from Radio 5 – some sort of decoy. Some woman basically left a message asking me to call her, which I never did because I didn't know what it was about and I couldn't be bothered.

Eventually my producer Ashley called back and it turned out it was Jeff Smith from Radio 1. Jeff said some nice things about the show, so we decided to meet up. We had secret meetings with Andy Parfitt in hotel bars. It was just kind of like psyching each other out.

The impression I got was that Jeff had heard the show and was a big fan. Consequently Andy had heard bits of the show and liked it as well. And they were just kind of like, 'We kind of like it.' They said, 'We think your show would work on Radio 1, possibly, one day in the future, what do you think to that idea?'

'It's a very interesting idea.'

Simon Garfield: Before he started on Radio 1 in July 1997, Chris Moyles came into the studios to get used to the equipment and record some trails and links. On my way to meet him I asked a producer how I'd recognize him: 'Oh, you'll recognize him. He has eaten all the pies, and the person that sold them to him, and the shop.' Moyles wasn't that fat, although he did have fat habits. He sipped warm Coke at ten in the morning and ate a Mars. He sweated heavily. He frequently brushed his curtains haircut back over his brow. He was twenty-three. He didn't look like the sort of man you'd pin your hopes on.

Chris Moyles: They were very careful not to say that there was something definite. So I drank a couple of free BBC drinks and that was about it, really.

They wanted me to do a pilot and I said, 'No.' And they

wanted me to come in and mock up a trail. I said, 'No.' And they said, 'Can you send us a tape of the show?' and I said, 'No.' Because, I mean, they heard the show and phoned *me*. And I thought, It's not too difficult to put a tape in the machine, plus then they get it warts and all, you know, you're not sending them a sugar-coated copy of yourself.

Any old time – Friday, Saturday night – stick a tape into a machine and they're going to get exactly what it is that we're doing.

Jeff Smith: I had heard him on Capital, where he was doing some brilliant stunts. I heard one he did with Lee Hurst where he phoned him up when he was on stage in Guildford, and he got Lee Hurst to ask the audience to shout Chris's name, a clever three-way thing.

I was talking to Andy about Chris, and he wanted to hear a tape. I thought I wouldn't ask him for a tape directly, because if you ask people for demos they go in and make one especially for Radio 1 and you can't tell what they're really like. I just taped him off air, and handed the tape around. But getting Andy and Matthew to listen to a tape sometimes is just like . . . sometimes it does annoy me because I would have thought that they would be desperate to hear great new DJs. 'Matthew, have you listened to it yet?' 'No.' So I sat him down and played it to him, and he thought Chris sounded good. They met at the Langham Hotel. They got on straight away because they both smoke and drink beer.

Chris Moyles: I was working at a station in Bradford when Matthew Bannister was announced as the new Mr Big at Radio 1. And everybody was saying, 'Doesn't make a lot of sense, does it, putting a bloke from what is essentially a BBC talk station in charge of Radio 1?'

And I thought, 'Well, GLR's produced some of the greatest, for want of a better word, radio personalities, modern day personalities. When Matthew was there it was people like Danny Baker and Evans. And Emma Freud, she was there.

Tommy Vance, yeah well, Tommy Vance. Gary Crowley. So, you know, obviously hit and miss. So I thought that if this guy's found a couple of them, I thought he'd be pretty good. And he looked like a friendly man.

Andy and Jeff had made an offer and I was still umming and ahhing about it. So they brought Matthew in to try to . . . Well, Matthew wanted to meet me and I was obviously quite keen to meet Matthew. We reminisced about old stories and smoked ourselves silly for about an hour. While Andy Parfitt and my agent Tony sat and discussed business, we were talking about rude e-mails we'd been sent in the past. Very casual, very kind of not how you would imagine meeting with the boss of BBC radio to be. It was kind of like going out with your mate's dad.

He said he just liked the show and that the show stood out like a gold ring in a piece of pig poo on Capital. That wasn't necessarily a compliment, just a statement of fact that it was different.

He said, 'Chris, you're just what we need to give the station a kick up the arse. For the past ten years, Chris, between you and me, it hasn't been working, no one's listening, you're the man to pull it back up, single-handedly. Forget Evans and Greening and Dave Lee Travis and Bruno Brookes, you're the man, Chris.'

And I said, 'Matthew, I think you're drunk.'

Jeff Smith: We knew that we needed more people, especially with Nicky Campbell moving on. We were losing a personality jock, so it made sense to replace him with another personality jock. I think Moyles is unique, but he is part of a family that also contains Chris Evans and Chris Morris. I think he fits our sound better than Capital's. Radio 1 has always picked people off, right from when we took the best people from Caroline and Luxembourg. It's like A&R – little labels sign good bands first, but then the majors just come along and take them, and the majors then get a roster of the best people.

Anybody who's offered a job at Radio 1 has to think about it seriously. He was very cool about it, but I think secretly he was excited. Capital certainly wanted him to stay, and he was offered a breakfast show on Kiss. I think Capital saw it as a big loss, but they won't admit to it. There's all sorts of propaganda going on that says they sacked him. But I'm sure they had in their mind that Chris would one day be a breakfast show presenter. Also, when he was on Capital in the evenings on Fridays and Saturdays, Chris was a serious competitor for us. He was on against our specialist shows, which meant that if you didn't like what we were doing at that time, you'd find the bands that Radio 1 would normally play, like Sleeper and Cast, on Chris's show. And our listeners might then stay with Capital.

Chris Moyles: Radio 1 is nothing like you imagine it to be. I'm from Leeds, and when you're a kid growing up there and you're listening you think, Radio 1 – that's the dogs, the be-all and end-all. When I started to discover radio, I heard Gary Davies and *Steve Wright in the Afternoon* with all these wacky bonkers characters and that was like the canine's testicles today. Fantastic stuff. I'm sure somewhere there are some really old tapes of *Steve Wright in the Afternoon* in my bedroom.

The other presenters are very shy here and keep to themselves. At Capital there was more of a boys' club, almost like a playground. Simon Mayo is very very quiet, Jo Whiley is the shyest woman I've met in my life. At Capital it was different: Dr Fox would walk in and say to me, 'Hey, Desperate Dan, you fat bastard!' People are genuine here, and friendly, but quiet, and they've got their own lives. Three years ago on my old station, the breakfast show jock and me used to go out for drinks, and then I'd go back to his place and talk about ideas and get drunk. Can't see myself doing that with Zoe Ball. And the man who does the evening show here is John Peel, old enough to be my dad, so I won't be going to the Wimpy with him.

Jeff Smith: I think the slot won him round for us. My original thought was to put him on overnights for maybe three months. That would have got him used to the Radio 1 format, bedded him in, and we would have been able to hear how he was sounding. But he had other offers and so we had to coax him, and we had to give him early breakfast, beginning at four and ending at seven. Essentially the appeal is being able to do six to seven, because you get quite a big mainstream audience then, especially from 6.30, his last half-hour. It's a good way to get a cult following, to get nightworkers or insomniacs who just tuned in by chance, to say to their friends, 'Have you heard this guy, he's quite good.' The plan is just to build up his name, and then in a couple of years who knows where we could put him. He's got everything in position to be a big star, if he wants to be.

Chris Moyles: The main reason I took the gig was Matthew's assurance that I wouldn't be straitjacketed. Most radio round the country is just far too restrictive for people who want to spill their brains out on the air. Stations get scared of it, they don't understand it, they think it's a personal thing against management, whatever.

For me now, Radio 1 is still the big thing. Not as big as it used to be, listener-wise, but more people still want to work at Radio 1 than anywhere else.

So potentially this can be great for me. The thing is, it could also ruin me, because if we go on the air and . . . On Capital, if the show didn't work, then it just didn't work in London. On Radio 1, if it doesn't work then it doesn't work everywhere. Everybody's heard you fuck up. One of the things I said to Matthew before I joined was that I want to make sure that when I go to Radio 1 it's the right decision. Because once you go to Radio 1, as far as I'm concerned, that's it, you ain't going anywhere else. The only way is – you know, if things go bad the only way is down.

So this is where the show starts to get taken seriously.

Jeff Smith: I programme the programme clocks with everyone, so I sat down with him and said, 'This is where you do your feature, this is where you're going to play music.' The format is: out of the news with a record, a segueway every twenty minutes, through the top of the hour with a sweeper [a jingle with a station ID], very basic. In Radio 1 you have to be so careful not to over-format and become just like a commercial station.

A programme clock is important at every time of the day, because it gives an audience certainty in knowing exactly where they are. It defines a station's sound. I would have clocks everywhere if I could, even on the specialist programmes. On the whole it should be fifteen records an hour if you can do it. Chris Moyles has fourteen records an hour because he talks more, Radcliffe and Lard work about twelve records an hour because they talk a lot, too much probably. People say that Chris Evans at the end basically played about one record an hour, but it depends on what you have to say, doesn't it? When Evans talked, time passed by a little quicker, but when Radcliffe and Lard talked a lot on breakfast it didn't pass by quite as fast.

The good thing about Moyles is that Capital softened him up a little bit. I don't have to beat up on him to respect the music policy and play the tunes. As he gets a bigger name it's going to get more difficult, but hopefully he won't let us down on that. But he knows he's in a good position and it would be silly to fritter that away.

We've had a lot of signings recently. Over the last few years, people like Clive Warren and Charlie Jordan have come on board, who are servicing the station correctly and playing the records, but not actually providing us with much on the image stakes, whereas Chris Moyles fits in with the image in every way.

We haven't had a talent like Chris for many years. We've either brought them in already really big, like Chris Evans, or we've brought in your record-playing DJs like Clive Warren, who is good at what he does, but even he realizes his limitations.

The important thing is to have DJs who enjoy the music. A lot of commercial radio DJs are good at selling it, but I think at Radio 1 it has to be a bit sincere. You have to go out and see bands, and be able to enthuse. You can't just read it from a sheet, like it used to happen.

He was paired with Simon Barnett because we were concerned that because he's young he should be with quite an experienced producer. Simon had the Lisa I'Anson show which he did excellent work on, making sure the programme was kept tight. Simon's aware enough to know that Chris needs space, but also to be told where to stop and start and remind him of the station format. Also, Simon was once a DJ himself, so he knows how they work. Being a producer you have to handle the talent and the ego and the needs of the DJ, but you also realize that the management want a certain thing. It's about diplomacy. The best producers get it right. He had a beer or two with Chris and clearly they worked together well.

Chris Moyles (Three months later): They gave me a producer and a couple of assistants who weren't the right people for the show. If someone works with me, they have to get inside my head very quickly. With Simon Barnett I could go down the pub with him, but I'd find that I came up with ideas for the show with other people. That's not right, is it? I brought everything to the party. If I have to have somebody, it should be someone who goes, 'Nah, that was shit, try this – stick a foghorn under it.' And then I'd say, 'No, you want the sound of a cockerel.' I don't know what's wrong with my head, but a lot of ideas float around there all the time, like sitting with someone and going, 'Right, here's a great idea: we'll get women to send in a photograph of themselves, topless, but they put their breasts through some plants, and we'll call it breast in-plants.' That's a good idea.

216

I am surprised how quickly things have happened. Two months in, we get the official word that I'll be filling in for the breakfast show. Phenomenal progress. It's never been heard of at Radio 1 before. That's very very flattering, but realistically who else is going to do it? Mayo's done it, Dave Pearce has done it, Jo Whiley can't do it, Mark and Lard have done it, Peel can't do it. So it's 'May as well throw the fat boy on, see what he does with it.'

Have you asked Matthew who his favourite jock is? Ask him. He loves me the most . . . I think the show I do is genuinely funny. It's different to what most people are doing – I'm doing it, Evans is doing it, to a certain extent Chris Tarrant is doing it – that type of radio where you come on the air and sell a bit of your soul. It works, but if everyone was doing it, it wouldn't. The reason me and Evans are doing well is because of format radio – that we don't sound like the rest of the formatted day. If everyone was doing 'Whe-hey, let's get the cleaners in!'-type radio, then Steve Wright wouldn't have stood out. Steve Wright was only different because Gary Davies was on before him, and Bruno Brookes was on after him.

But I think I've been hired because I'm good, basically. I don't think the show is shocking or outrageous, I just think it's funny. I'm really crap at being a DJ in the sense of 'twenty to eight, Radio 1, the low is down to 22, but it will be a warm day tomorrow though, if you're getting ready for the big Bank Holiday weekend . . .' I can't do that. I used to be able to, but I just got bored with it. I've got lots of respect for people who can do that, and somehow make it sound interesting.

[*A trailer for Zoe and Kevin is audible in the background.*] 'I wrote that!' says Moyles, turning it up. 'I fucking did!' [*It goes, 'Zoe Ball . . . with her sexy legs, she is such a babe . . .' Another advert goes, 'New Music, New Breakfast, New Britain.'*]

Yeah, and new fucking time! [Moyles has lost the last half hour of his programme, from 6.30 to seven, to the new breakfast show.] It pissed me off, a real pain in the arse. It's a shit cunt bag of bollocks. It was the selling point of me taking the bloody job. Seven o'clock – yes sireee, I'll have that! The figures just fly up between 6.30 and seven.

Matthew Bannister: What he wanted from me, I think, was an assurance that I understood his humour and I understood his act and I understood his motivation in being on the radio, and that I wasn't going to subject him to an iron discipline that took all the initiative and spontaneity out of him. And I pointed to my track record for appointing broadcasters and letting them have a certain amount of free rein.

Our conversation was not just about whether you could say 'arse' on the radio, it was more about how much the format would be stretchable to allow him to be spontaneous and different, rather than, 'Can I say "fuck"?' or anything like that. Clearly we're in the business of succession planning, and you could see someone like Moyles being a potential future breakfast show host, so we wanted to try him out early in the morning, and then we gave him the Saturday breakfast show so we can hear what he's like on that. We felt that the early breakfast show, to be frank, was a pretty straight offering with Clive Warren, and that we should do something better and stronger at that time in the morning. Obviously I think he's going to be one of those people who probably polarizes the audience.

We did talk about putting him on the breakfast show as the replacement for Mark and Lard, but we decided that he wasn't ready yet. He's very young and although he's been in radio since he was about two, as far as I can work out, we thought that it wasn't . . . it was too much of a risk.

Jeff Smith: Now, I think he's fine. He's doing all the things we want him to do – he's funny, naturally funny. He's the closest we've ever got to getting someone like Eddie Izzard on the radio – someone who can do freeform stuff. Our only problem is that he is displaying elements of Evans in the sense that he wants to drop records to talk. What he says tends to be rather entertaining, but he doesn't really know when to stop. What he needs is really solid production, and probably a couple of better slots as well, so that more people can hear him and start talking about him. It's a building process, but the idea is to one day get him ready for a really big slot.

At the moment he's still not ready for breakfast. At one stage Matthew and Andy were arguing to put him on the breakfast show to replace Mark and Lard, but I was against it, because he's not ready. He's twenty-three, twenty-four, and a little immature about things and he just needs more time to just get better and be funnier. I do feel responsible for him, and I do want him to do well, but you can't do it too fast. What he would perceive as doing well could possibly ruin him – getting too high a profile too fast. Say he did replace Mark and Lard, and the audience was still plummeting, and he was on doing his act, and he was talking a lot and we'd all be getting annoyed with him, he'd end up on Thames Valley 210. He's so close to it – he loves the business and being on the radio, but something like that could really fuck him up. In a Simon Dee way.

John Peel: From what little I've heard of him, Chris Moyles does seem to be DLT in waiting.

Zoe Ball (Disc Jockey): I think the important thing with Chris Moyles is that people don't give him too much praise. Otherwise he will become the egomaniac that Chris Evans has become. It is so dangerous: as soon as people start saying to you, 'You are so good . . .' you do start to believe it and you start to treat people like shit. My other thing about Chris Moyles is not to let the tits thing go too far. Already a lot of my friends are going, 'I wish he wouldn't talk about tits so much.'

Simon Garfield: I once asked Matthew Bannister to comment on each of his DJ's particular qualities, and he said he liked to have people on the radio who don't sound like anybody else. Students would ask him how to get on the radio, and he'd always tell them just to be themselves. 'People who are false are found out, and particularly on Radio 1 we're not in the business of projecting a false image, we're in the business of real people doing real things.'

Simon Mayo was someone who didn't sound like anyone else, he said. 'He's not a slick DJ, he's a real person with a lot of technique. The key thing about Simon is that you get this sense of somebody talking to you, and a real companion, and it's quite difficult to do that.' In all the turmoil, Bannister was proud that Mayo's mid-morning slot had never changed.

Jo Whiley had similar attributes. 'Jo Whiley is real, there is no artifice about Jo, genuinely passionate about music, but she talks to you like she's your sister, she doesn't come on in the overtly, terribly sexy way that so many female DJs do on commercial radio. She can talk about music with a passion, and she's another communicator of reality, and I think that's very powerful.'

Bannister said that Mark and Lard were also 'real.' 'Okay, so they're acting a bit on air, they're sort of acting northern tosspots, but it's become so much them that they're sort of like it when you go to the pub with them. In the pub they're slightly quieter and less boisterous, slightly more thoughtful and serious. Mark used to pre-plan a lot more than he does now, but the material that really seems to come off are the spontaneous reactions between the two of them.'

With Dave Pearce, Radio 1 has 'spent too long trying to turn him into a personality presenter. I don't mean that he hasn't got any personality, but turning him into somebody who might be a Chris Moyles or a Chris Evans or a Mark and Lard is not the right way for Dave. Dave is a music presenter, and he's very good at getting away the music, and at drivetime we've finally found a place where Dave feels comfortable.'

Steve Lamacq was a tale of growth. 'I think his presentation style has got warmer and more engaging than it used to be – it used to be a bit uncompromisingly dark, and now Steve's lightened up quite a lot, and I think that's partly the influence of John Peel, who he's clearly turning into in many ways. It was really interesting to hear him on New Year's Day doing a mainstream show, because he's a witty man, he was very entertaining on the subject of the January sales. There's no doubting his knowledge or his credibility.'

Mark Goodier was also genuinely enthusiastic about music and the art and craft of putting together radio programmes. 'I don't think he'd be very upset if I said Mark is an excellent midfield player. He's not one of those snazzy strikers who's always scoring a spectacular goal, nor is he a sort of dull clogging defender, he's somewhere in between. He's an incredibly competent presenter, certainly a lot less faceless than some people one hears.'

And Moyles was a unique talent, Bannister repeated. He related well to his listeners, and manipulated the medium in a novel way. 'He's got things to learn yet, but he shows every sign of being an interesting property for the future.'

Andy Parfitt: Because of what Chris Moyles has done with us, other people have taken more note. He's upped his ante. There are so many radio stations out there, and there is so little distinguishable talent. It's relatively easy to hire the best specialists, but when you're talking about the mainstream and finding people who are genuinely in contact with the audience and genuinely entertaining and intelligent and giving more than your average sort of presenter, it starts to become very difficult.

If you go and hire from the area of journalism you find that very few people come with the sense of how to make music radio work. They haven't been schooled since the age of fifteen in their bedrooms, mixing music, talking over music. You may get people with the right credentials in terms of their mental approach and the content of what they say, but then they miss out on the sort of aural sensibilities you need.

But if you just go and get jocks from commercial radio, it's a screaming nightmare. The reason that ILR has such heavy formatics is because they don't want their DJs to go and bugger up their brand value because they'll say things that are . . . There are some notable and wonderful exceptions, but generally speaking you want to contain these people because they're going to embarrass you.

I think that one of the reasons Chris Moyles came to us was because he felt that this was an opportunity to grow up, grow as a broadcaster in a way that would be encouraged.

Chris Moyles (on air, February 1998): My agent is coming in later, at about six. He should worship the ground that I walk on, kiss my feet, because he makes 15 per cent of everything I earn, and so he'll soon be a millionaire. Because at the moment I'm the hottest property on the radio.

[*Later in the show his agent hadn't appeared, but Moyles announced there was a 'sexy slapper' on line four.*]

Woman: Hello?

Moyles: What's your name?

Woman: Hannah.

Moyles: Where are you from, Hannah?

Woman: Aberystwyth.

Moyles: Describe yourself, then.

Woman: I'm nineteen, lovely body, brown hair, big boobs.

Moyles: Are you single?

Woman: Of course.

Moyles: You're every man's dream. Why are you single?

Woman: I'm keeping my options open.

Moyles: And the top two buttons of your blouse, I bet.

Woman: I'm not wearing a blouse. Pyjamas.

Moyles: Do you have fantasies about me?

Woman: Of course, darling.

Moyles: Will you do anything for me?

Woman: Yeah.

Moyles: Will you come in here and bare all in the studio?

Woman: Sure.

Moyles: Tomorrow?

Woman: Okay then.

Moyles: Will you crawl around naked on your hands while we ride around on your back?

Woman: If you like.

Moyles: My producer has gone all quiet. Normally he laughs, but he's just gone quiet. See you tomorrow, Hannah.

[*The following day, Hannah came into the studio.*]

Moyles: It's coming up to twenty-five past six, I'm Chris Moyles, in our hidden studio, which is now covered in newspaper on Hannah's wishes.

Hannah: Thank you.

Moyles: Hannah's our listener from yesterday who phoned up for *True or False* and said that she'd come down to our studio today and maybe strip naked for us. Why, exactly, would you, maybe, strip naked?

Hannah: Because I love you, obviously.

Moyles: But you're not scared of me?

Hannah: No I'm relaxed. Cool as a cucumber.

Moyles: Okay, so we're now sitting in this studio which has a massive window to the front and a window to the side which looks through to the breakfast show studio. These are now all covered with bits of newspaper. Even the tiny little peephole in the door is covered with newspaper so that nobody can see in. It's like being in an air-raid shelter. So we'll do *True or False*

223

and Hannah will be line four, and we'll just find out what happens. *True or False* line one, hello?

Caller: Cummmon, Chris!

Moyles: Cummmon you, what's your name?

Caller: It's Mark from Birmingham.

Moyles: Mark from Birmingham true or false: Ben our producer is a very excited bunny this morning.

Caller: That's true, Chris.

Moyles: It *is* true! Question number two, true or false: Ben hasn't had it for a long time.

Caller: It's gotta be true, Chris.

Moyles: It's false I'm afraid. He had a Ribena yesterday, his favourite drink. Line two, hello?

Line Two: Cummmon!

Moyles: Cummmon! What's your name?

Line Two: Keith from Sleaford.

Moyles: True or false: Beavis and Butthead are to join Radio 1 to present our new weekend jazz music show.

Line Two: True!

Moyles: False! Sorry, bye-bye. Line three, hello?

Line Three: CHRRAAAGH!

Moyles: I've got no idea what you just said, but it was very loud. What's your name?

Line Three: I'm Hercules.

Moyles: Of course you are. And where are you calling from, Hercules?

Line Three: I'm from Hertfordshire.

Moyles: True or false: John Peel invented the wheel.

Line Three: Oh, that's false.

Moyles: It's true, bye-bye. And now line four, live in our studio is the lovely Hannah! Hello, Hannah!

Hannah: Hello!

Moyles: So you were on the phone yesterday and you said you'd come in and strip naked for us.

Hannah: Yeah.

Moyles: You also said you'd show me your tattoo. And that you'd let me draw a tattoo on you.

Hannah: Yeah, all of those.

Moyles: We've covered up all the windows because you're a little bit shy.

Hannah: Only a little bit.

Moyles: Bottling it a little bit?

Hannah: Only a little bit.

Moyles: And your friend's giving you grief. You want to do it, but I think your friend's putting you off.

Hannah: You reckon?

Moyles: So there's you and me in the studio, your friend, and Jude and Ben and Clive. Now if that's too many people for you we can kick them out.

Hannah: No, it's fine.

Moyles: If you just want it to be you and I, I'd be quite happy with that.

Hannah: No, because Ray has to show her tattoo too.

Moyles: Okay. So where is your tattoo?

Hannah: It's kind of above my left buttock.

Moyles: I've got to see this. And you've both got similar tattoos?

Ray: Do you need mine as well?

Moyles: It's up to you. Look at this! They've now got their backs to me and . . . oh my God! They're very nice.

Hannah: Thank you.

Ray: Thank you.

Moyles: I bet when you had that tattoo done it took longer than it should have done. I bet that bloke was enjoying himself when he did your tattoo. It would have taken me four hours. So where do you want me to draw a tattoo on you?

Hannah: On my shoulder.

Moyles: She's coming round to my side of the desk. Oh my God, she's taken her jacket off, and she's not wearing a bra. We've got a completely topless woman in the studio! It's fantastic! I'm enjoying this moment. No the thing is, we couldn't find any special paint pens, so I've got some paintbrushes and paint.

Hannah: Could you not use Biro?

Moyles. Okay, Biro. Wow, look, I'm drawing a tattoo on her shoulder. Chris . . . was . . . here. I'm going to play this record while I finish off this tattoo . . . of the entire population of China.

Chapter 10

The Overmarket

Tim Westwood: 'It has so much support from the ladies . . .'

Jeff Smith: I'm not sure that Radio 1 is ever fully appreciated. For all the work we do . . . I don't think we get enough support from record companies or the industry as a whole. What happened with Oasis, yes, was a classic example.

When the new album came out [*Be Here Now*] we were promised the worldwide exclusive first play. We trailed this for several days, but when it came down to it their management said they were going to give four tracks to all the radio stations, but that we could have two extra tracks. Thanks a lot. So we played the six tracks, and the next day the band's management called up and complained that we hadn't played jingles between the tracks to stop piracy, something I'd never agreed. On the programme, Steve [Lamacq] had said that he hoped that the following day he'd be able to play the remaining tracks, but Oasis said no. The following day he had to go on the air and apologize to the listeners.

I was pissed off. There should be a special relationship between Radio 1 and bands like Oasis, because we kicked it off for them. Radio 1 had played the first ten Oasis singles, on the playlist every one of them, bar none. We played a demo on the C list before they'd even released a record. We get behind new bands, and are they just going to blow us out in the end? We build them up, and they don't really want to stick with us. With Oasis that was a useful experience, because it makes me cautious for our future. To be honest, it makes me doubt playing these new records at all.

We're a radio station that needs supporters, because we're always going to be criticized for doing things wrong. When the government begins looking at charter renewals again, Radio 1 will be continually chased after. We break all this new music, and then commercial radio stations get to play it when it's a hit, and then we get accused of sounding like a commercial radio station. In the end I wonder what the defence will be for us when you don't get support even from bands like Oasis. That's my common complaint to record company MDs – they take us for granted, and I don't think they support us in the end. When the axe is just about to fall it might dawn on people that they need to shout about Radio 1, and realize that Radio 1 is the most important radio station in the world for breaking new music. We make an absolute difference.

Simon Garfield: Jeff Smith was born near Blackpool in Lancashire, and grew up doing all the usual musically obsessive things. He used to like Radio Caroline, and sent in requests. His dad liked the Beatles and Simon and Garfunkel, his mum listened to Nat King Cole and Dean Martin. He was fascinated by the packaging of the *White Album*; his first single was T Rex, but he also bought Lieutenant Pigeon.

He ran his own little radio station at home, and then worked in a record shop and did a mobile disco, which he saw as a good way of building up the record collection. He did communication studies at college, worked on the college radio station, and sent off tapes to Radio 1, tapes of him as a DJ. No one liked them much.

He got his first proper job as a studio manager for the World Service at Bush House, and then went to TFM Radio in Stockton-on-Tees as a programme manager. There he learnt about pop radio formats, programme clocks, computerized music, scheduling. He joined Radio 1 in 1990 as a producer, and helped establish the *Evening Session*, first with Mark Goodier, and then with Jo Whiley and Steve Lamacq at the birth of Britpop.

He remembers arriving at 'this enormous personality station packed with what the Americans call "gladiator DJs" – send them into battle and they're going to win in every market.'

Even the producers were big names, and initially he was in awe of them. 'But after a while, and this sounds arrogant, you begin to think that you know more than they did. All they knew was the BBC, their little world, and they had never seen the greater commercial world. They didn't see that everything was changing. I used to go to awaydays with management and tell them that Bob Harris, although a great broadcaster, wasn't fitting into the sound of now. But the station was completely absorbed with growing old with the audience rather than having to lose some of them at some point. The idea of shedding any audience was never considered as an option, it was an awful thought. If ever you brought up the idea of pruning the station, losing a bit but then bringing it back stronger, they would just regard this as a failure.'

Smith worked as music manager for a while, but regretted his lack of influence. So he joined Wise Buddah, Mark Goodier's fledgling independent company that signed Pete Tong and made several shows for Radio 1 and other networks. He came back to the station at the beginning of 1997, taking over from Trevor Dann as head of music policy, one of the most influential jobs in music radio. He now controlled the sound of the radio station by chairing the weekly playlist meetings, scheduling all mainstream programmes, dealing with the record companies, helping to develop the turns. For a music lover it's a great job, and a terrible job.

Jeff Smith: I was talking to the head of promotions at MCA Records, and he was saying that Woolworths and WH Smith now don't stock records unless they're A list Radio 1. So that puts a huge commercial pressure on what is public service radio. I try not to think too much about the implications for the music industry on the decisions we make for the playlist, but clearly they are huge. Essentially, if me and the producers don't think a record is right for us, then it won't get into a lot of shops.

The shops will get a marketing sheet from the record companies which will say, the new Pulp single: Radio 1 A list, *Top of the Pops*, *TFI Friday*, MTV. When they see the A list entry, that's the one that pushes them over, because we're still the only national radio outlet for this sort of music. Okay Virgin, but they tend not to play the leading edge stuff.

It used to be that it was enough just to be on the Radio 1 playlist, but now it really has to be the A list – the rotation can be around thirty plays a week. The audience for that is almost 10 million. You can't buy that sort of exposure. [A record on the B list gets about ten to fifteen plays a week, the C list perhaps five.]

Sometimes when the promotions people come in here I can feel the huge pressure behind them to have a hit. You sense the marketing budget behind them, and the pressure they're under perhaps from America to make a record sell. Someone will say to them, 'This has been Top Forty in the Billboard charts, you must do the same in the UK.' And if it's a country song, or a slow adult ballad, they're going to be in trouble.

Simon Garfield: Each week about thirty pluggers – record promotions people – enter Smith's small office for five or ten minutes and sit on a fat chair to flog him their latest greatest new thing. They talk about their priorities, a little bit of background if they're pushing a new artist, and they give Smith two or three songs to play on the CD player behind him. They get a pretty instant response. It's a nervous thing to watch.

One Tuesday morning in November 1997, Steve Morton (husband to Jo Whiley) and Nigel Sweeney (known as Spanner) from an independent company called Intermedia started the plugging day.

Steve Morton: Because a lot of our records are doing well, I've got some stuff way upfront for you to be aware of. So . . . Bernard Butler, his first solo single since leaving Suede [*hands it to Smith*]. The *Evening Session* are giving it it's first play on Monday – Steve Lamacq absolutely loves it, but it's not out for about six weeks – January 5th. He's signed to Creation. NME have said 99 per cent certain front cover for the first week in January.

Jeff Smith [*putting it on, a slow-building request to stay, and not to go*]: Nice voice . . .

Steve Morton: He surprises everybody.

Jeff Smith: The time is just right for him. Today is about songs, isn't it? He's always written great songs, and because he can sing as well, that sounds perfect for now.

Steve Morton: It's epic, epic.

Jeff Smith: It's a Vervey type thing.

Steve Morton: That's it. He wants to put a band together. Mark Cooper [producer of *Later* with Jools Holland] has already gone mad about the album. Bernard has to find out whether he can sing live now – you know, live, live, live. Right. Next, Space and 'Avenging Angels'. This comes out last week December.

Jeff Smith:
'If we carried on the way we were going, we would just evacuate the radio station'

[Jeff Smith puts it on: a big airy sound, lots of guitar and harmonies, but a strange section in the middle where the singer finds a megaphone, and starts singing like a fairground barker, a vaudeville sound.]

Jeff Smith: I've never been a big Space fan, so I'd have to chat to other people. My initial response to that is that it's all right, but I don't like that funny little bit in the middle.

Nigel Sweeney: Could you do me a favour and live with that for a couple of plays? Because I was also worried about that . . .

Steve Morton: So was I.

Nigel Sweeney: . . . but I timed it, it's thirty-five or forty seconds, and actually because it's odd, it does work. Christine Boar [former Radio 1 producer, now MTV] was the one who first held us back when we first brought 'Neighbourhood' out. She was the one who went, 'Spanner – this is fucking awful.' She held us off the playlist. In hindsight that was good. We weren't ready to be on the playlist and have a hit record, because at the time they were playing live and playing and playing and developing. And then what happened was 'Female of the Species' came out and she went, 'Wow', and then she went back to 'Neighbour-

232

hood' and said, 'Now I see . . .', and she went completely potty about it and it was a hit. At MTV she's gone completely potty about Space, because they are so unusual.

Jeff Smith: I thought 'Dark Clouds' was quite a good song. I thought 'Female of the Species' was all right.

Nigel Sweeney: Actually I think that was brilliant, 'Female of the Species'. But that break in the middle . . . it did worry me, but as a radio person you need to listen to it a couple of times.

Jeff Smith: But if you and me are worried about it, once it gets to producers and further down the line, people are just going to spot that again and again.

Nigel Sweeney: Maybe what we should do is a trial edit for radio, but we wanted to leave it in just in case people didn't find it odd.

[*They leave.*]

Jeff Smith: The record company may well do a radio edit, which the band may not be happy with, and they'll blame Radio 1 for interfering in their creative control.

[*Next up, Julian Spear, head of promotions at A&M.*]

Julian Spear: I wanted to say thanks for supporting our records. I've always said about you that if you hear a good song you'll support it. Particularly with the Adams, which I think is one of the best pop songs he's ever written [Bryan Adams, the sincere Canadian rocker whose new song, 'Back to You', surprisingly made the B list the previous week.]

Jeff Smith: There's a nice sound to it.

Julian Spear: I think it's freshened him up a bit. It's an absolute pop song in the best traditions.

Jeff Smith: Yes, it's cheerful, light – gives us what we need at this time of the year.

Julian Spear: He's coming in for support – he's doing the breakfast show, and doing a Mayo session. I was obviously hoping that we might go up from here [to the A list].

Jeff Smith: I don't know. It's a gradual process, because these producers over the last couple of years have not felt so free to get involved with pop music as they do now. They find it a little difficult when Bryan Adams is on the playlist, or Jon Bon Jovi or Mariah Carey, because we haven't really done that in the last couple of years. I think it's a case of making sure that they're comfortable with it. If they are, then I don't see any reason why not. But we have to chip away, and build up a pop sensibility that the producers have sort of lost. It's a negotiation I have to have with them, especially with a singer like Bryan – just because of his name, unfortunately. But I am trying to change what's happened here over the past couple of years with the music policy, and make it a bit more mainstream.

Julian Spear: It's essential for the station. Individually the producers I've talked to are fine with that – it's just when they're in front of each other. My concern is that B list records can sometimes get very little play on the breakfast show.

Jeff Smith: I wouldn't worry about that.

Julian Spear: No?

Jeff Smith: You'll definitely get breakfast show plays. If they want Bryan in, it seems silly of them not to play it. If they drop it I'll have to have words with them.

Julian Spear: I know that Zoe is a massive fan . . .

Jeff Smith: I wouldn't worry about the *quality* of plays – it's just that I don't know if you'll get the higher rotation. But it's a very solid B list record, and hopefully we can move it up later.

Julian Spear: Well, if you've got the openness of mind to do that . . .

Jeff Smith: Well, If I didn't have an open mind I'd be working on another radio station.

Julian Spear: Thanks for your support on that. And for Sheryl Crow. I've never been involved in a Bond song before, but it's unbelievable. I can't turn on anything without hearing about 'Tomorrow Never Dies'.

Jeff Smith: It's such a fabulous song that.

Julian Spear: It *is* a fabulous song – she's a clever girl. She co-wrote it with Mitchell Froom, and I wouldn't want to under-estimate his influence. There's little bits in there – that guitar riff – that's a little bit of 'Watching the Detectives'. I know Mitch is a big Costello fan.

Jeff Smith: It's good for now, because we have a lot of intro-spective ballads, but this is a power ballad, and there aren't many of those around.

Julian Spear: The only other record I wanted to mention, and you must credit me with not giving in . . .

Jeff Smith: Not Del Amitri . . .

Julian Spear: Del Amitri. We're on about forty stations around the country, Virgin have playlisted it, and I heard it on the radio and I thought, Fucking hell, this is a really good little record. I'd like to ask you, if I could, we're out next week, I mean I don't expect . . . the best I'd ever expect at this point would be a C list. So I'd ask you if you'd be open enough to hear it again for me.

Jeff Smith: I will listen to it again later.

Julian Spear: We've got about five TVs coming up. We're on forty stations. We're on Virgin. I think we're going to go eas-ily into the Top Forty.

Jeff Smith: Leave it with me.

Julian Spear: It's a well-made record. I think we're just about to clinch *TFI Friday* today.

Jeff Smith: Great.

Julian Spear: I can't say more than that.

Jeff Smith: No, you can't.

Jeff Smith [*later*]: A few years ago we absolutely wouldn't tolerate having Bryan Adams on the B list. When Trevor was doing it. And it was right in some ways because there was a job to be done for those two years to clear out some of the old audience as well as clearing out some of the old staff.

But now we have to consolidate our position as the UK's leading contemporary music station, as we like to position ourselves, but if we are going to be that we have to play a good range of music. A lot of our older audience will like Bryan Adams and Mariah Carey. If we just concentrate on that cool, credible, student, cutting-edge-type audience, we'll have no listeners within a year. If we carried on the way we were going we would just evacuate the radio station. Then the BBC would have no public service arena for a younger audience – there would be no way in. And the BBC cannot afford for that to happen, so Radio 1 cannot afford to be just a cutting-edge radio station.

Simon Garfield: One plugger said that on his way up to your office he heard 'Drive' by the Cars, a classic soft oldie of the sort Radio 1 doesn't play any more.

Jeff Smith: That must have been the 11.33 spot. A record chosen by the listener, always a mistake.

[*Next in, Alex from Size Nine Promotions, a small independent. She brings in the new Gala single, a follow up to their big hit 'Freed From Desire'.*]

Alex: What's happening with it?

Jeff Smith: I'm not getting a positive view one way or another at the moment. I'm very much open-minded on it. If we could garner a bit more support . . .

Alex: I'm not sure if I can, really. The producers here don't like the song, in the same way that I don't like it. All I can do is let them know the plot that's behind it. Pre-sales are already over 100,000.

Jeff Smith: It came up at the playlist meeting last week, and we did talk about it. I was thinking about it as a C list, but you can't force producers to play it.

Alex: I shall do the rounds with it again, but I can't get people to like it.

Jeff Smith: That's pop music, isn't it?

Simon Garfield: Jeff Smith says he listens very carefully to every record he playlists, partly to ensure no one takes great offence from a track. Occasionally he will demand a radio edit to eliminate swear words – there is an approved radio version of Radiohead's 'Creep' without the 'fucking's, an alternative version of Black Grape's 'Get Higher' without the references to Nancy Reagan smoking pot. His biggest recent dilemma came with Prodigy's 'Smack My Bitch Up'.

Jeff Smith: The song is complete nonsense, really, nonsense words. It could be any words, really, but the problem I have is that it's those four words in that particular order.

[*He calls Scott Peiring, the band's promotions man.*] Scott, hello, just a quickie really. The Prodigy, the first single – is it going to be 'Smack My Bitch Up'? Just so you know, the track was played [from the album] on the *Evening Session* and we've had a few calls. I'm just worried that it might brew up into something more if it's a single, and if it goes out with that lyric. It will be seen as an anti-woman type song. I can imagine that's the last thing the Prodigy really want. If you can provide me with any ammunition, or tell me if there's any chance of a change of title or a re-recording of the lyric . . .

[The problem is daytime plays. Smith says he doesn't want it to appear as though Radio 1 has banned the record.] We would never do that. I believe in artistic freedom, but when it comes down to something which could be seen as abusive against women, which wouldn't be seen as our view either, then I obviously have to make a bit of a stand. In the past we would have reacted differently. Mike Read, who banned Frankie Goes To Hollywood's 'Relax', would have just gone on air and said, quite proudly, 'Oh we're banning it.' But nowadays we're more attuned to our audience.

I'm sure the Prodigy would be the last people to go down that non-PC line, because they're quite a PC band. I think one of the samples they use in it is based on an old Ultramagnetic MCs track, who were American hip-hop originators, and a lot of that music was not very right on. So maybe the Prodigy is making some tongue-in-cheek reference to that, but if you don't get the gag, which most of our audience won't . . . They'll just hear it and think it's really out of order. And if we did ban it, a lot of our audience would be on our side. But then again we have a lot of listeners who are Prodigy fans, so it's a difficult one. If it was someone else but the Prodigy they would have re-recorded the lyric for us, just to get on Radio 1. Prodigy and Oasis are in a position of some power, so they won't change it, but anyone else . . .

[Then Helena McGeough comes in, from Parlophone. She has the new Paul McCartney single.]

Helena McGeough: Could you just give this a blast? I know it's Paul McCartney, but all the same . . .

[Smith plays it, a song about some people going fishing, and how nothing feels so fine as being together with you.]

Jeff Smith: It's a nice song.

Helena McGeough: Pretty, isn't it?

Jeff Smith: It's distinctively older McCartney type stuff. It's not as if I could say, 'If that vocal was Noel Gallagher doing it, we'd necessarily love it,' because it's not the sort of thing Noel would write. But I imagine McCartney could write a song for us one day that we could get really excited about.

Helena McGeough: I certainly hope so.

Nigel Sweeney (*a few days later*): I promote Ash, Babyface, Björk, Bernard Butler, Garth Brooks, Elvis Costello, Janet Jackson, Jamiroquai, M People, Kylie Minogue, Rolling Stones, Simply Red, Space and U2, amongst others.

Before the changes at Radio 1, each of the main programmes seemed to be quite separate from each other, and did what they very much wanted – little empires in a bigger empire. They seemed to have much more say in what records they played and the playlist was often ignored.

When Trevor Dann came in and said, 'Nothing before 1990,' most promotions people felt, bloody hell, he can't do this, but you get used to it pretty quickly. We all had to adapt to a different system. Trevor completely focused the playlist, and it championed Britpop. It was no coincidence that all the major record companies then ran around trying to sign up all the Britpop bands they could find.

It used to be an open-house policy, a shambles and very Arthur Daley. The skill was just trying to catch producers in corridors, and bursting into offices, and trying to get as many people out to lunch and the pubs. But I have never seen anything dodgy going on. There was lots of talk about white goods going to producers' houses, but no evidence. The best thing they get out of us is free CDs. Lunches and drinks – that's just a business thing.

My job mostly involves information – bringing a flow of information between radio station, artist and the record companies. Releasing a single is dreadfully expensive in this country, because the videos cost so much, and the rest of the promotion and marketing. So I have to let a record company know that Radio 1 will support a single or not.

When Sinead O'Connor had recorded 'Nothing Compares 2 U' she had just left her manager and came in with her lawyer and said, 'Radio 1 have *got* to play this single.' I explained that I want them to, but they don't have to.

She said, 'No, you don't realize – they *have* to.' I told her we would make sure everything was done properly. So we serviced that single, and the first person I spoke to was Ric Blaxhill, a producer who's not there any more. He said, 'This is tosh – absolute crap!' I sat there comatose, not knowing what to do. This producer had no personal contact with the artist, but I had serious pressure from Sinead, and I did think it was a fantastic single.

I went off to see other producers and a couple of them were fifty-fifty. Then I went to see Fergus Dudley, who produced Simon Bates. He got it 100 per cent – loved it. So he went off to Bates and said, 'I think this is fantastic,' and Bates trusts his producer, and soon he's on air going, 'This, loves, is a number one record!' And off the record goes, and more and more people recognized it as a great record.

Radio 1 still offers the music industry the best chance of breaking a new record. It's very hard to have a hit with certain types of bands without being on the Radio 1 playlist. Very hard. Getting on to the playlist is a big event for everyone – the artist, the record company, the plugger, and it's an exciting day if you're on. I still sweat until that Friday morning at ten – we get it from Radio 1 reception. And I must see the actual piece of paper. Once I was told by a producer that my new Simply Red single was on there, and what a great record everyone thought it was. So I told everyone, the record company, the management, Mick Hucknall, and then I got the list and it wasn't on. The man who told me had made a mistake.

With Space, when Jeff didn't like that megaphone bit, I had already timed it as forty seconds. I try not to play singles more than four or five times before I start plugging them, otherwise you get blasé about it. But playing it in Jeff's office I also felt that bit in the middle was too long. So I went off to the record company and then the management.

You have to talk to the MD of the company, because it's an important decision. So I said to the MD of Gut Records – we share the same building, but it was a telephone call, not me going down the corridor – I said, 'Edit. Don't muck around. Radio 1 definitely want an edit on that section, and I want it almost halved.' I saw that Jeff had definitely squirmed at that bit, and I thought we had to do something quickly. Hopefully they trust me.

The record company said, 'Okay we'll get it sorted.' Space's manager didn't disagree with me. So I saw Jeff on the Wednesday, and by the Thursday the MD has gone up to Liverpool, and the edit is done, and that bit is now nineteen seconds not forty-one seconds, and the band actually prefer it.

I had the edit in my hand by Friday. The video will be done to that new version. The record company then had to go to the expense of producing more promotional copies, but it had to be done.

Jeff Smith: People always ask me, when they bring in early cassettes, 'What do you think of this mix for the next single?' And I'm loath to tell them in a way, because you don't want to be their A&R, but you do have a bit of responsibility to do that. Some of these new bands, if they come up with a new record and it's not right for us, we've got to make sure it gets right. In the past people have said, 'Well, you go away and you edit how you want – it's your problem.' But I think it's a problem for all of us. If we decide to get behind a band we don't just go on one track, but we check they have two or three good singles or see them live. In the past we've put a band's record on the C list, and their next one comes out and it's crap, and it feels as though you've sold the listener and the record company the wrong story.

I've always felt a great responsibility, especially towards the artist. Our prime responsibility is to our audience, but quite a lot of our audience are artists anyway. I've always been told, 'You have to be careful what you say about Oasis because Radio 1 is the station they listen to.' It's more comfortable for Radio 1 to have that relationship with an artist than it is to have that relationship with a big record company.

Simon Garfield: On the day it was announced that Ball and Greening would be the new hosts of the breakfast show, a weekly playlist meeting took place in the first-floor conference room to decide which records they should play. It was a rolling affair through lunch: producers of the mainstream shows would drift in and out with a pile of new CDs, and Smith would go round the table asking for their favourite new tracks, and then everyone would chip in to say not bad, better than Bryan Adams.

But first the current list had to be cleaned up. The existing playlist was passed round, a three-sheet listing of artists, songs, release date, how long songs had been listed, and the number of weeks the records had been playlisted by Virgin and Capital.

Once a record had been on an A list for seven or eight weeks it would be time to move it off, irrespective of its chart position, to make room for something younger. Records usually appeared on the lists about four weeks before appearing in the shops, and although the record companies were told only about lists A, B and C, the true categories were rather more complex: Super A, A1, A2, B1, B2, B3 and C. Smith has studied American books on formatics, and has produced some theories of his own. These days, he says, you have to be very sophisticated to compete in your delivery of music: a vague A list record is no longer sufficient – you have to know where you're going to put it, and how you're going to rotate it. And you have to know that you're playing a new A list record in a set of music that's familiar: more than 80 per cent of Radio 1's current playlist is non-chart, and Smith believes they have to be cushioned by familiar favourites.

'We get our popularity in the way that we frame our unfamiliar tracks,' he says, while admitting that the way to really build up an audience is to play a very few familiar tracks very often. While

Radio 1's Super A list was giving the Verve's 'The Drugs Don't Work' thirty plays a week, Atlantic 252 was giving All Saints' 'Never Ever' and Chumbawumba's 'Tubthumping' about ninety plays.

Soon Smith would replace the C list with the 'As Featured' list, which would enable him to play just about any track he and his producers fancied. 'No set rotations, so that we can go earlier on some records, perhaps two months before release, and include album cuts or perhaps import-only records. Take Blur, the Andy Wetherall mix of "Death of a Party" that was only available in Japan: I would have put that on the C list, but to put Blur on the C list would have carried a stigma and would be seen as a slap in the face. So it's an As Featured.'

The definitions confuse some producers. Before new records are played, Smith rattles through his suggested amendments. 'I thought we should take the Kavanagh record off, I thought we could move up the Propellerheads to the A list. And the Coolio record to the A list. And Backstreet Boys to the A. And Monaco off, and Tina Moore to B2 and Roni Size off. I've been looking at taking off the Bentley Rhythm Ace record, the Ocean Colour Scene record and the Finley Quaye record, because I think we've done quite a lot with those. The question is, do we put those on the B list, or, I think the better option, because we're going to be short of space this week – put them on to B2?'

Pat Connor (Jo Whiley's Producer back from leave): Is B2 a new phenomenon?

Jeff Smith: B2 is basically what we did with the D list for a while.

[*Pat Connor gives Smith the top CD from her pile – 'Everybody Loves a Carnival' by Fatboy Slim. Smith snaps it into the machine behind him. It's a Big Beat record – lots of sound effects, up and partyish, some shouting, some trumpets and traditional instruments mixed with electronic effects. He plays it loud, and the producers in the room tap pens, rock back, nod heads. He plays four-fifths of it.*]

Jeff Smith: Barrie?

Barrie Kelly (Breakfast Show Producer): Ace.

Jeff Smith: It's fantastic, isn't it?

Chris Humphrys (Music Programming Assistant): I like it, but I'm not sure whether it's a radio record.

Anna Bowman (Producer): Oh, *what*?

Jeff Smith: I know what you're saying, because there's that difficult bit in the middle, when you go, 'Oh dear . . .' Whereas the Propellerheads has got it right for us because it's got *all* the bits. I can just imagine us having Propellerheads on the A list, this on the B, and Pierre Henry on the C list, and the Lo-Fidelity All Stars, and that would be our Big Beat representation, and I think that would be very cool. Shall I put it in the frame for a B?

Producers: Definitely. I think so. It's a great build.

Jeff Smith: Thanks for that, Pat. Barrie?

Barrie Kelly: Catatonia – they put horses' heads in people's beds. The song is called 'I Am the Mob'.

Jeff Smith [*playing it*]: I'm not so sure about the bit about putting bullets between people's knees.

Barrie Kelly: Well, they have got a big fan-base.

Jeff Smith: If we were Xfm, or only London-wide it might be okay, but for the whole country . . .

Barrie Kelly: I'm just putting it forward . . .

Jeff Smith: It's a good tune, but people won't get the cleverness of it. The irony. They'll just see it as sick.

Jeff Smith: We should play this 2K record [*He puts it on, an operatic, shouty record, using bits of 'For Those in Peril on the Sea' and lots of submarine-type blips.*]

Producer: I think they're just taking the piss. It sounds quite dated.

Jeff Smith: I think it's a spot-play record. I just think people won't want to hear that an awful lot. The KLF [2K under a previous incarnation] – that was then, and we don't really play much of that. They think people are still interested in them, and I'm not that sure that people are. But am I wrong? You saw them last night, didn't you Barrie?

Barrie Kelly: The best bit was waiting for them to come out. You didn't know what was going to happen. They had a dead swan on the stage . . . when they came out there was a brass band, and then they come out in wheelchairs, like old men. And then there was this preacher in a gold lamé suit.

Producer: What did they do with the swan?

Barrie Kelly: Well they had an axe, and you thought they were going to cut its head off, but they didn't.

Jeff Smith: I just can't hear it on rotation.

Producer: They're very good at getting the press releases out.

[The rap DJ Tim Westwood arrives with his selection. He holds up a CD from Busta Rhymes.]

Jeff Smith: We've talked about it.

Tim Westwood: I appreciate that. But this is like a defining moment in hip-hop. This is what it's all about at the moment. This record. He was certainly the star of Notting Hill Carnival, alongside Lil' Kim, and the vibe on this record is incredible, and the way he rhymes over this record – this is just what it's all about at the moment.

Jeff Smith: We had this conversation before you came in, and more or less came to the same conclusion, but it's great for you to tell us.

Tim Westwood: The strength of this record . . . I was in a club the other day, and there was a fight going on, and the DJ put this record on and everyone started dancing. Any record that can stop violence is an incredible record. There were guys with their noses bleeding . . . He's running things in the clubs at the moment, and that's going to sound so good on the radio, man.

Jeff Smith: Yeah, it does work. We're probably going to add it on the C this week, and see how it all goes for us.

Tim Westwood: Oh definitely.

Jeff Smith: And we played that album track with Erykah Badu, which I think is going to be the next single, so we can sort of build it with Busta.

Tim Westwood: Oh, excellent. [*He hands round a new CD.*] Lil' Kim. I know this has been up before, but we can't afford to miss out on this artist. This is the one that takes Lil' Kim to that whole new level. Biggie Smalls is on it. This is a great record on a radio and club level. She was another star of Carnival. In fact there was more vibes on her coming over, and the girls love her . . . [*The single plays.*] This positions Kim where she really is. 'Ladies Night' was very much on that pop level, but this has already taken her to that overmarket. At Carnival, when she performed, because the crowd was getting out of control, the police had to cut short her act, and this was going to be her finale, and she couldn't do it, and she was in tears. If we miss out on this we've really missed out on what Lil' Kim represents.

Jeff Smith: We were saying that this is where we want to move to in hip-hop and rap – away from the karaoke popness of it, where singers just use an old pop sample and put new lyrics on – Puff Daddy and 'Missing You'. But this is the real deal. And when they give us soft, embraceable records like this I think we should try and embrace them if we can. But where, though? Is it B, or is it C? Given that we've got Coolio and Foxy on – do we wait a week? We'll look at it.

Tim Westwood: It has so much support from the ladies . . .

Jeff Smith: Coming out of those meetings, the producers have to be broadly happy, because they're the ones who have to go into the studio with the freelance presenter and cajole them that these are really good records to play. The presenters are not always that convinced about it.

Simon Garfield: 'Avenging Angels' got to number six in the charts, selling about 180,000 copies. The next single by Catatonia, called 'Mulder and Scully', got to number one. A collaboration between Space and Cerys Matthews of Catatonia, 'The Ballad of Tom Jones', got to number four, and sold 230,000. 'Smack My Bitch Up' was released as an EP, thus enabling DJs to play other tracks on the same record. The title song was played mostly at night. And within a few months, Busta Rhymes reached number two.

Jeff Smith: When we're compiling our list of records we have to bear in mind not only what's cool, but also what's just great pop. If we niche ourselves too much then our audience will decline even more. I think in some meetings I'll have a too mainstream view about things. I'll come in some days and I'm just thinking about attracting an audience, but someone will say, 'We have to have a maverick tendency,' and they're right. We have to go out on fliers. Sometimes we just over-analyse everything we do, the precise content of every record we may or may not put on the playlist. But that's the way the BBC would prefer it to happen, because it is a public service.

*

Steve Lamacq (Disc Jockey): We got a call the day before saying, 'Noel Gallagher would like to break his radio silence.' We didn't know that Liam was going to be coming to the interview, but they turned up together. They'd obviously stopped off at a hostelry along the way.

Liam Gallagher (on air, 23 October 1997): We've just done a cover of the Stones' 'Street Fighting Man', just to piss them off ... I'm gonna shoot my mouth off here – all these snakes coming out the closets, all these old farts, I'll offer 'em out right here on radio. If they want to fight, be at Primrose Hill, Saturday morning, at ten o'clock. I will beat the fucking living daylight shit out of them. That goes for George, Jagger, Richards and any other cunts that give me shit ... They're jealous and senile and not getting enough fucking meat pies. If they want to fight, I'll beat them up ... We play for the people who fucking bother to listen ...

Steve Lamacq: Strangely, you get used to people swearing. After a while it has no effect. After they'd done it a few times, all I wanted to do was to get them to say something interesting, which I think they probably did. Noel said there won't be another Oasis album until 2000. Things that Noel was saying about Liam being his inspiration – that was new. The whole interview went through so many stages, and seemed to be a condensed version of what Oasis were – from the arrogant swagger and confidence, to the rivalry between them, then a certain paranoia, and then finally a morose, frustrated Noel saying the band's a bit boring at the moment.

[On air]: What was your reaction when you first heard the Verve album?

Noel Gallagher: Well, I thought it was about time that those guys done it. When he got on the stage and played a few songs before we played this gig in New York a long time ago, he played 'The Drugs Don't Work' and 'Bitter Sweet Symphony', and they're actually songs that do touch you. But I will say that drugs do work.

Liam Gallagher: It's the truth, though. Either that or he's got a shit drug dealer. I know what he's saying, but drugs do bloody work, Richard. He knows the score. The last time I bloody met him I chopped him out one ...

248

John Peel: There was a lot of *language*. The frequency with which the word 'fuck' appeared . . . several hundred times. And the C-word as well. It was a fairly fraught evening, which Steve handled extraordinarily well. I should have burst into tears.

Steve Lamacq [on air]: Are you going to have kids?

Liam Gallagher: Yeah, next year I reckon. I'm gonna have a bang at it. I'm gonna have a go.

Steve Lamacq: Would you be a good father?

Liam Gallagher: I'll be wicked! I'll be the best father in the world. I'll be shit at paying the bills, but . . .

Steve Lamacq: Has it made you less protective of Liam? Knowing that he's got someone there for him?

Noel Gallagher: What? I'll tell you what, man. He can look after himself. He's my younger brother right, but . . . How old are you?

Liam Gallagher: Twenty-five. You didn't get me a present, you cunt. Oh, you did . . .

Noel Gallagher: Yes, I did. He's twenty-five. I'm thirty-four. I don't need to look after him.

Liam Gallagher: Nobody needs to

Steve Lamacq:
'Strangely, you get used to people swearing'

look after me. I look after me fucking self. Don't fucking speak for me ...

Polly Ravenscroft: We knew that Noel was coming in, and I said to Paul [Simpson, press officer] that we should get as much PR as we can, and so he was sitting in, and we got a PA photographer as well. I happily went home, and then I got a call about a quarter to seven, sounding very panicky.

Paul said, 'Are you listening?' I wasn't. He said, 'Liam has turned up unannounced, he's on with Noel, it's all going very wrong and they're swearing a lot.'

My first question was, 'Have they said "cunt"?' He said, 'Yes, about three times.'

I said, 'Is it still going on?'

Paul said, 'Yeah, and now they're saying, "Paul McCartney is surrounded by a bunch of fucking lesbians."'

I said, 'I'll call Andy and I'll call you straight back.'

He said, 'Shall I get this picture taken or not?'

'Yes.' I knew it was going to make the papers, so I thought we might as well have a Radio 1 picture.

I phoned Andy and said, 'Are you listening?' He said, 'Yes.'

I said, 'It's a disaster. You do realize that the shit really is going to hit the fan and they've said "cunt" quite a few times? The *Daily Mail* will be phoning me any second.'

Andy Parfitt: I went for a run at about seven-thirty. I came back, had a bath, and switched on Radio 1 to hear someone say, 'Cunt ... fuck ... the drugs do fucking work ...' I got out the bath and phoned the studio, talked to the producer, who was in a pretty shocked state of mind: 'What the hell's going on?'

The interaction between the two brothers, and some of what they said, was bloody fascinating if you cared about Oasis, and I think the swearing was getting in the way. Steve could have said, 'Look, this swearing is not getting us any-where,' and then played a record, and seen whether between him and the producer and Noel they couldn't have asked Liam to leave.

In that interview Noel Gallagher said, 'I don't think the album is very good, there won't be another Oasis album for two years,' and that he thought the production of the album was overcooked . . . He said some extraordinarily important things. He apologized to people for the hype. Unfortunately his brother also came on and said, 'Fuck, cunt' and switched the attention.

Polly Ravenscroft: By now, all the papers have called. Matthew's deputy Jim Moir [controller, Radio 2] phoned me up. Other people were saying we should have an enquiry. We had to put out a statement, and I usually take a couple of calls from the papers to see what line they're going to take before deciding what we're going to come back with. First we apologized, obviously, then said that Liam wasn't expected, and that on air they had asked him to stop swearing – so we put the blame on them rather than us. I then spent the next four hours on the phone – it's important to talk to the journalists individually.

In one way it was good publicity for us, but I think a lot of Oasis fans were shocked by it. Also, I didn't think it was a very good interview, where other people did. I do disagree with Matthew and Andy about this – I think we should have pulled it. The question I kept getting asked was, 'Why didn't you pull the plug?' I went into a story about, 'It's not as simple as that.' The good thing is that the tabloids don't really understand how radio works, so you can quite easily spin things like that. Actually it is easy to pull a live broadcast – you just put on the emergency tape. The next day Liam punched a journalist, which was fantastic, because then all the attention was back on them.

Andy Parfitt: When I talked to the producer and Steve the day afterwards I was pretty convinced that they had done all that they could to control it. We all think there is a gallery full of people, and lots of security people, but it's just Steve, a producer and a BA [Broadcast Assistant]. But I think that removing Liam, having warned him sufficiently clearly, saying, 'This has got to stop,' would have been the ideal thing.

It happened to me as a young producer, a live phone-in with a footballer on Danny Baker. When it happens you have to have an action plan. You have to have options. Option one: what can I do to stop it completely? I could go into the next studio, I could get Steve into it, give him his records and lock the door. Second option, stop it for a bit and talk to them and hopefully carry on.

My view of the whole incident will inevitably be tempered by the question: Did our procedures go according to plan, and were the right referrals made at the right time? Because with the amount of live broadcasting we do, we are often close to the edge in a way that other BBC outlets aren't.

It's a clear demonstration of the responsibilities of the BBC. It raises all sorts of questions within the Corporation about what's important. You know, 'We can tolerate this sort of swearing from important playwrights, but when it comes from pop musicians . . .'

Thankfully, the number of very young people listening to Radio 1 at that time is virtually nil. I think it was an important interview, and I'm glad they chose Radio 1 to come to. But I don't believe that all publicity is good publicity. Ultimately all the swearing gave us some credibility with some sections of our target audience, but I'm not proud of that. I don't think headlines which read something like 'Radio 1 gives thumbs up to foul-mouthed louts' are particularly helpful.

Matthew Bannister: I was on holiday at the time, in true BBC fashion. I was on Necker Island with Richard Branson. Polly rang me up, but obviously I didn't get the full impact of it until I got on the plane to come back and got the *Daily Mail*, in which somebody was asking for me to be fired from my job.

It was my view that it should have been pulled sooner. But

it's very easy for BBC managers to sit in judgement with hindsight when you've got a young woman producer and a young woman researcher on duty with Steve Lamacq and two of the biggest rock and roll stars in the world live in the studio and they're big blokes as well. Trying to physically eject them from the studio or have an argument with them would have been extremely difficult.

It's one of those things where it's what I believe is called, what Jeeves calls, a concatenation of circumstances. We booked Noel Gallagher to come in in very good faith. Noel's done a lot of live interviews on Radio 1 in the past and been perfectly responsible, a very intelligent guy. Liam turns up and he's had a few, a few of what we don't know, but a few. And he's asked and told to behave himself but it's not in his nature. If you've ever seen them live, you know that he's not able to speak for longer than a sentence without a few F-words and so on.

I'm afraid to say we had ninety-one complaints, which is pretty significant, even for Radio 1.

Chapter 11

A Particularly Vicious Tackle

John Peel and Polly Jean Harvey at Peel Acres:
'At one point a combine harvester drove by'

Simon Garfield: People said that you could tell it was a serious party because senior management had their collars turned up. After exactly thirty years of Radio 1, its current staff visited a brasserie in west London to drink some beer and tell jokes about Dave Lee Travis. None of the old guard were invited. There was really nothing to remind those present of where they worked, apart from their colleagues. There was a tarot reader, some dancing, and the DJ was a friend of a friend.

At the bar, Simon Mayo was talking to Zoe Ball, who had yet to start at the station. She says the doorman wouldn't let her in at first. She's rather nervous about her first pilot next week. Mayo says, 'All the bits that go wrong – use those as the trailers.'

The day before, Mayo had been on the front page of the *Sunday Mirror*: 'I Stole From No 10'. 'Last week I was on the Jack Docherty show,' he explains, 'and I told him that I had nicked some stationery when I went to Blair's party – just a dare I had with Eddie Izzard and some others. He only asked me about it because I had already mentioned it on the radio several weeks before, and there had been this little follow-up item in the *Sun*.

'So the *Sunday Mirror* must have assumed that no one could remember the *Sun* piece and that nobody watched Jack Docherty. So they doorstep me on Friday night, but we're at Oasis at Earl's Court – which was boring, really. The babysitter tells them to come back the next day. The next morning they come round and I'm out. Then later they get me, and ask me the story, and I tell them what I'd already said on television. They ask me to pose with the stationery, which I refuse. When they leave they say, "We're just trying to fill the paper." I tell Helen, my wife, "Well I think I've quashed that one," and then next morning at the newsagent's there it is – the whole of the front page. How desperate are they?'

Matthew Bannister approaches, wearing suit trousers and white shirt, but with a leather jacket on top. He introduces Mayo to Chris Goldfinger, the dance DJ. Chris has been with Radio 1 for about a year, but the two DJs have never met.

'I often listen to your show,' Goldfinger tells Mayo.

Mayo thanks him, then says, 'And when do you start with us?'

'You idiot!' Bannister says. He turns to Goldfinger, 'You have to excuse Simon. He never stays up late. He's got kids.'

Mayo talks about Zoe. 'The thing about her is that she's like Meg Ryan: men fancy her, and women want to be her – she's great looking and strong. Women don't want to be like Claudia Schiffer, not my wife anyway. Zoe and Kevin are really our last chance. If it doesn't work with them we may as well all go home. They can't just last months – they need to last two years.'

Simon Willis, Mayo's producer, says that he thinks the Mark and Lard breakfast show will be like *Monty Python* – baffling at the time, subsequently recognized as something very special.

Bannister gave a little speech. Radio 1 is a more accurate representation of young people than it has ever been. The changes were painful but necessary. Thank you for your loyalty and professionalism.

Bannister looked around the room and noted that most people were not yet born when Radio 1 began. 'There are, of course, some notable exceptions, including John Peel ... The lesson we can learn from John is that wallowing in nostalgia is not the way ahead.'

A few days later, Radio 1 threw a surprise party for John Peel at the ICA. Many old friends showed up, and many musicians spoke of 'if not for him . . .' Among several presents, John Birt sent a pineapple.

John Peel: In thirty years there has genuinely never been an attempt by management to exert any control over my programmes, not beyond the occasional comment like, 'Ah, John, you still playing that bloody awful rubbish?'

Someone from management did come down when I was playing a lot of hip-hop, and then later when I was playing jungle, to inform me that I shouldn't be playing this music because it was the music of the black criminal classes.

Simon Garfield: A few weeks after the party, I arrived at his desk at the time of our appointment, and he was asleep. Someone said not to wake him if I could possibly help it, but at this he woke up, and started to open his post, a thick pile of brown cardboard with vinyl inside. I gave him a shiny Liverpool Football Club sticker, a swap from my children's Merlin collection. Peel said, 'I can make use of this. I've been trying to complete my Spice Girls album, because I reckon that if I live another fifty years, which is of course extremely unlikely, it could be worth about £6.'

I asked him to take me through those key times when he thought, 'Oh, they're really getting rid of me this time.'

John Peel: I've thought that the whole time, really. I think insecurity probably makes you do your job better. I was initially employed for six weeks. It was a programme called *Top Gear*, introduced by two DJs. Initially they thought the notion of one DJ alone introducing a three-hour programme was madness, like walking to the moon. Tommy Vance was one of the others, also Pete Drummond and Mike Aherne.

Simon Garfield: Not the person who was arrested recently for alleged paedophilia?

John Peel: No, unfortunately that was Chris Denning, who lost his job here very early on because he said – and at the time this seemed rather magnificent, but given his subsequent history it was not quite so wonderful – he said, 'God I felt great this morning, I woke up feeling like a sixteen-year-old boy. But where do you find a sixteen-year-old boy?'

There was a kind of healthy paranoia at Radio 1 at the start. There was this assumption that the station wasn't going to last very long, and then there was the assumption that even if Radio 1 continued, you as a DJ would very likely not.

I think I was a handy safety valve for some time. If people called up to complain about the safe and predictable nature of the station's playlist, someone could always tell them, 'Well, you can always listen to John Peel. He plays strange discs.'

I'm very grateful to a man called Teddy Warwick, who, if you wanted to translate Radio 1 into the current New Labour set up, would be the sort of John Prescott figure. He was management, but also sympathetic to whispered left-wing philosophy. He presented the cause of my programme very persuasively in management meetings for many years.

One controller, Derek Chinnery, disliked me intensely, and took every opportunity to let me know that this was the case. He was persuaded to keep me on largely by John Walters, who was my producer for about twenty years. Walters was a brilliant debater, or rather arguer. He could see through all the bollocks to the core of any argument, and would fix his teeth into it and never let go. There have been times in the history of Radio 1, and this will no doubt surprise you, when the controllers have not been people of enormous intellectual stature. And these men would just get so fed up with arguing with Walters that they would just roll over.

Once Derek Chinnery called Walters into his office after he had read something in the papers about singers with spiky hair who were spat on by their adoring audience. He said something like, 'We're not playing any of this punk rock, are we?' and Walters gleefully replied that the last four programmes had consisted of nothing but. No doubt Walters will be able to tell the story far better than me, and at far greater length, and in a way that reflects far more glamour on himself.

John Walters: There's no doubt that various people in power would have liked to have got rid of us at some stage, but the trouble was that we were the ones that people used to come from Finland or Los Angeles to see. We were once asked to represent the BBC at a broadcasting conference in Spain. Derek Chinnery, who was the controller then, went with us. But previously he had sent a memo to the organizers saying, 'I can bring John Walters and John Peel, but why would you want to talk to them? They're not at all typical of Radio 1.' I think it was the nicest thing he'd ever said about us.

The great and the good knew John Peel, so the thought of management going, 'Oh, he's run his course, we'll bring in a bright new hairdresser,' – they couldn't have done that, there would have been questions asked at governor level.

We did tend to know what we found interesting, like the Slits, who obviously couldn't play at all. But I had a fine art degree, and once you'd come to terms with a white square on a white background, you weren't going to be thrown by the Sex Pistols. Peel was like the water diviner, walking across a field with a stick. Suddenly – boing! – he'd say, 'It's here,' and then I'd have to get the spade out of the car and dig and make it happen.

In Room 316, where we were, we knew what our audience was and hit it, perhaps better than any other music programme in the world, as far as I know. I think that a very strong case could be made for John Peel being the single most important individual in the history of British rock music. People say, 'Oh, what about Lennon?' but I think over the years it holds true.

Andy Kershaw: Yeah, Walters's office, it was just like a broom cupboard and there wasn't even room for a third chair when I arrived, so I used to sit on an upturned wastepaper basket.

When I arrived, Walters described it as like an elderly couple in their twilight years, him and Peel, sitting across the hearth from each other in a pair of comfortable armchairs and suddenly, against all medical probability, having this unexpected child. A role which Walters played up no end. He was huge fun to work with. And somebody once came in and noticed the parallel between our office and the House at Pooh Corner. There was Walters, who was rather portly and pompous, so he was Pooh Bear. And then there was Peel who was Eeyore in the corner of the field, Oh it's drizzling again, no thistles. And then there was me who was jumping up and licking your face and trying to shag your leg, and I was Tigger. And we also had a secretary who was small and pink and she looked like Piglet.

Walters, like Peel, had an enthusiasm bordering on the juvenile. As Walters famously said of Peel, although it could have been said the other way round as well, 'The day Peel reaches puberty, we're all in trouble.'

John Peel: I'm fifty-nine in August. I always say I look like a minicab driver. These days I find that a lot of people working here, young people, come up to me and make rather un-British little speeches about how they grew up listening to my programme, which is lovely to hear, and then you can think to yourself, Well, perhaps you wouldn't even be working here if it wasn't for me, and I quite like the thought of that.

But even the younger ones stopped listening to the programme at some stage. It seems that people listen to the pro-

Simon Mayo:
'If it doesn't work with
them, we may as well all
go home'

gramme for a while and then stop, and often listen to the programme later on in their lives. I get letters from people who say, 'I hadn't listened to your programme for twelve years, and I was driving home the other night and heard something I thought was fantastic. I've listened every night since, and it was just how it used to be.' Sometimes kids write in and say, 'I was listening to your programme in my bedroom the other night when I was doing my homework, and my mum came in and said, "What are you listening to?" I said, "John Peel," and she said, "Oh, I used to listen to him when I was your age."' It's nice being woven into people's lives in that way.

As a young lad I used to listen to the American Forces Network in Europe, coming out of Stuttgart, and to Radio Luxembourg, and the signals were always satisfyingly feeble, so that you really felt you were participating in something quite exceptional.

The record that genuinely changed my life was on *Two-Way Family Favourites* on the BBC. It may be hard now to understand how frustrating it was to listen to the radio then, because you could often sit and listen to a programme for several hours and not hear a single record that you liked. You'd listen to things like *Housewives' Choice* in the morning – based on the premise shared by Radio 1 when it first started, that house-wives were some sort of subnormal minority group, as if perfectly sensible women would walk down the aisle but then return as gibbering idiots. So you'd listen to that, and get many Glenn Miller records, and always something called the 'Nun's Chorus'.

Two-Way Family Favourites was a show that reunited our boys overseas with their families back home, on a Sunday lunchtime. One afternoon I heard them say, 'Lance Bombardier Higgins has requested the first record by the new American singing sensation Elvis Presley.' On came Elvis, and it sounds idiotic to say it now, but at the time 'Heartbreak Hotel' was just a revelation, like being transported immediately to another planet. The only thing that came close was when I heard Little Richard a few weeks later. It was genuinely frightening, as if something had been unleashed on the world that would never go back in the bottle. It turned out to be the case, wonderfully.

John Walters: John is obsessive in his listening. There was one important Peel birthday when they invited me and my missus out for a meal and then back to stay the night at his cottage. The following morning I came down early with his present, and he was sitting there having breakfast at the kitchen table, and he had his cans on, and was listening to a tape, and was writing down something like, 'Three minutes ten, one star.' He never stops, trying to catch up with this vast backlog of records and tapes and CDs that gets bigger every week.

John Peel: I listen to bands' demo tapes almost exclusively in the car, in the two-hours' drive back home. The ones I don't like get thrown on the floor in the passenger's area and by the end of the week they swill about. The ones I do like get thrown over my shoulder into the back seat, and then harvested at the end of the week. I know that I'm going to die trying to read the name of some band in the headlights of a car behind me, and then drive into a truck in front. People will say, 'Oh, this is the way he would have wanted to go.'

On the radio I listen first to Xfm, and then when I'm out of the M25 area I listen to the strangest programme on the air at the moment – Keith Skues. Yes, Keith 'Cardboard Shoes' Skues, who used to work at Radio 1. It's on Eastern Counties Radio – Bucks, Cambridgeshire, Northamptonshire. He still has a serious feature called *Keyboard Cavalcade*. 'Sedate 78s' feature in each programme, along with military bands playing hymns, and an anagram competition. You simply don't know what he's going to do next. One day he broadcast an hour-long interview with himself by somebody else. He'd gone up to Hallam, and some mate had interviewed him about his career and life and times, and he brought the tape back down and then broadcast it. An interview with Keith Skues on the Keith Skues programme.

Simon Garfield: At the Radio 1 Sound City week in Oxford in October 1997, Peel and Steve Lamacq took part in a lunchtime forum at the Union debating chamber, a cold building with statues and stained glass. Before it started, Peel, in his thick country jumper and green Doc Martens, had been asked in the bar if he had ever considered writing his autobiography. 'Every now and then I have an expensive lunch with a literary agent, but I think I'm too lazy and there are too many records to play.' Someone told me later, 'Oh, actually I think he regards it as his pension.'

About 150 people turned up. Peel and Lamacq spoke a little about their lives, and then answered questions from the audience: How did they choose which bands to feature in session? What advice did they have for fledgling DJs? How important, truly, were the Stone Roses?

Lamacq said that he and Peel both listened to demo tapes in the car in the same way. He also cajoled Peel into telling his Noel Edmonds 'Gotcha' story, which Peel resisted for most of the session. Finally, when there appeared to be no more questions, and some people were heading towards the bar, a man shouted, 'Come on now, Noel Edmonds!'

John Peel: Noel Edmonds? To me he's a showbusiness phenomenon. What is it that Noel Edmonds does, what is it that makes him such a big figure? Not a big figure physically – he could walk under a table with an umbrella up. The only gift he has really is extraordinary confidence, and obviously he's done extremely well with this. This idiotic 'Gotcha' thing he does – for some reason he's determined to get me. This has made me slightly paranoid. Any invitation I get I think, Is Noel behind this?

In a few years this will probably drive me barking mad. The only attempt to get me that I know about . . . He genuinely thought that I was stupid enough to want to take part in a nature programme, in which the idea was that I would stay up all night on a badger watch. The joke was that they weren't going to be real badgers, they were going to be people with glove puppets. I thought, Is that the best you can do?

Simon Garfield: At the surprise party, Peel was presented with a precious set of CDs, a one-off collection of some favourite tracks and sessions. There was a message from Tony Blair, a curry from Billy Bragg and some live music from Dreadzone, a current rave. When he arrived, he genuinely appeared not to know what on earth was happening.

John Peel: I'm unbelievably gullible, and I'm quite ashamed. How could I have believed that something had really gone so wrong with the studios that I had to decamp to a van outside the ICA? But I thought, Well, they've told me this, so how could it be otherwise? And it was a very touching occasion, a bit like being at your own wake without having to go through the business of actually dying. Everyone was watching me because I cry very easily, but the only time I came close was when I realized that my children had been brought down, including the two that are at university in the North of England.

The pineapple, yes, very strange. There was a reason for it. Occasionally I'd be invited to these rather serious BBC events at TV Centre. I used to dread these things, but you had to go.

Quite often I was the only person from Radio 1 who was invited, probably because I had been to public school. You'd go along, and everyone who was there you knew, but only from the television. And everyone else was going, 'Marvellous to see you, Peter!' And, 'Where was it – *Cannes*? . . . Got back from Turin okay, I see . . .' The whole establishment. So actually I'd never know anyone there. Once I found myself sitting across the table from the Two Ronnies and thinking, What do I say to these bastards?

On another occasion I had just recorded *Desert Island Discs*, so I went along with Sue Lawley. When we sat down I was at a table which included Nicholas Witchell, P.D. James and Jonathan Powell. I turned to the bloke sitting next to me and said, 'Hello, we haven't met – I'm John Peel.' And he said, 'I'm John Birt, and actually we were introduced five minutes ago outside.' You don't really recover from that. After about an hour of non-conversation I said to him something about football, and he said, 'Didn't you break your wrist playing five-a-side in Holborn about ten years ago?' I said, 'How did you know that?' He said, 'I was the bloke that tackled you.'

John Birt: It's the only time playing football all these years that I'd ever injured somebody badly . . . I don't think it was anything dirty, it was just one of those things that happened. And I, in the way that you give people flowers or something, I gave him something which at the time, it seems odd now . . . well it was a slightly exotic thing, a pineapple. It was the first time I ever came in to Broadcasting House.

John Peel: It was a particularly vicious tackle. Why a pineapple? Have you got any other suggestions as to what to bring someone when you've just broken their wrist? So for this party he sent me another pineapple, which I took to be a strangely touching gesture from a man who has a reputation for being a slick Dalek.

At the party I also got a letter from Liverpool Football Club, with a nice message about my anniversary. One assumed it was signed by all the players, but on closer examination it had been signed by the groundstaff and the people from administration. This told me quite a lot about modern football. Sammy Lee was the only player, and he only played in the seventies. I was quite wounded.

I'm not conscious of great change over the years, though I occasionally hear tapes of early programmes and swoon with embarrassment. I had an absurdly affected voice – terribly laid-back in a sub-Scousy way. But that was how I spoke at the time. Now my voice has changed, from living in East Anglia, and the fact that Sheila my wife comes from Bradford, and my kids for some extraordinary reason sound as though they were born in Thurrock – you know, 'Awright dad, how's it going, mate?'

Perhaps my presentation now is a little more urgent. Now I'll talk over the ends, the fades, of records, because there are so many records I want to get in.

But I probably make the same number of mistakes as ever. There is this body of opinion which thinks that I do them to be cute, but I think that being cute in my condition would be being not far short of offensive.

Steve Lamacq: There is always some speculation that John will one day introduce a band on stage, and he'll put them on at the wrong speed.

John Peel: The changes in technology have worked against me. There is now so much more that you have to do. Before, the studios contained a bored engineer, the chap who crawled out on to the wings and stuck his chewing gum in the hole of the petrol tank to keep the show airborne. But now of course he's not there, and since the building's been crammed with consultants, and engineers and genuinely useful staff have been disposed of, we now have to do it ourselves. There are some people who work here for whom technology is an end in itself. They kind of retune the studio, so that when I get in I find myself wishing that I could just press a button that would get it all back to normal. It means that I can't sit back and enjoy the music as much as I used to, because there's more things to worry about.

Happily my producer has a technique – she just comes in and finds the unit that appears to be posing a threat to life, and just presses all the buttons until the right thing happens, and so far it's always worked.

John Walters: At one point Peel would come to our house after the show on a Saturday and we had this thing going – the late-night movie. We used to try and pick a meal that tied in with the late film on BBC2. It began by chance when all we had in the cupboard was bacon and beans, and they were showing a Western. After that, when they showed *Footsteps in the Fog* we had pea soup, you know, a pea-soup fog. We did one once which was *Foxhole in Cairo*, about people going across the desert and they keep seeing these beers. We went out to get the hottest vegetable curry, served it up. So Peel said, 'This is jolly hot, can I have a glass of water?' No. And then he'd go into the kitchen for some, and I'd turned the water off at the mains. We did it for a year or so. Quite amusing, but then it passes.

John Peel: I live in Stowmarket in Suffolk, and rather than return every night after a show I spend some nights in London hotels. The last one I was in, I got to bed at about 12.15 and fell asleep immediately. At about four o'clock I woke up as we middle-aged gentlemen do, and I thought that the bed was a bit cold. Then I realized it wasn't cold, it was damp. Then I realized, it's not damp, it's wet. And it couldn't have been me, or it would have been warm. The mattress – the previous occupant had had some sort of misadventure in it. But the problem with hotels in central London is the night staff – they employ people who are prepared to work for 25p an hour. The thought of getting dressed at four in the morning and saying 'I demand another bedroom' seemed futile. So I stayed in that bed. But in the morning I had the longest shower I ever had in my life.

John Walters: Peel does tend to rewrite history a bit. He still surprises me with stories from his youth. He once told me he had an aunt who went out with an arctic explorer, which is quite possible, but he then stretched it by saying she kept huskies in the spare bedroom. He once told me that his grandfather used to get champagne on the National Health. I questioned him on this, and he said, 'Yes, champagne on the National Health.' Eventually he said to me, 'Oh, I asked my mum, and I muddled it up. It wasn't champagne, it was morphine.'

He told me that years ago his first appearance in showbiz was on stage with Frankie Howerd singing 'Fuzzy Wuzzy'. He said, 'Every year we went as a family to the Liverpool Empire, to the pantomime. And because we were quite well off, father being a cotton broker, we always had a meal at the Adelphi and then went to the show and we sat down right at the front. Whenever they said, "Right, all the little boys, you come up on stage and sing along."' Peel said he was so used to the idea of prep school, that when a grown up told you to do something, you did it, for fear of being soundly thrashed. Often he was soundly thrashed if he did it or not.

So although he was very shy, he said he went up and stood there petrified alongside Frankie Howerd. I said, 'Well what did you sing?' Because I've very rarely heard him sing anything, he's got no ear for music, like Kershaw – terrible. He said, 'I sang "Fuzzy Wuzzy Was a Bear".' I thought, Okay, they often have 'Fuzzy Wuzzy' at pantomimes, either that or 'There's a Worm at the Bottom of the Garden (and his Name is Wiggly Worm)'.

Then a while later I was at a surprise buffet lunch for Ned Sherrin's sixtieth birthday, and one of the guests was Frankie Howerd. Kershaw arrived late on his Harley Davidson, came banging at the door and then came in wearing his leathers, carrying a crash helmet. Frankie Howerd looked at him and said, 'Who's that!!??' We said, 'Oh that's a disc jockey – Andy

Kershaw.' Frankie Howerd said, 'Shame – I hoped it was a kissogram.'

I was standing near him, and I told Frankie Howerd this story, about how John stood next to him and sang 'Fuzzy Wuzzy Was a Bear'. He said, 'No. No, it wasn't.' I said, 'Well John is sure.' He said, 'No, I never did "Fuzzy Wuzzy Was a Bear". It was "Three Little Fishes".'

So I told this back to John, and he said, 'Oh yes, perhaps it was "Three Little Fishes" then.' So you have to be a bit careful with him.

John Peel: I used to run a record label, catastrophically unsuccessful, called Dandelion. Named after a hamster – that's how things were in the late sixties. We put out about thirty LPs using other people's money. There were one or two I quite like to listen to, and one or two atrocities. Stackwaddy were fantastic. They had an album called *Bugger Off* which Annie Nightingale used to play a lot. They were punks before there were punks – these very primitive lads from Manchester who played a rather violent and inaccurate R&B.

I managed to get them booked on to the *In Concert* programme on Radio 1 – a big mistake. It wasn't necessarily pop music lovers in the audience – you'd get people from the Darby and Joan club in Leicester who'd turn up because they'd got tickets for an unspecified BBC show. When Stackwaddy turned up they must have been horrified. The lead singer, enormously drunk, staggered around amongst the elderly audience asking if they'd got any favourites.

Once, we got a person over from the States to see a whole load of Dandelion bands at a college in London. We made the mistake of putting Stackwaddy on first. The singer was a deserter from the army, and wore this improbable wig all the time. He sang with his head pointing upwards. They turned the treble up on all their equipment so it was like listening to a kind of buzzsaw.

The singer was very drunk, and the first thing he did at the start of this gig was just walk to the edge of the stage and piss on the students.

Simon Garfield: Peel often says that he doesn't get to see many bands play live, partly because of where he lives, and partly because of when he broadcasts, three nights a week from 8.40 p.m. So occasionally bands come to his house.

P. J. Harvey came down one summer day, and at one point a combine harvester drove by, but failed to make it on to the recording.

Then Blur came down, a fact that he managed to keep completely secret. He called up the parents of five friends of his daughter Flossie. 'Your daughter must not go to school today,' he told them. 'She must come to our house, but I can't tell you why.'

Blur chatted with Peel in his front room. The talk came round to what it was like hearing early tapes of their work.

John Peel: There's nothing wrong in doing embarrassing stuff. I used to play *Melanie* records on the radio. Do you remember Melanie? Have any of you ever heard Melanie? What was that song she did? She did a song about bicycles . . .

The point is, she came and sat on my bed when I had jaundice, because her manager thought it would be a good idea, and played songs. Just her and me and this New York manager in a nasty dark blue shot-silk suit which I shall never forget – I still wake up screaming in the night. She'd got these two voices, one very quiet, and she'd suddenly go terrifically loud and you'd jump back. But of course what do you do when somebody's sitting on the end of your bed and singing songs? At the end of a number do you go, 'More! More!'?

Damon Albarn: Was she a prototype P. J. Harvey?

John Peel: No, no, P. J. Harvey would be a far superior artiste. Flossie, can you go and get a Melanie record? Just go and look at my files – it's under M, astonishingly. [*To the band*] I think you should hear Melanie before you disappear into the afternoon. She had this song about bicycles – 'My Little Bicycle' or something . . . unspeakable stuff. Here we go . . . [*reading* *tracks*] What shall we have? 'Animal Crackers'? 'Christopher Robin is Saying his Prayers'?

Members of Blur: *No way!*

John Peel: Flossie, do you want to go and be DJ for the day?

Flossie: I'm not sure how to work your record player. I'll have a go, though.

John Peel: Okay, I think Christopher Robin is the one, number three. [*To Blur*] So who would you have playing in *your* garden?

Blur: Can I have Inner City Unit? And the Butthole Surfers?

John Peel: Really? Like, even the 1997 Butthole Surfers?

Blur: Well, the 1988 Butthole Surfers.

John Peel: Yes, that would be quite good.

[*Flossie puts the Melanie record on. It sounds very strange.*]

John Peel [*to Blur*]: Just like her dad, she plays records at the wrong speed! It's genetic damage. [*To Flossie*] Thirty-three and a third, my angel! Imagine what it's like for my children. Unless they get into contemporary country and western I don't know what they could do to really piss me off. There was one golden moment when William was younger and he came to me with his younger sister when I was playing records in my room. They said, 'Dad, do you mind turning the music down, as we can't hear the television.' I said, 'I'm supposed to say that to you.'

At Radio 1 I try to keep myself to myself. I've always thought that avoiding office politics was a rather shrewd thing to do. I feel a bit like a person who lives in a cottage while a new estate is being built around him – so long as I can tend to my bees I'm perfectly happy. On the few occasions I've talked to Matthew I've found him rather affable, rather a nice bloke. But I think it would be rather awful to phone up and say, 'Matthew, we must go and have a drink' – arse-kissing, really.

I don't socialize that much with people here. I occasionally go to the pub or the wine bar with some of the women, because obviously they don't see me as a threat. I'm not likely to try to get off with them.

I do still see the Radio 1 thing as being what I do – the occasional TV and other radio is not the priority. Radio 4 is still seen as being the senior service, so when a couple of impeccably middle-class women call up and ask me to do a programme I'm always hugely flattered. You go off to very low-key places like Coventry to interview a family who have nineteen children, and you think, Oh no, but then you meet them and you come away quite heartened by it all. Sometimes if you're a regular reader of the newspapers and watch TV news programmes you can whip yourself up into a froth of despair. So going out and finding that not everybody wants to kill you is kind of reassuring.

I still like doing my programmes, however crap I might have felt during the day. Recently life at home has been rather complicated. Sheila had a brain haemorrhage about twenty months ago, obviously that was unimaginably terrifying. It appeared she got through all that without any lasting problem, but her eyesight has deteriorated dramatically over the last three months. Her mum died just before Christmas, and her father now lives with us. He's a sweet man, and he's tired and getting old and does rather funny things. We put him to bed last night, and took the dogs to the top of the hill for a shit, and when we got back Grandad was in the kitchen fully dressed. He'd been in bed for about an hour, woke up and thought it was morning, and then got up. So we had to escort him back to bed again. So life has been complicated, but it seems to be all right again when I come in and start mispronouncing the names of songs.

I'm a great believer in getting your priorities wrong, setting your sights low so that you don't go through your whole life frustrated that you never became prime minister. Really, it's playing and listening to records that I like.

Chapter 12

Zoe Ball Gets Tighter and Tighter

Kevin Greening and Zoe Ball:
'I am not your hold-the-jackpot-winner-cards girl'

Jeff Smith: The original plan was to give her a forty-five minutes sports show on Saturday lunchtime. Matthew and Andy really wanted her on the station.

Zoe Ball: In about March 1997 there was rumour in the newspaper. I got a phone call from Jo Whiley's husband, saying, 'Are you really going to Radio 1?' I had no idea what he was talking about.

I was doing a pretty bad but fun show on Liberty, once every four weeks, sharing a slot with Emma Forbes and Karon Keating, very middle of the road. I rang Peter [Powell, former Radio 1 DJ], my agent, and said, 'What are these rumours? If they do ring, tell them I'd be interested.' But they didn't ring.

Several months later there's a call which says there's a chance of a show combining music with football. I felt I didn't quite know enough about football to talk about it on air, and we never got very far with it. There was another vague idea about doing an entertainment show – you know, what's coming up. Two weeks later I was driving back from a week in Devon and Peter calls to say, 'Do you want to do the Radio 1 breakfast show with Kevin Greening? Be at this hotel by six tonight.' A crash-the-car scenario.

I'd never even met Kevin Greening. I walked into the hotel in a daze. The White House. They were all in the bar and I was late. Matthew and Andy were there and Peter. It's horrible when you first meet people you might work with and you're the new girl, hideously intimidating. You have to impress, but also be quite cool. I was smoking heavily. Then Kevin came in in his biker gear, and the first thing I said to him was, 'Hello, I'm Zoe, what sort of music do you like?' Embarrassing.

My initial concern was Mark and Lard. Do they know? Why is this happening so quickly? I had a mixture of feelings: This is madness, this is fantastic. And I'd had a bad experience before with a male co-presenter when I did the *Big Breakfast*. I'll never let anyone treat me the way I was treated on the *Big Breakfast*. Already on Radio 1 I've been like, 'I am not your hold-the-jackpot-winner-cards girl. I am not going to lie across a car on the front page of the *Sun* every week.' But I'm not very good at being tough.

Matthew and Andy were saying to me that they need more women, and that the breakfast show had to be more of a family thing and younger. They said, 'Because you're on the cover of this and that, and you talk a lot and like your music, you seem like the perfect person.' But what are the chances of something like that working?

Kevin Greening: At the beginning of 1997, I was firmly under the impression that my star was fading at Radio 1, and I was looking elsewhere. I started at weekend breakfast, was moved to weekend lunchtime, which was billed as a promotion, and then moved back to weekend breakfast, so make of that what you will. There were certainly no whispers going round about me being the next big thing.

Barrie Kelly: It was clear that Mark and Lard weren't going to be around for ever, and there were a few stories. I heard the rumour about Kevin taking over on the Friday, and I talked to my girlfriend about it over the weekend. We said, 'It's silly, isn't it, the thought of him doing it? It's not like he's a personality DJ.' She said, 'Don't worry, there's no way, you won't have to get up at four in the morning.'

On Monday Kevin came in to do the normal drivetime show, and was leaving a few subtle clues. 'Oh, a big meeting going on tonight.' 'Really? With who?' 'Oh, Matthew wants to see my agent, don't know why.' The next day it was, 'I've got this important meeting at one today at this hotel. So I might be a little bit late to do the prep for the show.'

The next day he said to me quietly in the office, 'I can't really say what's happening, because I've been sworn to secrecy, but something big's happening.' Not the best thing to say. He said, 'I can't tell you,' but then he said, 'Come outside.' We had a cigarette. He said, 'If I was given the breakfast show, would you want to do it?' Bang. The jaw goes down. I thought, 'The breakfast show? They've actually given you the gig?' Obviously Kevin's a great presenter, but . . . he's always been the supply DJ. All the other breakfast DJs, with the exception of Mark and Lard, have all been huge personalities. And going from Mark and Lard to Kevin was strange – they're both similar, in the way they treat the media, a little bit distrustful.

But he didn't tell me anything about Zoe. I read about it in the *Sun*, as I've done in the past with Radio 1 – you know, the people who work there are often the last to know, they're so frightened of leaks. When I read about Zoe coming my heart sunk to the bottom of my stomach. I knew I could do Kevin, but Zoe was this far more famous personality that I'd never met, someone always in magazines and on the television, and I had no idea what she was like, and whether we'd get on, and how the hell I was going to build this programme around her and Kevin.

Polly Ravenscroft: I got a call at home, where I was off with a migraine. Andy Coulson from the *Sun* called me at home, which he would never do normally. He's good in that he always tells me they're going to run a story in advance. He said that he had this story that Kevin Greening was going to do the breakfast show and that Mark and Lard had been given the sack. He asked if we want to make a comment, and said, 'I've got it to myself, it's quite big news, and it's going to go on the front page tomorrow.' I said, 'Andy, let me call you straight back.'

I then spoke to Matthew. At that point I knew about Kevin, but not about Zoe. And I knew that Mark hadn't been told yet. Matthew said, 'Fantastic news, we've got Zoe as well.'

I said, 'Great, but what are we going to do? We're going to be on the front of the *Sun* tomorrow, but it's the wrong story.' Matthew said, 'Mark and Lard haven't been told yet, so can't we get them to hold off?'

At first I went, 'Don't be ridiculous.' I phoned Andy back, and said, 'It's a different story to the one you've got now, but it's fantastic, better than the one you've got, and I promise you I'll give it to you exclusively if you hold off for twenty-four hours.' I said I couldn't tell him what it was, because the deal hadn't been signed. Eventually I also told him that Mark and Lard hadn't been told yet. Andy said he'd have to think it over. But then Andy was on the phone to me every half an hour saying, 'Who is it?' And you really want to tell them. Eventually Andy said, 'It's not Zoe, is it? I promise you I won't run it tomorrow.'

At that point Andy Parfitt had phoned me and said, 'There's a slight problem Peter Powell has told me about. Zoe has a contract with the *Mirror* whereby apparently they get all her stories first.'

Zoe had signed a £100,000 contract with the *Mirror* to do a lot of promotional work for them, and give them any exclusives. I said there was no way that the *Sun* was not going to get this first.

I called Andy Coulson back at the *Sun* and said, 'Yes it is Zoe,' and he said, 'It's a complete nightmare, because we won't be able to do anything with her. I'm really worried.' I kept on promising him that he would get the exclusive. Later that night, we had to get Peter Powell to give Andy his word that he wouldn't give it to the *Mirror*. But Peter Powell was beside himself with worry that it was all going to go wrong. By this time I was thinking, 'It's a job, it's not a matter of life and death.'

We did the photo shoot with Zoe and Kevin and Andy Coulson the next day. Andy Coulson said he was getting paranoid because he knew someone from Peter Powell's office would phone the *Mirror*. And of course that day the *Mirror* called me, saying, 'Is it true about Zoe?' I didn't want to lie, so I did something that some would say was more nasty – I didn't speak to them. The *Mirror* kept wanting confirmation, and I had a stream of really abusive messages on my mobile answering service, with Matthew Wright saying, 'I can't really believe you're doing this, Polly. It's a *big* mistake.' In the end I got Sue Lynas [Chief Publicity Officer, BBC Network Radio] to call Matthew Wright and say, 'It will be fine for you to run with it, but Polly can't speak to you until tomorrow.'

The next morning I woke up and it was on the front of the *Sun* and *Mirror* – great for us. When I get into the office I call the *Mirror* and say, 'Look, I'm really really sorry,' and the showbusiness editor is really furious with me. He said, 'I can't believe you didn't speak to us. I thought we had a bit of a personal relation-ship, and you were a real shit to us.' I sent them some flowers, and Piers Morgan, the *Mirror* editor, sent them back with a note saying, 'Put these where the sun don't shine.' Really horrible.

Matthew Wright: It all became very personal. Previously we had made a conscious decision to champion Mark and Lard as best we could. Piers and I both thought it would help us build a long-term relationship with Radio 1.

It would have been very easy not to have had any Mark and Lard coverage in the paper at all, but we were being positively discriminating, and Radio 1 were very appreciative and con-stantly told us how appreciative they were.

So you can imagine how fucked off I was when I discov-ered through other contacts in the radio industry that a deal was going down with Zoe Ball, and a deal was being done to give it all to the *Sun*. I was fucking furious.

I had no idea that she was joining until lunchtime the day prior to the paper coming out. And by four o'clock I was con-vinced she was joining, but no one would confirm it. Polly went off radar, Matthew Bannister went off radar, no one would answer any calls or return calls. Talk about having the door shut in your face. It was unpleasant and it won't be forgotten.

And in the end we just strongarmed one of Zoe's people. I won't identify who, because it would be unfair. And he basic-ally said, 'I'm afraid a deal has been done with the *Sun*.'

But Radio 1 was wrong. I can appreciate that deals can be made between Zoe Ball's agent and the *Sun*, I can appreciate deals have to be made, but considering the support that we'd been giving to what was effectively a losing show with Mark and Lard, as an act of goodwill, I took it personally very badly. The breakfast show had come full-circle, had become very showbiz again like on the old Radio 1, and just as this was happening, we were being squeezed out.

It also seemed unfair because Zoe Ball was signed up as this notional *Mirror* girl. That deal was done a long time before the Radio 1 deal. At that time she had *Live And Kicking*, having left the *Big Breakfast*, not a lot else going on, and I think it was quite a shrewd deal by her agent to ensure that her profile didn't just remain in Saturday kiddie land.

From our interest it was like, after one of our think-tank conferences there was this feeling that New Labour should be reflected in a *New Mirror*. There was this feeling that we should be looking for some kind of thing to encapsulate that, and rather than *Old Mirror*, the image of cloth cap-wearing blokes, it was felt that young, trendy, in touch, sensitive nineties girl or woman would be a better direction to go in. So Zoe would be wheeled out for various promotions as representative of the *Mirror*, or if you wanted to take the *New Mirror* woman's view on something then Zoe Ball would make herself available.

Matthew Bannister: So we got on with our plans to announce Kevin and Zoe, and the day before the news broke, with the contracts all signed, and the photographs done with the *Sun*, I came back to the office at about five o'clock, and Chris's agent Michael Foster rang up.

He said, 'Hello Matthew, would you consider Chris Evans for the Radio 1 breakfast show? I know you're thinking of making a change.'

I said, 'Frankly, your timing is appalling. I've made a commitment, and I've got a team that I'm committed to. And I've told the papers.' He said, 'Well you could say it was a pack of lies – think about it. I'll be in the office until seven if you want to ring me back.' I rang him up almost immediately and said, 'There's no question of me even considering this. But if Chris would ever consider doing a bank holiday show or weekend shows for us then please pick up the phone.' He said, 'I want to make it clear to you that there's no chance of Chris doing anything but the breakfast show.'

So I was slightly hurt when I picked up the *Sun* a few days later to read Chris saying, 'Matthew asked me to come back, but I said fuck off, fuck off, fuck off.' In fact all that had happened was that after he had left, about a month afterwards, I rang his home and left a message on his answerphone which he never replied to. Then within a couple of months I spoke to John Revell, who was then his managing director, and said, 'This is loopy, John. You and Chris and I have worked together for years. It's crazy for us not to be talking. If Chris wants to do any bank holiday shows or weekend shows then I'd be happy to talk, and in any case we should have a beer.' But the breakfast show was the one thing that was never at issue.

Zoe Ball: There was all this press building me up, and people must have thought, Who does this girl think she is, she's never deejayed before. Because Barrie had worked with Kevin before they already had their idea of how the show would be, it was, 'Right, we need to find vehicles for Zoe . . . Zoe must do an entertainment report.' Matthew had already said to me, 'Zoe, you go out there partying and we want you to come in the next day and say, 'I've just got out of a lift with Ewan McGregor . . .' The plan was that Kevin would be very strict and slick and drive the desk, and I'd come in and be fluffy.

They were going to call one of my bits *Ball's Update*, you know, balls-up date, but within a week it was clear it wasn't going to work, that it was going to be like showbiz reporting on GMTV. I was getting very anxious, worried about how much input I was going to have. At the time all they were making me do was press. I said I'd rather be sitting in the office coming up with some ideas.

We did three pilots, and it was clear I needed a lot of work, but the show was starting to take some shape. Management were very hands on, but we expected that. Management used to come down and say, 'We want this, we want that,' and after they'd gone we'd all go, 'Urrgh!' [*puts fingers down her throat*]. But obviously they knew what they wanted and what worked. Everyone else was apparently saying to management, 'You've just got to let them get on with it and stop interfering.' Anyone can sit on a radio show and say, 'Here's the news, here's the weather, here's a record, here's another record.' At one point I was like, 'Look, you've employed us to do this. If you just want someone to play records and not speak, then get someone else in.' I want to talk, that's the whole point. That's what everyone's always loved about Mark and Lard and Chris Evans – they've got things to say. Anybody can go on and say, 'Ooh, there was a gig last night and now here's this . . .' – that terrible middle-of-the-road radio, where you just think, Oh shut up and say something interesting, which is what I'm sure people think about me . . .

We just had this 'keep it tight, keep it tight', so in the end we started saying that on the radio: 'Keep it tight, keep it tight . . .' And then after each pilot management would say, 'You've got to keep it tight . . .'

Kevin Greening: The first three pilots were shite. Because I'd never worked with Zoe we tried to get to know each other between the records, but it was rambling. I know that management were extremely worried, and Barrie protected us from the worst of it. There was no doubt that after the huge turnaround in the last few years we were under great pressure to get it right. But I think management also knew that neither me nor Zoe really needed to be doing this breakfast show, and they couldn't bully us or make us unhappy. I had genuinely felt that if the breakfast show was offered to me I would refuse it, because I loathe getting up at five in the morning, and I really don't need everyone's expectations on my shoulders. I hope management knew that both me and Zoe felt that if things didn't work out we would just walk away from it. But if the first show had been as bad as the pilots we would never have recovered.

I have always been genuinely pleased that Zoe is getting all the attention. I never wanted my picture in the papers. Personally it means there is slightly less pressure on me. I was aware that if the show failed all the criticism would be 'Zoe Ball's show fails . . .' Very unfair on her, of course.

Zoe Ball: Then a few days before we start we find out that Chris Evans is going to Virgin and that he's going to launch on the same day as us. On the Friday that I found out, I was doing rehearsals for *Live and Kicking*, terribly tired from all this running around and press, and my initial reaction was just to laugh, saying, 'I don't believe this,' and then by lunchtime I was in tears, thinking, This is going to be like my experience on the *Big Breakfast* all over again – the big hypey build-up, and then it not working, and being ridiculed and blamed for it: She can't do it, she isn't up to it.

I was going, 'I don't want to be involved with this tit for tat. How could I compete with Chris Evans? I'm friends with him in as much as I sometimes run into him and we end up getting very drunk and having a laugh. But I can only go out getting drunk with him twice a year because it ends up being so messy. About this time a story appears in the *Mirror* that says I hate him, a complete fabrication.

Matthew Wright: There erupted a war of words between Zoe and Chris Evans.

Well, there wasn't actually. It was an implied war of words – this attempt to turn two people who I know to be friends, to try and put them head to head as bitter rivals.

Evans started it by making various comments about Zoe, basically saying that the BBC was using her as a publicity stunt. And then there begins an area that I'm not prepared to talk about on the tape . . . basically, having Zoe Ball complain on Radio 1 about an interview in the *Mirror* being made up is a PR disaster as far as I'm concerned. That's just bad, makes everybody look bad.

Polly Ravenscroft: It didn't help the *Mirror* when they ran this piece with her slagging off Chris Evans – totally fabricated, and Matthew [Wright] didn't have anything to do with it. But a few weeks after the show began, me and Piers Morgan and Matthew [Bannister] all went out together, and we got on fine. The next morning I got some flowers from Piers with the message, 'Put these where the sun does shine.' And overall I was very pleased with the publicity – you couldn't buy that sort of coverage.

Matthew Bannister: The official line was that the competition was 'good for radio', which I genuinely believed. Previously, there had been all sorts of stories about Chris going to Talk Radio. I heard from Tina Ritchie, the newsreader, that she was thinking of going to work for him at Talk. Then she came back to us and said, 'It's all fallen through, I'll stay with you and do the new breakfast show on Radio 1.'

I first heard about Chris doing the show for Virgin when Robert Devereaux, the former head of Virgin Communications who is an old friend of mine, rang to say, 'Just out of courtesy you ought to know that Chris is joining us.' Clearly it makes life more difficult, but it also makes radio more interesting, especially national radio. It meant we had to work harder and we were all going to be under a spotlight, and we had to be very surefooted. And it put a lot more pressure especially on Zoe, which is not what you want when you're trying to make a good creative show.

The best shows establish themselves over time. During the pilots we said things like, 'the timing of that didn't quite work,' or 'You have to explain the rules of this quiz a bit more clearly,' or 'You have to get the contestant on faster,' or 'You have to get in and out of the news more tightly.'

Zoe Ball: I've always been wary of management, because they've got to make you feel good about yourself and boost you. So whenever they said, 'You'll be here for a year,' I was thinking, Yeah, right, three months down the line it'll be like Mark and Lard. I did think, Yeah, feed me as many lines as you want, but I'm not going to believe them because I've done that before and I've been shafted. But I did like Matthew a lot, and he was quite sincere, and he had a good ability to provide genuinely positive criticism. He would say, 'Just try this . . . give this a go . . .'

But it wasn't Kevin and I getting the grief – it was Barrie. I could see him getting more and more stressed, and it was like, 'Barrie, don't listen, do what you want to do, don't feel you have to do everything they say, at the end of the day this is our show.' Having been a presenter I know how much you get in the ear. I felt, Yes, I am not seven years old, I have worked in television, I was a researcher, I do know how this works. I've learnt how to switch it off. But I saw that Matthew genuinely cared, and how important this show was for him, and I thought, God this poor guy has been up against a wall.

Barrie Kelly: The first show was an absolute circus. I came in the day before, on the Sunday, and everything fell through. Kevin and Zoe were supposed to go to Rome on the Saturday to see the Italy–England World Cup qualifier. They did not want to go. We had been working really hard on the pilots, but then they were told they had to go out to Italy just to hang out and do some interviews. We arranged to talk to Skinner and Baddiel out there so that we'd have something on tape for the first show.

Kevin went out on the Friday, and Zoe was supposed to have gone out on the Saturday, after *Live and Kicking*. But she got to the airport late, and missed her connecting flight. Quite sensibly, she turned back, but it wasn't the greatest of starts. Kevin was in Rome not knowing what the hell was going on. Baddiel and Skinner didn't have a hotel because their tour operator had fucked up, and so there was no Baddiel and Skinner interview. We didn't have a footballer, we didn't have a pop star, so we had no interviews for our first show, and all we had were features that were not finely honed. The only thing we looked like having was the Spice Girls on the phone from Istanbul, but that wasn't definite.

On the Sunday at midday it was looking a disaster – very far from the big event Matthew wanted. But then Chris What-mough, who also works on the show, hugely experienced, knows everyone, confirmed the Spice Girls.

It's hard to explain why this was so important. But Chris Evans can just go on the radio and do what he does, but Kevin and Zoe didn't really know each other, and we needed all those props to work the show around. We got Teddy Sheringham confirmed at eight o'clock on Sunday evening – he was back in Manchester, and was going out for a beer with his mates, but Chris had pleaded with him to do this phoner. So we had a footballer. And then from nowhere Ian Broudie [singer with the Lightning Seeds] became available. We slept up the road at the George, so we'd be in at a minute's notice.

I was in the office at about five on Monday morning, and when Zoe arrived, all you could see were camera flashes – a relief that she'd turned up, but you felt, Poor girl. A scrum outside Radio 1 at 5.30 in the morning, many journalists and TV crews, a foretaste of things to come. Flowers came from record companies, people sent us food – a huge display basket of muffins, ridiculous. About two minutes before we went on, we had a group hug – just me, Kevin and Zoe. It was like, 'We're going to do this.'

The show was a dream. Nothing drastic went wrong, it was fast, funny, you could hear the production. I thought, The whole nation is listening, so we really tried to hammer it out, threw the kitchen sink at it, the best show we could. Then afterwards we heard a tape of Evans's show, and he hadn't tried. He did all his old stuff, had all his old Radio 1 jingles. One jingle even had his own Radio 1 time on it, seven to nine, as opposed to his new Virgin time, seven to ten. He hadn't made an effort, but Evans can do that – he just goes in and talks, that's all he had to do.

After the show Zoe looked so happy, I'll always remember her face then. Then all the press people came in, and Matthew arrived with flowers and seemed really relieved. Then all the cameras again, and the show was no longer ours.

Simon Garfield: After the first show, after he had delivered the flowers, Matthew Bannister stood outside Yalding House having a smoke. 'I think we won,' he said. 'It was just really alive. Fresh. Young. It was in colour! Certainly the people who only liked Mark and Lard will probably go elsewhere.'

Kevin Greening joined him. 'That was the worst show we'll do, and even then it wasn't bad.' Bannister congratulated him. With Zoe Ball and Polly Ravenscroft they were driven the 400 yards to the Langham Hilton press reception.

They sat behind a table, from where Zoe was asked to give the thumbs up sign, and to show her bra. 'I got her arse,' one photographer said. After it's over, Zoe Ball says, 'Fucking hell, that's that then.' She then did the *Richard and Judy* show and an insert for *Live and Kicking*. As he left, Kevin Greening was hugged by Peter Powell.

The Chris Evans show was still on air. In one feature he saluted those he said are in his imaginary Radio Hall of Fame, an unironic item. He recited their names – Johnnie Walker, Stuart Henry, Kenny Everett, Chris Tarrant, Steve Wright, Noel Edmonds. After each one John Revell said such things as, 'Radio 2', 'Capital' or, if deceased, 'Radio Heaven'. Evans said that he was not yet part of the hall of fame himself, but hoped to be.

The critical reaction at the end of the week was mixed. Tracey MacLeod in the *Mail on Sunday* found Evans 'like a kid in a sweetshop, rejoicing in his newfound freedom from the playlist and settling a string of old scores ... Over on Radio 1, there was no respite from degrading banter – the difference being that this time it was served up by a woman at her own expense. Zoe Ball has obviously decided to base her persona on *Loaded*'s pin-up babe rather than on the nice girl we've seen presenting children's TV.'

Paul Donovan in the *Sunday Times* found both shows 'inane', but also one or two redeeming features. 'The funniest person on either show is Radio 1's new flying spy, Major Holdups, who speaks like Colonel Blimp as he barks out information about the blocked westbound A25 between Dorking and Guildford, and the tailbacks on the A38.' He noted that Virgin's breakfast audience trailed a long way behind that of Radio 1. '[Evans] will probably put on listeners, but it will be an uphill struggle. There are nine minutes of commercials an hour, interrupting him constantly. He also

285

has to stop for three traffic packages and two news bulletins an hour, and, as a result, seems to be starting and stopping all the time. Outside London, he goes out only on unfashionable and booming medium wave.

'Ball and Greening may have the advantage of FM and the absence of commercials but they, too, have their problems. Greening is less flaky and verbally more acute, though he did make a dreadful mess of a two-part Manchester United "joke du jour". But Ball seems the star so far. She has that indefinable blend of glamour, ego, energy and individuality, with a squeaky, coveted, ultra-contemporary female voice. What if she gets all the attention and Greening none, which, given her looks, is a distinct possibility?'

Zoe Ball: The first show had a few cock-ups, but for the first day I thought it was great, and afterwards I was on a complete high. But then at the Langham there are all these very negative and aggressive questions from journalists, mostly about Chris Evans, very sneery, waiting for us to fail. Someone asked me if I fancy footballers.

Peter Powell [former Disc Jockey, now Agent]: Now radio is right back in the headlines where it should be. Radio is the most exciting medium in entertainment by miles.

I left in 1988. Now Radio 1 is the right station for the right period. It is not for anyone of my age to question whether it is better or worse than the one for the generation that I appealed to. It was a completely different musical platform that I stood for, and one which was in tune with that time. But now there is a new time, a new generation of presenters. But it's no revolution, it's evolution.

Zoe Ball: Someone sent me this fantastic card of Peter when he was about twenty-five, and he was really pretty. I forget that it's him sometimes. He used to be this massive DJ.

I think I've come on a lot in a short while. I make fewer mistakes and fluff fewer lines. Me and Kevin understand each other more. At the beginning we were guessing and both speaking at the same time. We know what doesn't work. We long ago abandoned that idea of Zoe goes to showbiz party with a microphone, which is just pants. It's much better to come in and say, 'Guess what? I ended up under a table with blah.' But there are still some times when I think that I'm guesting on Kevin's show.

I used to read the e-mails, including the crap ones, ones that said, 'Look, you're great on the telly but you're shit on the radio.' Ones that said, 'Oh shut up, stop screaming, stop rambling, I hate you, bring back Mark and Lard,' and I got really down. I thought, Why am I doing this job? I'm obviously useless. But Chris Evans then said to me, 'For Christ's sake why do you read them? Don't read them – you'll destroy yourself.' Chris said, 'God, the amount of people who don't like me . . .' But then I realized actually some people do like me and I do have some things to say.

Barrie Kelly: Matthew said, 'This has got to be a huge show, we want lots of newspaper coverage, lots of events that blow everyone else out of the water.' We all wanted that. But I also wanted an old-school sort of show, going back to Simon Mayo, not so shouty, more relaxed, warm, bringing people in.

We've got *His and Hers*, the Major doing the traffic, *Headline Makers*. *His and Hers* – well, you need a competition, some interaction between the listener and the DJ – a very simple mechanic, win His or Her stuff. *Headline Makers* – another simple thing, making up puns. We had *60 Second Cinema* with Mark Kermode brought over from drive, we have *60 Second Sport*. We have the *Voiceover Men*, another Steve Wright thing, we have Mitch who is our showbusiness correspondent, sort of doing what Zoe was down to do.

And we have *Shop 'Em or Drop 'Em*. This was designed to get the show in the papers. It was a question of whether you either dropped your trousers, and the cameras would all go off with the tabloids there, or you'd tell a story which could, again, get in the papers. The biggest one was probably Helen

Mirren, who shopped Harrison Ford for being a terrible kisser. A newspaper then rang up his agent to get a quote. It was in the *Sun*, the *Mirror*, the *Independent*. They were asking other actresses what they thought of Harrison Ford's kissing. Not earth shattering, but it got stuff in the papers, you know. Who else was there? We had Jack Dee who said that Terry Wogan wore three wigs. That got in the paper. Bryan Adams dropped everything. Robbie Williams dropped everything. It's strange being in a show where you're watching all these famous people drop their trousers. You think, What the hell am I doing, looking at Sting with his trousers round his ankles? But it seems to work, people seem to like it.

Kevin Greening: I've never made a big thing on air about being gay. I'm not camp and I don't fit into any stereotype, I think. It's a part of my life with many others, like being a biker. There's been very little adverse reaction, beyond the *Sunday Express* running a story with a headline like 'Zoe Ball and Me by Gay DJ', and then only five paragraphs in do they even mention my name. Chris Evans now has his Queer for a Year thing where he goes to the gay clubs and supposedly has gay relationships. It can be a bit patronizing, although I think it's well intentioned. Chris sang his own version of Billy Bragg's 'Sexuality' at my GLR leaving party.

Matthew Bannister: I went to the *Q* music awards [November 1997] and Chris was there to present an award. I didn't speak to him before the ceremony, but when he got up on stage he said, 'I haven't got anything to say except that if Matthew Bannister's here, life's too short, let's go for a beer.'

Which was a great relief to me, I have to say. We just went round the corner to a pub with Danny Baker for a pint or two. And it was as if nothing had ever happened, really. We just talked about how much we'd enjoyed working together in the past, how much we'd enjoyed ourselves at GLR. Danny Baker did his impression of Alan Partridge for half an hour.

I told Chris I had got a present that I'd been waiting for

months to give him of the artwork from *Viz* of him and Danny and Gazza on the razzle. And I said I hadn't dared to send it to him because I knew it'd just get in the papers. And he said, 'Oh, I'm sorry about that.'

I talked to him about Virgin and whether he was going to stay. He said, 'Well, I'm definitely not staying if Capital take over, I don't want to work for them. But maybe I'll try and buy the company.' I thought, Don't be silly.

And we're now friends again, I think. Chris is just somebody who switches like a light switch. I think all the things he's said between leaving Radio 1 and now he meant at the time. And now he's decided that he doesn't need to behave like that and he'd rather have me as a mate than not, I suppose.

Danny Baker said, 'This is very funny, you're going out with two people you fired.' And I said, 'Well some people might put a different interpretation on things, Danny, but the truth of the matter is that we should be bigger than all that.'

No doubt some time down the road me and Chris will fall out again, but during that drink I didn't feel I'd ever fallen out with him. And of course, in typical Evans fashion the reconciliation is not a question of picking up the phone quietly and going for dinner or anything like that, it has to be done on the stage in front of the Prodigy and Patti Smith and Paul McCartney.

But I've made it absolutely clear to Kevin and Zoe that the one thing that's not at issue is the breakfast show. I think they needed to be told that.

Funnily enough, I kept bumping into Chris because I often go for a drink after work to the Langham Hilton, which is across the road and one of the places you can usually find a quiet corner to have a chat with colleagues. Chris was living there, because for some reason he decided that his four houses weren't good enough and he'd fallen out with Suzi or something [Aplin, his girlfriend/producer], and so Chris kept coming into the bar.

I went in there for an early evening drink with Polly, and as I walked in there was Matthew Freud and John Revell and

David Campbell [chief executive of Virgin Radio] having a drink. There was nobody else in the whole bar. They were obviously about to make some sort of announcement, and I'd kind of known that all these shenanigans were going on, and I joked, 'Oh, I wouldn't announce anything now,' and went to sit at the other end of the bar to let them get on with it. And then Chris bounced in and came storming over to me and said, 'I've bought the radio station, I'm just going to have my picture taken for the *Financial Times*, for the first time in my life!' And he was just full of himself, ordered Dom Perignon, and we all had a drink together and he was really, really excited about it.

Then I saw him again on the night of the Radio 1 Christmas party, he came into the Langham again, a bit three sheets to the wind with Gazza.

To be honest with you, radio is almost a more sexy medium now than television. It's just getting talked about in a really high profile interesting way, and for Chris Evans to come in and persuade people to lend him £83 million to buy into radio . . . great for the medium. I wish him luck but not too much luck . . . as long as we're both doing well, then that will be fine.

The one thing that I like about it now is that it's not personal any more. For eight and a half months it sort of felt personal, and now it's just business. I'm nice about Chris in public, he's nice about me in public, he's nice about Zoe in public, she's nice about him in public, so the long day wears on.

Zoe Ball: There was all this stuff in the press, and I was quite excited, and I was wondering, 'Oh I wonder if he will . . .' There would be nothing more flattering than Chris Evans calling up to say, 'Please come and work with me,' but he didn't. I'm happy here now, but there were a couple of weeks when I was a bit unhappy, and I did think, This isn't going to work – Kevin and I are too different, and our humour is too different, and I'm not good at this and the pressure's too much. I was thinking, like, Have I made a big mistake? But also the thing with Chris is, I love him to pieces, but how much could you trust him? Can you imagine, I'd leave the BBC, I'd have to cut all my ties with BBC television, and then what if it didn't work? What if one day he woke up, as he does, and says, 'I don't like Zoe today, I'm going to fire her!'? My career would be over.

At the beginning everyone shouted about the fact that we had such good Rajar figures. I was like, 'Don't shout about this, don't do it, because they're going to go down.' I thought, I'm not getting into this, because this is going to come back in our face in three months' time when they go down, which they did. I knew everyone was going to go, 'See, she didn't do it! She's not the saviour of Radio 1.' Because I'm the one who gets it in the neck. Kevin doesn't have to do all these things, and I just get so tired of it. You can't go round shouting, 'We're the best radio show in the world,' because we're not.

One of my biggest faults, and I'm trying to put this right, is that I've always been very self-deprecating, and I really do take things personally. I've always been very 'I'm sorry'. But things do get to me, and I get angry and say, 'I don't give a shit about the figures,' because everyone does go on about them. They say, 'Oh, you can't go on holiday then, because it's Rajar.' But everyone is saying that Radio 1's figures have dropped so dramatically, and everywhere you go people say, 'No one listens any more' and it's a constant gag.

Around Rajar time I do find it quite scary. We'd had this brilliant skiing trip before Christmas, and we get to the airport and Polly mentions Rajar, and I was so angry. I just sat on this trolley and thought, Don't talk to me about this, I don't want to know about Rajar. I turned to everyone and said, 'Look, *you* don't have to be interviewed by people saying, "Oh, Chris Evans, Chris Evans" every day of your life. And I had that before with Gaby Roslin. The pressure all the time. How can you compete with someone like Chris? If he was on FM, would we still be on?' But I also feel like turning round and saying, 'Okay, who are you going to get if *we* don't work? Who's the next?'

Every time I get in a taxi they're listening to Heart, they're listening to Capital, they're never listening to Radio 1.

One of my friends, who is such a cynical old cow, turned to me and said, 'You two are all right, and I thought you were going to be terrible. I even laughed a couple of times.' But the amount of people who come up to me and say, 'I'm sorry, I listen to Chris.' I go, 'Cool.' I'd probably be listening to Chris, if I was listening to the radio.

Simon Garfield: In February 1998, another Rajar spin meeting took place to discuss the audience figures for the last three months of 1997. This was the first opportunity to measure the success of the Ball–Greening breakfast show, and to judge its performance against Chris Evans, and the results were fairly encouraging. The Radio 1 show now had 5.41 million listeners per week, while Virgin's had 2.27 million. Proportionately Evans had outperformed his rivals, putting on 750,000 new listeners nationally, compared to Ball and Greening's 400,000. Overall, Radio 1's reach went up from 10.8 million listeners aged four plus to 10.9 million, but its share of total radio listening fell from 10.2 per cent to 9.9 per cent.

Among its key target age range of fifteen to twenty-four year olds, Radio 1 put on 80,000 to the breakfast show, but it lost audience in this age group overall. In London, the Radio 1 figures looked less good. Radio 1's total breakfast audience in London was 602,000, while Virgin had 617,000. Both were dwarfed by Chris Tarrant on Capital, who increased his poor showing the previous quarter by 16 per cent to 1.95 million.

This was the top line, but the rest was media manipulation. There was a rumour that Chris Evans would show up at the next day's press conference in his capacity as station owner, and boast about his strong performance. But there were always ways to handle this.

Sophie McLaughlin [*reading aloud from draft press release*]: As you can see, BBC Radio continues to hold its own in the highly competitive radio market . . . narrowed gap on the commercial sector . . . over the last two and half years more than forty new commercial stations have been added to the Rajar measurement list, including Xfm in the highly competitive London market . . . a testament to the strength and appeal of the BBC brands.

The news everyone wants to hear is how Kevin and Zoe performed in the new breakfast show. We're delighted to announce that they've added 400,000 listeners to the slot. The programme has more than twice as many listeners than any breakfast show on any commercial radio station.

Matthew Bannister: Is Chris Evans's breakfast show now the biggest show on any commercial station?

Jo Watson: It is.

Matthew Bannister: So it's bigger than Capital's? So can we say, 'The Radio 1 breakfast show now has five and a half million listeners, sorry, has *gone up* to five and a half million listeners – more than double the . . . is Zoe and Kevin the biggest breakfast show in the UK? What's *Today* got?

Jo Watson: They'll be round about the same as last time.

Matthew Bannister: Okay, '. . . gone up to five and half million listeners, more than double its biggest commercial rival.' Why don't we say 'more than double Chris Evans'?

Sophie McLaughlin: I don't think we should say Chris Evans . . . [*reading again*] Another fantastic quarter for Radio 2 . . . record share continues . . . reach was strong . . . Steve Wright doing very well . . .

Matthew Bannister: Do we want to throw in the Wogan line here? The latest thing we're thinking about is that we might do a Zoe and Wogan picture story for the papers – you know, 'These people have 10.5 million listeners, and Terry's put on 160,000.'

Sophie McLaughlin: Right . . . a pleasing quarter for Radio 3, with the network registering its highest ever quarter share figure at 1.4 per cent, and reach up by 300,000. Radio 3's drivetime programme, *In Tune* with Sean Rafferty, has had an extremely successful quarter . . .

Matthew Bannister: I think it should be Radio 3's new *afternoon* programme. I don't think we should talk about *drivetime* in the context of Radio 3.

Sophie McLaughlin: Radio 4 . . . steady over time, though reach and share down very slightly year-on-year. But another very good quarter for 5 Live with yet another record Rajar quarter with a share of 3.6 per cent with more than five million listeners per week. And BBC local and regional continues to perform well . . .

Polly Ravenscroft: Do you want me to give you a rundown of what's been happening today? All the papers have called – the *Daily Mail*, the *Mirror*, the *Sun*, the *Express*, the *Star*. They've all had the figures leaked, and they're all saying we've only gone up 280,000, using the fifteen plus age range. So pushing the line of 400,000 will be quite hard.

Matthew Bannister: The story really is 'Five and a half million people plays two and a half million people.'

Polly Ravenscroft: I think the story tomorrow will be that it's quite good for both of us.

Matthew Bannister: That's the story I want.

Polly Ravenscroft: And clearly there's the rumour that Chris Evans is going to show up at the press conference tomorrow. The *Mirror* had that.

Sophie McLaughlin: What if he turns up and says, 'But you've lost 1.5 million since I was on . . .'

Matthew Bannister: Say, 'Yes we have.' Let's talk about our tactics here. Chris will try to get his picture in the papers. The question is, do we have a better shot of us getting a picture, anywhere, of us looking really pleased? Do we try and do it with Zoe and Terry together, or just with Zoe? I like the idea of them being together, because it gives the impression of Zoe being part of the BBC family, and gives Terry a platform as well. That gives us the chance of saying, 'We haven't only got one audience that's double Chris Evans, but two.' So we have them both having a glass of champagne together, in the Langham perhaps. I think that's a good idea, don't you?

Sue Lynas: Since the figures are going to have leaked tomorrow, I think we should talk about how Zoe and Kevin handle it on the show.

Polly Ravenscroft: I don't think they should talk about it. It's not interesting to the listener.

Matthew Bannister: It will be all right for them to say, 'Fantastic result – we've gone up by 400,000.' No, actually they can't say that, can they? Because of the embargo. They can say things like, 'the even bigger breakfast show' and all that kind of stuff. Whatever it says in the paper, they can say, 'We're very confident and proud, and what a fantastic thing, thanks for tuning in.'

Then we get to the press conference, and we have to decide what to do about Evans turning up.

Sophie McLaughlin: There's definitely an advantage in that I know him. He's not going to be rude to me. I could greet him with a kiss.

Matthew Bannister: It could be all out of control. We were just talking about whether I should go. I could go with a big bunch of flowers and give them to Chris – sort of nice.

Polly Ravenscroft: Oh no, you don't want to do that.

Matthew Bannister: But you don't want to get into a fight with him. If he's going to get up and ask difficult questions about Radio 1, we need to defuse it.

Sophie McLaughlin: If he's there . . . I'm cool about it.

Polly Ravenscroft: The only thing is if he says something like: 'When I was there we had a million more listeners.'

Matthew Bannister: That's exactly what he'll do. I'm afraid to say, that's why he's going.

Sophie McLaughlin: I'll say, 'Well, don't under fifteen year olds count?'

Matthew Bannister: The thing that worries me about it is that it's just going to be incredibly confusing for the journalists. And I know whose message they're going to listen to. We've made no secret of the fact that the audience has been falling since before Chris Evans left, and it continued to fall when Mark and Lard were on the air, but has now recovered and started to go up. That's the truth. The audience began falling during Chris's last quarter, and then continued to fall with Mark and Lard, which is why we've made the change, and since the change we've put on 400,000.

Polly Ravenscroft: How's Xfm doing?

Jo Watson: 234,000. They were after about 400,000.

Matthew Bannister: Makes GLR look good!

Liam Keelan: How have Mark and Lard done?

Jo Watson. Well. They've held their share. Thirteen per cent.

Matthew Bannister: Exactly the same as Nicky Campbell had in that slot, which is amazing.

Polly Ravenscroft: How have Capital done?

Jo Watson: They're up about 300,000. The breakfast show is about the same. Chris Tarrant has clawed back what he lost last time.

Sophie McLaughlin: In reserve, can I use the line about how this is about more than just ratings?

Matthew Bannister: The key line to keep hammering away at is that we have five and a half million listeners, we've gone up by 400,000. We have the biggest breakfast show in the UK. I think we should claim the biggest breakfast show. If it's touch and go with the *Today* programme I don't think they'll get very upset. We are double the size of the Chris Evans breakfast show, and our breakfast show is a million bigger than Virgin's whole station. That's it. Just keep saying that.

Simon Garfield: The following morning, before the press conference, Kevin Greening told listeners the Rajars meant a lot to him. 'We're incredibly happy this morning, but our happiness is embargoed until twelve o'clock.' Zoe Ball said, 'Even though it's in the papers!'

Chris Evans said that he had been drinking with his team since lunchtime the previous day, and he was one of the few staff to have made it in that morning. He told his listeners not to be misled by what they read in the newspapers. 'Radio 1, in the first month of the new breakfast show, put on 750,000 listeners. Over the three months, because the first month was so good, they've shown a gain. Actually, their figures are going down, and that's the truth.'

A listener phones in with an example of a common confidence trick – the theme for the day. He begins by congratulating Evans on his listening figures. Evans says, 'If just one more person had listened to our show we would have got 4 million! Virgin got 3,998,000, but one person they interview represents actually 2,000 listeners. So they're not very accurate, but they're far more accurate than the TV ones, right?'

Caller: Yuh.

Chris Evans: They have people keep what are called Radio Diaries, so there's no way that we can figure out if there are 4 million, 6 million or 8 million – we don't know how many people are listening – we just base it on this multiple of 2,000 per person who has a diary.

Caller: Right, anyway, I have a con for you. You know how if you want to get something fixed and the warranty is just about to expire and you take it back to where you bought it and the dealer says he'll have to check with the manufacturer . . .'

Sophie McLaughlin did her bit at the press conference, going through it with the pages from her computer. There were only two questions from the floor. A woman from the Press Association said, 'Now, Sophie, why have Zoe and Terry Wogan got the champagne out this morning, when year-on-year listening at those stations has gone down quite substantially, especially at Radio 1?'

Sophie said that Zoe and Terry had a lot to celebrate. 'Zoe and Kevin have seen a 400,000 increase on the breakfast show in just three months, and Terry continues to do a fantastic job for us at Radio 2. If you combine those together it takes BBC breakfast listening to just over 11 million every morning, so that's fantastic.'

Press Association: Sorry, but year-on-year is a significant comparison isn't it?

Sophie McLaughlin: But quarter-on-quarter we've seen reach on Radio 1 stabilize, and as I've said, we've added to breakfast show listening, which is great news. Year-on-year, yeah, we've seen a decline in the past year, and we've never made any secret about that. It's a highly competitive market, but we have added listeners this quarter, so it's looking up.

The man from *Broadcast* magazine had a tricky one: 'Just following on from that, if there has been this improvement at breakfast time, but nevertheless Radio 1's share is down from 12.4 to 9.9 in a year – that implies some very serious defections, doesn't it?'

Sophie McLaughlin: The breakfast show has done disproportionately well for us, which is great, because as we all know that's where the battle has been hardest fought. But quarter-on-quarter, as I said, the reach has stabilized, so the schedule is actually performing well.

Man from *Broadcast*: I was talking about share. I wonder if you could tell me, compared to a year ago, which part of the schedule has suffered?

Sophie McLaughlin: We can talk about that afterwards. You need to talk in detail to the Radio 1 press officer about that, in terms of specific figures.

There were no further questions. Neither Matthew Bannister nor Chris Evans turned up.

The following day, the national papers had decided not to print any pictures from the Ball/Wogan photocall. However, the *Sun* did run an interview with Zoe Ball, in which she said that she didn't like to think about ratings too much, and that she had once snogged Chris Evans when both of them were very, very drunk.

Chapter 13

A New Machine

Jo Whiley: 'I looked at Matthew, and he was apoplectic'

Simon Garfield: On 25 February 1998, staff arrived back from lunch to find they had a new controller. They received a memo from the old one, too: 'I am delighted to announce that we have appointed Andy Parfitt as Controller of Radio 1 . . . As you know,

Andy has played a major part in the repositioning of Radio 1 over the last four years. He is passionate about the network, about talent and about music. I know he is the right man to lead Radio 1 into the twenty-first century.'

Matthew Bannister wrote that he was sure he was leaving the network 'at the leading edge of modern music . . . with a highly talented team well prepared to take on the challenges ahead'. Later that day, at the formal announcement, he told people that he'd miss their friendship and loyalty and hard work, and that he'd still keep in touch as much as he could. In truth, he'd been drifting apart for a while.

Matthew Bannister: It's really impossible to do both jobs, impossible to be director of BBC Radio and to run a station that is as demanding as Radio 1. It was becoming increasingly clear to me that running Radio 1 was becoming a part-time job, and I didn't think that was fair to Radio 1. Also, after four and a half years, I think it's time to move on and let someone with fresh ideas and fresh energy take over. The timing was about trying to get Radio 1 into a period of stability, launching the breakfast show and making sure it worked, and getting the first figures.

With Andy there is continuation of mission . . . I would expect that, as with the other networks, major changes to the schedule or major changes of policy would be discussed with me before they came in, but it's his job now. I'm responsible for the co-ordination of the networks, their overall strategy, the allocation of funds between them and the co-ordination of their marketing and making sure they complement each other and don't bump into each other.

The most important thing to remember about it all was the question that was asked of me at my interview, about being Mr Nasty in the press. When I answered it I had no idea what it would be like, but I still believe in the answer: If we believe we're doing the right thing, then we'll take all the flak. And I believe we did do the right thing, and made Radio 1 into a modern radio station. We've turned it into something the

BBC can be proud of, and something which has credibility with young people. And that conviction saw us through some stormy times. I'm incredibly proud of it.

John Birt: If you say to me, would I have predicted [the dramatic loss of audience]? No. Was I surprised by it? No. So it was somewhere between those poles.

I thought that, very broadly speaking, if you could wind back the clock, you'd have made more incremental change earlier over a much longer period of time. But given the position we were in, do I broadly think we did the right thing? Yes, I broadly think we did. We've kept Radio 1 within the BBC. We have a station we're proud of.

You have to have a sense of proportion about this. We've still got, in this crowded marketplace, we've still got a station which remarkably reaches out to very large numbers of people. If you compare that figure with the sort of figures we used to get when we had a monopoly, it's not as high. But have we managed to maintain its broad appeal whilst maintaining a public service perspective on it? Yes.

Was I relieved when the steepness of the graph started to steady off again and our audience started to stabilize? Yes.

Do I, over time, expect, with further competition . . . do I think those figures will maintain forever? No.

No Radio 1 controller has ever heard me say, 'I'm going to judge you by how many listeners you attract.' Even before I was director-general I only ever pressed on the Radio 1 controller to be really clear about his purposes. And his purposes are to reach out to young people with a beguiling mix of music and other information that they need, with public service in mind. This means exactly the same as it does everywhere else at the BBC – exposing people to things they might not otherwise encounter. Obviously it's tough, because you have to speak to people in a language that they will identify with and understand, in an entertaining and intelligent way that widens their horizons.

Chris Moyles: It's been about three months now. It's nothing like you imagine it to be. When you're a kid and you're listening, you think, Radio 1 – that's the dogs, the be-all and end-all. You think everything will be perfect at the ultimate place to work. But as a place to work it's really just like any other station. Comparing it to Capital where I worked before, building-wise Radio 1 is a shit-hole, an absolute fucking pit of a place to work. The studios are quite nice but not as flash as Capital. The reception area here is horrible. It would be very nice to walk into the flashiest reception in the world, a reception that goes, 'Whey! Look at us! Fuck off!' This *is* Radio 1, for God's sake, the best radio station to work at in the world. The licence fee-payer can be happy with the knowledge that none of their fee has been squandered on wasteful things such as paint or nice furniture.

But when you're on the air it makes no difference. It wouldn't matter if I was broadcasting from a box – getting lost in your own little world.

Three years ago I was working at Chiltern Radio. If someone would have said in two years I'll be at Capital and then a year after that I'll be at Radio 1, I would have said, 'Sure, and my arse plays the trumpet.'

John Birt: The big theme in the BBC at the moment is getting ever closer to our audiences, and we're trying to do that. It's not a new thought. The last five years, I think, have been marked by a really serious effort to understand our audiences better, how they're changing, what their needs are.

Chris Moyles: Wow, look, I'm drawing a tattoo on her shoulder. Chris . . . was . . . here. I'm going to play this record while I finish off this tattoo . . .

John Birt: There's no part of the audience that's changing more rapidly than young people. Understanding them, understanding what their tastes are, what their musical tastes are, what their personal needs are, the world in which they're operating, a less secure world, a world where both main parties are moving on a path towards self-reliance, where a lot of the old securities have gone . . . Helping, albeit in a predominantly entertainment environment, being aware and alert to their needs and their interests and their passions and their concerns is something you can never do enough of . . .

And that's Andy's job. We're not looking for a revolution now, we've had the revolution.

It's terribly important that the licence payer understands what they get in return for their licence fee from the BBC. So we have to say to young people, as to other groups, the BBC is an organization which can bring you things like Radio 1. What we find in our research is that people say things like, 'Well, I think it's a bit of a stuffy organization, but I love *Shooting Stars*, Radio 1, *Alan Partridge* and *Match of the Day*.' And that is a manifest contradiction and we've got to . . . align people's feelings about the BBC with the programmes we actually make.

Do we have a sort of masterplan for people to first listen to *Newsbeat* and then the *Today* programme and finally *Panorama*? Nothing as crude as that, but certainly as a generality – why were we so keen to keep Radio 1 in the charter debate? Answer: we wanted to be able to offer young people something that they associated with the BBC. A different vision of the BBC, which was a sort of Olympian heights BBC of Radio 3, Radio 4, which was culturally, socially and age specific, was not to me at all an attractive vision. In my view it's simply wrong to collect a licence fee from everybody and then invest it in programmes for a few.

But I was really keen to hold on to Radio 1, Radio 2, so that we were able to do things for young people and frankly, yes, to introduce them to wider experiences, I'm not embarrassed to say it, and a different tone of voice, a different way of looking at the world. And yes again, I'm not embarrassed to say that you do hope that by introducing them to the BBC in that environment, as they get older, they will move on to Radio 4 and watch more programmes on BBC2 and so on.

Jo Whiley: There was one night when Christopher Bland, the

Chairman of the BBC, had a dinner in his suite at Broadcasting House with the theme of Youth. Youth from everywhere, so there was someone from *This Life*, someone from the TV music shows, someone who did young stuff from all the stations. I was Radio 1's representative, and Matthew was there as well. We all had to give little speeches, and say what we liked and didn't like about the BBC.

It went round the table, and after three speakers a theme developed, which was about cuts and having no money. When it got round to me I said, 'Yeah, having no money – I have to share a BA, a researcher, with Nicky Campbell's show.' I said it was very hard to make a good show with half a BA. I looked at Matthew, and he was apoplectic. After he said, 'I didn't know about this.' He was horrified that I'd just told everyone that we weren't properly resourced at Radio 1.

After this meal I went with him to Soho House, and we left there at four in the morning, absolutely plastered, and Matthew gave me a lift home. That's when you have the best conversations with Matthew. I got in the next day, and had all these phone calls from people wanting to fix all the problems, putting it all right. God knows how he remembered with the astonishing amount he drank.

Matthew Bannister: There's a certain amount of sadness in stepping down, because Radio 1 in 1998 is my baby, and it's been a consuming passion, and the people who work there I feel a great deal of empathy with and I've enjoyed working with them.

Given my time over again, I wouldn't have rushed in and thrown everything out. I don't think we got clear what we thought Radio 1 was for when we set out, and we only did that after about a year. Once we got it clear, it was easier, but we were to a certain extent trying a whole load of things without a proper understanding of the purpose of the station. I think we can be forgiven for that, in the sense that I don't think anybody else had a clear idea of what Radio 1 was for either, or should be for. It was Andy Parfitt's Wire Free Radio 1 – youthful values and new music – which really crystallized our sense of what it was for. It was only when we saw that that we stopped this pragmatic thing of trying to keep on a programme for the over-thirty-fives here, and keep on a programme that would appeal more to thirty-fives to forty-fives here, and so on, which was a bit of a mish-mash to be honest with you, and which I regretted afterwards.

I think the other thing I regretted was that a number of very great friends of mine, and performers who I really like, suffered badly in the process because they were ill-cast by me and they didn't feel comfortable. They were the standard bearers of this new regime and went out in front and got hammered by the newspapers . . . a very painful procedure, a really awful thing to put people through.

And even after we got our focus, we then took a long time to focus the music policy around that, because we were under such pressure from the falling ratings. To have confidence in your own judgement and your own focus against a constantly dropping audience is quite a difficult thing to do. It's quite difficult to arrive at that when every month and every quarter you're getting, 'Another million have turned off – what are you going to do about it?'

There are fewer young people in the population than there were, and they're certainly a minority group compared to the rest of the population, but focusing on them is a public service, and that's what we finally got ourselves round to doing. And I'd argue now that if we hadn't changed that quickly and had all the rows and the hoo-hah, I'm not sure that Radio 1 would be as strong and as clear as it is now, because we'd still be in the transitional period, rather than in a consolidation period. But I can tell you it wasn't a pleasant experience to go through for me or for the people who worked with me, and it was unnecessarily bruising for the audience. So I regret all those things, and I think that they were wrong, but I think we had the courage, and the BBC had the courage, to support us to get it right. And the end result is a station that is a happier place to work, and a more cohesive listen for those who love it.

I don't want any more huge upheavals, but there is more tuning to do to the machine to make it fire on all cylinders. We've got the luxury of thinking about the margins now rather than the middle, but there is some more to be done just to make sure that every single thing is bolted down.

Simon Garfield: A day after his appointment, Andy Parfitt chaired another regular strategy meeting in his office. The mood was little changed, though every now and then some flowers arrived, or some champagne from the staff. The meeting covered the usual things, an upcoming Drugs Night with a documentary and a poll, how they'd handle the Oscars, but it was set apart by a more visionary interlude, during which Parfitt discussed his plans for the future. He referred to the presentation booklet that he used during the interview that secured his job.

Andy Parfitt: I talked about how much I knew about the current radio market, and told them all about how most listening is to music radio, and that there are on average sixteen stations to choose between if you live in metropolitan areas.

I talked to them about our positioning statement, saying I think it's a brilliant lever for public service presentations, about how unique we are, and our great portfolio of specialist programmes. But I said that the weakness of it is that it's not about the audience, it's not about people. And it lacks any sort of dynamic, aspirational quality, in my view.

I also said that as a positioning statement it leads you towards male specialisms, and then showed them that we have a huge great bias in our audience towards men, and we don't succeed with women at all, and why was this? I then showed them that we were in decline, even despite Chris Evans being on board for that period. Not a steep dive, but there we go.

These are my strengths and weaknesses [*he holds up his booklet*]. I said, okay, we are on national FM, which gives us a quality advantage over some of our competitors, but we don't exploit localness, like ILR do – they really make their area their own. We've got these household-name presenters – I said that we have these personality DJs with complexes most of the time. They don't want to be DJs. They have this anti-DJ personality. I said we've got cutting-edge DJs, but they're isolated and not part of the network as a whole. I don't know if you saw that brand stuff: the BBC research showed Radio 1 DJs separate, as a brand, from Radio 1 itself, i.e. Tim Westwood and Judge Jules were seen as cutting edge, and gave value to the audience, but Radio 1 itself was seen as the parent. I said we've got music radio expertise, but we've got lack of discipline in delivering music all over the shop that we need to sort out.

We've got this huge range of live music and speech, but it's on a schedule that's so rich that you'd never know what's on.

We're part of the BBC family, which brings great benefits – Radio 5 Live, *Live and Kicking*, the *O Zone* and so on, but we're also a youth brand that is at odds with the sober BBC institution.

Then I gave the depressing part of the presentation. All BBC presentations have to have a really depressing part where you say that the future is going to go mad. The prediction is for fifty new analogue licences within the next three years (five to ten regional licences, forty local licences), an increase in the average competition in metropolitan areas by about two or three new services – so the average choice goes up to eighteen services. And they're very likely to be Top Forty stations, because that's not what people have got – 40 per cent of areas do not have Top Forty stations. That's serious shit for us. In the digital world, local, regional and national multiplexes mean that there could be up to twenty-five different music channels all with the same quality as Radio 1, and all aimed at fifteen to thirty-four year olds, because that's where the listening is.

The question I asked is, What sort of station should we be in five years' time, and what sort of Radio 1 did I want to be controller of in five years' time? How could we position Radio 1 to meet the competitive assault and yet retain our public service credentials? And then the second question was, Can we do better?

So this is the diagram for my vision of Radio 1. I had fifteen minutes to do this whole presentation. This line across reads: We Are Young. And then it's got New Music First, Contemporary Pop, Specialist and Live Music here, and then our style values here. I said that if you thought about a BBC radio service for the young, in five years' time it would equal a music radio service. In other words I was trying to get away from New Music First as being the first thing you thought of.

I said I wanted Radio 1 to be a place where there was a real and proper understanding of what it means to be young in the UK, for males and females. I really sense that now there is not a proper understanding of what the audience is like. Now we make huge assumptions about what they think will be trendy, or what they think about the movie *Titanic*, or what they think about Celine Dion. I said that we want it to be an exciting celebration of the young experience in the UK, but also a guide to life in a complex world. There are things that we can do that ILR will never do, things about leading people forward.

I think Radio 1 should be a strong, focused, tightly managed brand. In terms of managing that brand, the target audience should be even tighter than fifteen to twenty-fours. I don't know if anyone saw that research about the epicentre of youth culture as being seventeen to twenty-one, that absolute time when you just blow up.

Then they said, 'Does this mean that you will completely cut back from New Music First?' and I said, 'Not at all, because New Music First is the way we argue our public service credentials, but concentrating on the young is something we do internally.'

I then said what we're going to do about our tactics for survival. I said we've got to change the personalities, these anti-DJ personalities of our DJs, and make them more outward-looking. I said we've got to be consistent about our music delivery. We have to have hard-disk playout systems eventually. And if we can't exploit localness then we have got to exploit what we can get – Kate Winslet, Madonna and big national things.

I've had some thoughts about the core schedule, but I want to be very careful about how we change it, and how we look forward to getting Moyles up to weekend mornings, and whether or not we should take him off early breakfast. I think we'll change it a little bit, we'll probably do Sunday nights and Monday nights in one little move, and then probably do the early breakfasts and weekend mornings at another time. And then I proposed a new structure for production.

And that was it. And they gave me the job on the back of that.

So there's loads to do. I want a series of team meetings with producers and DJs, and I want to set up something that I want to call Music Radio Masterclass, which would be a training session for a week so that all the BAs and all the producers can learn what I know about music radio – about briefing DJs, the fact that they're in charge, the fact that they have to know the law, lots and lots of stuff. There's libel, the commercial policy ... when I went down there yesterday and saw everybody who looked about eighteen, I thought, Why do we assume that they know all this stuff? It seems to me that sometimes we just plonk empty vessels in the schedule, and then we expect them to perform. We don't work with them enough to make them do it like we want to. There is loads to do. So I'm going to try to get out of a lot of things now to concentrate on this, but I need all your help to get them to understand what we understand, and to play the fucking records when they're scheduled.

Simon Garfield: A few weeks later, in the audience figures for the first three months of 1998, Radio 1 recorded an increase of 240,000 people to 11.1 million, but its share of all listening fell from 10 per cent to 9.6. Year-on-year listening was down by 700,000, while share had fallen 1.6 per cent. At breakfast time, Greening and Ball had lost 82,000 in the last quarter, while Chris Evans had risen by 234,000. At the press conference, Virgin was keen to point out that in London, the only city where it broadcast on FM, Evans had a quarter of a million more listeners than Radio 1 – to which Radio 1 responded that it still had well over twice Virgin's total national audience. These minor, short-term skirmishes concealed the fact that since June 1993, Radio 1 had lost over 8 million listeners, and more than half of its share of the radio public.

Yet at the beginning of May 1998, Radio 1 had a magnificent night at the Grosvenor House Hotel, venue of the Sony Awards, radio's annual celebration of its best and brightest. Here the programmes counted, not the size of their audience. Jo Whiley was named DJ of the year, *Blue Jam* was comedy programme of the year, and Mark and Lard won the best daytime music award. There were silver and bronze awards for Chris Moyles, Dave Pearce, station branding and coverage of Glastonbury.

This was by far the station's best performance since the awards began, and was marked by much revelry. But it was an old Radio 1 employee who won the most prestigious trophy of the night: Chris Evans picked up the special Gold Award for his services to radio. 'Radio is where it's at,' he announced, as he thanked all the DJs who had inspired him since he was a boy. 'I was asked to a seminar on the future of television,' he said. 'Well, the future of television is radio.' No one quite knew what that meant, but they seemed to like the sound of the words.

Matthew Bannister: There was a very moving evening after I left, when my wife persuaded me that I had to go to dinner with some of her colleagues at the Metropolitan Hotel, and I didn't want to go. I turned up, and of course the first person I saw was John Birt, and then Andy Parfitt, and then a procession of DJs, and it was very touching, because I thought I was going to slip away quietly. I sat between Emma Freud and Zoe Ball, and Jo Whiley was there, and Simon Mayo and Liz Forgan, and it was very moving. The *Sun* sent along a crate of wine, and, far more important, they also sent me a broken piece of banister and a note which said that the banister was now officially dismantled and will never be used again. There was also a cartoon, drawn by the man who had originally drawn me sliding down the banister, and now he had me in white tie and tails going on to higher things. Very touching.

I think what I enjoyed most about the whole thing was giving a platform for talented people and talented musicians to go on the air and talk eloquently about things they loved.

John Peel: There's nowhere else I could possibly do the sort of work I do other than Radio 1. For a period I was paid what they called a loyalty payment for not allowing myself to be seduced by any commercial station, but they soon realized that no company was trying to seduce me, or could possibly want the sort of programme I did, so they quickly removed it.

I always compare a good programme to surfing, not that I ever surf. I always imagine what it must be like – when a programme goes well you do feel you're riding along the crest of something. You go out of the studio at the end and say, 'Wow, what a great programme!' and they say, 'Oh, it sounded like all the others to me.' But some nights you can come away feeling so desperate because you've made so many mistakes, and you go out and say, 'That was just a disaster.' And people say, 'Oh, it sounded just like all the others to me.'

A lot of people who have been writing to me have been doing it for almost thirty years, and some of them have become family friends, and we've been to their weddings. And all I want really is to operate on that sort of level. But on my fiftieth birthday I wrote to about thirty of the people who have been in touch with me over the years, a lot of whom I haven't met. I told them I was having this party, nothing fancy, not a showbiz event, we had a field across the road and you could pitch a tent there or have some floor space in the house, and I'd be really pleased if you could come, and bring a mate. But only five of them came, which I thought was terribly sad. A lot of them admitted to me subsequently that despite everything I said, they still thought they'd get up there and find Cilla Black and all but one member of Genesis. So even the people who know what you do still think it's glamorous showbiz.

Postscript

When the first edition of this book appeared in October 1998, readers had three questions. They wanted to know what I had been obliged to leave out, how people at Radio 1 had reacted to the book, and who my favourite DJ was. Perhaps we can cover these in reverse order. My favourite DJ – apart from *everyone's* favourites John Peel and Mark and Lard – is Simon Mayo. I appreciate this may be an extremely uncool choice, and may shock some of you so deeply that you resolve to throw this book into the ocean and never buy any book ever again lest it disappoint in a similar way, but tough. It is a choice brought on by aging, and it may happen to you one day as well. I didn't much like Mayo when he was an eager break-fast show upstart, but in the last two years he's been sounding like someone who's not really trying, which is a fantastic thing to hear on music radio. Having spent a fair bit of time with him – including an emotional session on the Roadshow – I am as saddened as he probably is that he features so fleetingly in these pages. Or perhaps he is pleased. I just don't know.

The response to the book from DJs has been muted. A couple of them mentioned it on air, and I did hear a new trailer for Chris Moyles which used a couple of quotes (something like: 'John Peel calls him DLT in waiting . . . Zoe Ball wishes he wouldn't talk about tits so much'), but apart from that, nothing. Not a peep out of Simon Bates or DLT. I did have a nice chat with Andy Kershaw, but not about the book. I got a pleasant note from John Peel, but not about the book. Inevitably, the Peel note concerned Liverpool Football Club. A year after I had first met him, and gave him that Liverpool team sticker, a new set of stickers came out to obsess young boys, and I managed to prise another swap from my kids. I sent it to him with a note that said, 'Absurd as it is, I thought you might need this . . .' He wrote back: 'It's now stuck on the front of my address book . . .' Even these few words boosted my day – just to think, a little handwritten note from a man who gave the first national exposure to Penetration's 'Don't Dictate'. I hope it may become an annual event.

There was more feedback from the suits. My editor got a letter from Sir John Birt, or rather his people. Or rather, the BBC Litigation Department. I had misquoted him. I had missed out one word from the following comment: '. . . if you could wind back the clock, you'd have made more incremental change over a much longer period of time'. The word was 'earlier': 'made more incremental change *earlier* over a much longer period of time'. How was Birt so sure he had said this? Because he was the only person I had interviewed to record our conversation. Anyway, he wondered if we could change it for a future edition, which, of course, I am happy to do. Several months on, I'm still struggling to find any material difference in the two versions, but I'm impressed with Birt's attention to detail and glad that my licence fee is being pushed as far as it can go.

BBC management seemed fairly happy with the book, or at least relieved. Readers said to me, 'I bet they regret letting you in . . .', but I'm not sure this was so. I think there was joy that I hadn't talked about the considerable quantities of drugs consumed by some Radio 1 staff and DJs. I wasn't really interested in this, as long as it didn't affect their work. I was aware that in the music industry people sued if you wrote that they were positively *not* taking drugs, but I was willing to take this risk. Sometimes I felt that Radio 1 would benefit from the consumption of even more drugs. More drugs *earlier*.

Trevor Dann kindly invited me to the BBC Entertainments Christmas Party, during which Steps mimed their greatest hits. Everyone was terribly drunk, of course, so I had a good chat with Matthew Bannister. Matthew said he had no problems at all with the book, and was pleased that it hadn't harmed his relationships with others in the Corporation. There was one gripe, however. As part of the promotion for the book I had agreed to write a profile of Bannister for the *Mail on Sunday*. Part of the story considered the possibility of Bannister succeeding Birt as Director General. The piece was okay, he said, but there was a problem with the photograph – his mother thought it made her son look arrogant. 'The one with me and Zoe she liked,' Bannister explained, 'but the main one . . .'

Bannister had asked me to remove two passages from the book when it was still in draft form. One concerned the future of the Roadshow, which looked like it was about to be axed and replaced by a series of weekend beach parties, and the other concerned some pointed comments he and others had made in one of those Rajar discussions about how best to present disappointing audience figures. Bannister feared that the comments might present the wrong image of the BBC to the outside world – someone, for instance, had referred to the afternoon slot on Radio 3 as 'drivetime', which was considered a very non-Radio 3 phrase. 'Oh God,' someone said, 'you can see it now . . . "Radio 3 dumbs down . . ."'

Not long after the book went to press, Matthew Bannister got a new job – Chief Executive of BBC Production. This is potentially the most creative job in British broadcasting, for it entails running the largest production studio in Europe, and making almost 75 per cent of the BBC's entire output – a remarkable feat for someone who had never made a television programme in his life. In the future, he told me, 'Power is going to be in the hands of the audience – new ways of making limitless choices.' He was referring to digital, and to the inroads made by the Corporation's rivals. He hoped the BBC would be an independent guide through the minefield, becoming more and not less important as a purveyor of impartial news and current affairs.

At Radio 1, Andy Parfitt brought in some changes of his own. Zoe Ball took over as sole presenter of the breakfast show, while Kevin Greening was relegated to weekends and something on digital television that nobody watches. 'I'm so excited,' Zoe Ball said. 'It's been great working with Kevin – he's a top guy and I'm going to miss him.' Parfitt said that this had been his vision for a while.

Zoe Ball has become one of the biggest stars at the BBC, and now adorns the backs of buses. Much to Radio 1's delight, she is rarely out of the newspapers, being linked to many emotional events in dance clubs. She has grown in confidence, and still misbehaves. Last year she apologized for using the F-word on the breakfast show. She had seen a Fatboy Slim concert in Newcastle, and considered it 'so fucking cool'. She was sorry, but she was still tired, and the word just slipped out.

Chris Evans went still further at Virgin. Virgin was fined £10,000 by the Radio Authority after Evans broadcast a photographer's mobile telephone number, inviting his listeners to 'hound him until he goes toes up'. The photographer had apparently been tussling with Liam Gallagher. The photographer said he had received hundreds of calls, including threats on his life. A few months later, Zoe Ball announced that she thought Fatboy Slim was still so fucking cool that she had decided to marry him.

Zoe Ball's show is on the radio as I write, and she has just asked a caller a quiz question. 'Who lives at 10 Downing Street?' Then she said, 'Call us if you have a funny laugh – we want to hear the most annoying or weirdest or just funniest laughs.'

Today, an unkind analyst would call Radio 1 deeply schizophrenic, but that would be to ignore the spirit of the age. Britpop and sleazy American guitars have been overtaken by very chirpy factory pop, and this creates a problem with coolness. Britpop was perfectly timed for the new Radio 1 – Mayo and Goodier and Nicky Campbell could play Oasis and Blur with no embarrassment and some delight, and even Chris Evans, who understood nothing about hip pop when he joined the station, could appreciate the appeal of 'Wonderwall'. More importantly, it was Britpop that eased Mark Radcliffe and Jo Whiley into mainstream, a point illustrated now by the audible squirming when either of them has to play a scheduled song by Five. Whiley joked recently about 'getting my hands cut off' if she failed to play a single by Bryan Adams.

But Bryan Adams is indeed on the playlist these days, along with Honeyz, Cleopatra, Boyzone and B*witched. Unfortunately for the increasingly young and hip staff of Radio 1, such trash-deluxe sells rather well, and they are obliged to reflect this. Recently in the *Guardian*, the comedian Sean Hughes berated the station for killing new music, and sounding 'like a toddler's party'. In fact, things have gone back to the old days: 'Ratings by day, credibility by night.'

The station is still pulling in several directions – to Ibiza for a long weekend of drugs and partying and the best dance music, and Lisa I'Anson not quite making it to the studio in time because of all the above – and then back the very next day for a wet broadcast from the Roadshow in Blackpool. And then back to live Blur and Ash gigs and some advice on depression and exams and how to get free tickets for the Brits by gargling Robbie Williams songs.

Can one station genuinely be all these things and be successful? Even now, almost six years after the start of the revolution, it appears to be the trickiest of balancing acts.

Of late, the formula appears to working well. Earlier this year, some new Rajar figures announced that Radio 1 had added over 200,000 listeners in the last quarter of 1998, and Zoe had added half a million. Total audience was up to 11.4 million. At the press conference, the Radio 1 people had some good news at last. The audience liked Zoe. Female listeners were listening for longer. Chris Moyles had truly become the station's saviour. Bannister was talking to Evans about coming back to the BBC. Jo Whiley had another baby. Virgin was down. There were crazy plans for the millennium. The *Mirror* might be doing a spread on Mark and Lard's catchphrases. The coffee machine had been fixed. Radio 1 was on the way back. It's almost 8.40, and here's Catatonia.

Acknowledgements

For permission to use the following photographs the publishers would like to thank:

The BBC: DJ's Christmas Party, David Lee Travis, Bruno Brookes, Sophie McLaughlin, Andy Kershaw, Andy Parfitt, Chris Moyles (photograph by James McCormick), Jeff Smith, Tim Westwood, Zoe Ball and Kevin Greening, Jo Whiley, John Peel, Simon Bates, Trevor Dann, Steve Wright, Mark Radcliffe, Steve Lamacq, Simon Mayo, Annie Nightingale

Rex Features: Chris Evans (photograph by Dave Hogan), Matthew Bannister (photo by Karen Fuchs)

News Group Newspapers Ltd: Chris Evans and Matthew Bannister

east west records: The Shirehorses (photograph by Jon Shard)

Corbijn: John Peel and PJ Harvey (photograph by Anja Grabert)

Lines from 'The Hapless Boy Lard' by The Shirehorses on pages 176–7 by kind permission of BMG Publishing

Extracts on pages 32–3 from *Harry Enfield and his Humorous Chums* by kind permission of Penguin Books Ltd

Index